ARCHEOLOGY OF VIOLENCE

ARCHEOLOGY OF VIOLENCE

PIERRE CLASTRES

Translated from the French by Jeanine Herman

SEMIOTEXT(E)

First published in French in 1980 as *Recerches
d'anthropologie politique* by Éditions du Seuil, Paris.

Thanks to Jeanine Herman, Lewanne Jones, Sylvère Lotringer,
Keith Nelson, Shack Paste, Peter Lamborn Wilson and Jordan Zinovich.

Semiotext(e) offices:
522 Philosophy Hall, Columbia University, New York, New York 10027
POB 568 Williamsburgh Station, Brooklyn, New York 11211 USA

Telephone: 718 387-6471   Fax: 718 963-2603

Printed in the United States of America.

CONTENTS

ARCHEOLOGY OF VIOLENCE

1

THE LAST FRONTIER

> "Farewell voyages,
> farewell savages..."
> Claude Lévi-Strauss

"Listen! The rapids!"

The forest still prevents us from seeing the river, but the roar of crashing water on great rocks can be heard clearly. Fifteen or twenty minutes of walking and we reach the canoe. None too soon. I finish my trek like my companion, covered in dirt, my snout in the mud, crawling in humus that no sun will ever dry.... Still, playing Beckett's Molloy in the Amazons is quite something.

For close to two months, Jacques Lizot and I have been traveling through Venezuela's southern tip, in the territory of the Yanomami Indians, known here as the Waika. Their country is the last unexplored (unexploited) region of South America. This cul-de-sac in the Amazon, part of both Venezuela and Brazil, has up until now resisted penetration through a variety of natural obstacles: the unbroken forest, unnavigable rivers (once one approaches their sources), the remoteness of everything, illness, and malaria. All of this is hardly attractive to colonizers, but very favorable to the

First published in *Les Temps Modernes*, No. 298, May, 1971, pp. 1917–1940.

Yanomami, certainly the last free primitive society in South America and no doubt the world. Politicians, entrepreneurs and investors have let their imaginations run wild, like the Conquistadors four centuries ago, seeing in this unknown south a new and fabulous Eldorado, where one could find everything: petroleum, diamonds, rare minerals, etc. In the meantime, the Yanomami remain the sole masters of their territory. At present, many of them have never seen the White Man, as we used to say, and only twenty years ago, almost all were oblivious to the existence of the *Nabe*. An incredible bonanza for an ethnologist. Lizot is studying these Indians, has already spent two years among them, which has not been easy; he speaks their language very well and is now beginning another stay. I am accompanying him for several months.

We spent the first two weeks in December shopping in Caracas: a motor for the canoe, a rifle, food and objects to trade with the Indians, including machetes, hatchets, kilometers of nylon fishing line, thousands of fishhooks in all sizes, cases of match boxes, dozens and dozens of spools of thread (used for tying feathers to arrows), beautiful red fabric with which the men will make loincloths. From Paris we brought about a dozen kilos of fine beads in black, white, red and blue. I was surprised by the quantities, but Lizot simply said: "You'll see when we get there. This will go faster than you think." The Yanomami are big consumers; these preparations are necessary, not only for us to be well received, but to be received at all.

A small two-engine sea plane picks us up. The pilot doesn't want to take all of our cargo because of its weight. So we leave the food. We will rely on the Indians. Four hours later, after flying over the savanna, then over the beginnings of the great Amazonian forest, we land 1200 kilometers to the south, at the confluence of the Ocamo and the Orinoco, on a runway built ten years ago by the Salesian mission. A brief stop, just long enough to greet the missionary, a large, friendly, cheerful Italian with a prophet's beard; we load the canoe, the motor is attached, and we leave. Four hours upstream in a canoe.

Shall we praise the Orinoco? It deserves it. Even at its source, this river is not young, but old and impatient, rolling forcefully from meander to meander. Thousands of kilometers from its delta it is still very wide. Were it not for the noise of the motor and the water sliding beneath the hull, it would seem as though we were not moving. There is no scenery; everything is the same, each section of space identical to the next: water, sky, and on both banks, infinite lines of sweeping forest.... We will soon see all of this from its interior. Great white birds emerge from trees and fly stupidly in front of us. Eventually, they realize they must tack and fly behind us. A few tortoises from time to time, an alligator, a large venomous stingray blending in with the sand bank.... Nothing much. It is during the night that the animals come out.

Twilight. Hillsides like pyramids rise from the dense vegetation. The Indians never climb them: evil spirits lurk there. We pass the mouth of the Mavaca, a tributary of the left bank. Several hundred meters to go. A shadowy figure wielding a small torch runs along a steep bank and catches the rope we throw him: we have arrived at Mavaca, inhabited by the Bichaansiteri. Lizot has built a house here, very close to their *chabuno* (collective living quarters). A warm reunion for the ethnologist and his savages; the Indians are visibly happy to see him again (he is, it is true, a very generous white man). One question is settled immediately: I am his older brother.... Already the night is filled with the songs of shamans.

We wasted no time. The next day at dawn, a visit to the Patanawateri. It is rather far: half a day of navigation, up river once again, and then a full day of walking, at an Indian's pace. Why this expedition? The mother of one of Lizot's young crew members is a native of this tribe, although she married into another. For several weeks, she has been visiting her relatives. Her son wants to see her. (This filial desire actually masks a completely different desire. We will come back to this.) It gets a bit complicated in that the son's tribe (the father's) and the mother's native tribe are arch enemies. The young man, old enough to make a good warrior, quite simply risks being pierced with an arrow if he shows up there. But the Patanawateri leader, the boy's maternal uncle, informed the warriors: "Death to he who touches my sister's son!" In short, we can go.

It is no picnic. The entire southern zone of the Orinoco is particularly swampy: we are sometimes plunged waist level into flooded lowlands, our feet tangled in roots, and have to pull away from the mud's suction — we must, after all, keep up with the others, who burst out laughing when they see a *Nabe* having problems. We imagine all the furtive life forms in the water (great venomous snakes) and forge ahead through the same forest, unexposed to sky or sun. Amazonia, a lost paradise? It depends on for whom. I find it rather infernal. Let us not speak of it further.

As night falls, we set up camp in the nick of time at a temporary site. We set up the hammocks, light the fires and eat what we have, mostly bananas grilled in ash. We watch our neighbors to make sure they don't take more. Our guide, a middle-aged man, has been graced with an incredible appetite. He would gladly finish off my share. He can wait.

The next day around noon, a quick bath in a stream. This is etiquette; the *chabuno* is not far off, and it is only fitting that we be clean when we present ourselves. We lose no time penetrating the very large gardens where hundreds of banana trees grow. Our two young boys paint their faces with *urucu.* A few steps away the great circular awning stands. We quickly make our way over to the section occupied by the maternal aunts of our friend Hebewe. A surprise: with the exception of three or four old men, there is not a single man. It is an enormous *chabuno,* sheltering more than one hundred and fifty people. Scores of children play in the central area, skeletal dogs bark weakly. Hebewe's mother and aunts, squatting, launch into a long litany of recriminations against their son and nephew. The mother finds him insufficiently attentive: "I've been waiting for you for so long. You haven't come. What misfortune to have a son like you!" As for him, stretched out in his hammock, he affects the most total indifference. That done, we are received, that is to say, they bring us hot banana puree (entirely welcome). In fact, during our three-day visit, Hebewe's mother, a fine and charming savage lady, offers us food at all hours of the day in small quantities each time: forest fruits, little crabs and swamp fish, tapir meat. Green bananas grilled in ash accompany everything. This is like vacation; we eat, we swing in hammocks, we chat, we fart. (The Yanomami are true artists in this regard, because of the favorable effects of the bananas. In the nocturnal silence, there is a constant fusillade. As for our own decibel level, ours are hard to hear, and hard for us to hear....) There are worse fates.

To be honest, the peaceful slowness of things is due in part to the absence of men. The women are much more reserved, less given to insolence than their husbands, who have all gone to war against an enemy tribe, the Hasubueteri. A Yanomami war is a surprise raid: they attack at dawn when people are still asleep, flinging their arrows over the roofs. Those injured, the rare casualties, are most often accidents, in the way of the arrow's fall. The attackers then flee as quickly as possible, for the others immediately counter-attack. We would gladly have awaited the warriors' return for it was, Lizot informed me, a very impressive ceremony. But one can never visit for long before becoming a nuisance, and moreover, our companions are rather anxious to leave. They have done what they set out to do, and are not interested in prolonging their stay. The day we arrived, Hebewe spoke with his mother at length. He questioned her about his relatives, wanting to know who his cousins were. But the rascal is hardly concerned with enriching his genealogical knowledge; what he wants to know is who is he not related to, in other words, which girls he can sleep with. Indeed, in his own tribe — the Karohiteri — he is related to almost everyone (all the women are off limits). He must look for them elsewhere as a result. This is the primary goal of his trip. He will attain it. At nightfall, his own aunts bring him a fourteen- or fifteen- year-old girl. They are both in the same hammock, next to mine. Judging from the commotion, the violent movements wresting the hammock, the stifled murmurs, it doesn't seem to be going well, the girl doesn't want to. They struggle for quite some time, she manages to get away. We make fun of Hebewe. But he doesn't give up, for a few minutes later, a darling twelve- or thirteen- year-old girl comes in, her breasts barely developed. She wants to, and their frolicking goes on all night, extremely discreetly. He must have had sex with her seven or eight times. She can't complain.

A few minutes before leaving, the distribution of presents. All those who want something get it, depending on our stock of course, and always in exchange for something else: arrowheads, quivers, feathers, earrings, or else a sort of credit: "Give me some fishing line. When you come back, I'll give you some fish." Among themselves, the Yanomami never give anything for nothing. It is fitting to behave accordingly. Besides, the exchange of goods is not only a transaction that satisfies both parties, it is an obligation: to refuse an offer of exchange (it is practically unthinkable) would be interpreted as an act of hostility, as a perpetration whose end result could be war. "As for myself, I'm a very generous man. And you?" people say when they arrive here. "Do you have many objects in your bag? Here, take these bananas."

An exhausting return, accomplished in a day. The boys are afraid of running into warriors on their way back; one never knows what may happen. One of them insists on taking Lizot's backpack: "Walk ahead with your rifle. If the raiders attack, you will defend us." We arrive at the river in the evening, without having run into anyone. But along the way, they point out a small area off to the side. Last year, a warrior who was injured during an attack died here en route. His companions erected a funeral pyre to burn the body and bring the ashes back to the *chabuno*.

Two days of rest at home. We need it. The Bichaansiteri make up a rather large tribe; they have divided themselves into two *chabunos,* one on the right bank of the Orinoco, and one on the other side. A Salesian mission (there are three in the area, all at the edge of the river) has been set up at the site of the first *chabuno,* and the second, on our side, is inhabited by a family of Yankee Protestants. They don't surprise me, I've seen their likes elsewhere: fanatic, brutish, practically illiterate. So much the better. It is a pleasure to confirm the vastness of evangelical failure. (The Salesians are no more successful, but the Indians tolerate them more easily.) The leader and shaman of the right bank tribe complain about the American who preaches incessantly against the use of drugs, claims that the *Hékoura* (spirits invoked constantly by the sorcerers) do not exist, and that the leader should give up two of his three wives. Amen! "That guy is starting to annoy us. This year we are going to rebuild the *chabuno* much further away to distance ourselves from him." We heartily approve. What torment for this peasant from Arkansas to hear the drug-intoxicated shamans dance and sing every night in the *chabuno*.... This proves to him the devil's existence.

Tumult. Shouting. A ceremonial procession in the middle of the afternoon. Everyone is on the steep bank, the men are armed with bows and clubs, the leader brandishes his axe. What is this? A man from the tribe across the way has come to abduct a married woman. The offended party's people pile into canoes, cross the river and demand justice from the others. And there, for at least an hour, there is an explosion of insults, hysterical vociferation, howled accusation. It looks as though they will kill each other off, and yet the whole thing is rather entertaining. The old women from both camps are veritable rabble-rousers. They encourage the men to fight with terrifying rage and fury. The cuckold is motionless, leaning on his club: he is challenging the other man to fight one on one. But the man and his mistress have fled into the forest. As a result, no duel. Little by little, the clamor stops, and everyone quite simply goes back home. Much of it was theatrical, though the sincerity of the actors cannot be denied. Besides, many men have large scars on the tops of their shaved heads, collected during the course of these duels. As for the cuckold, he will get his wife back in a few days, when, exhausted from love and fasting, she reenters domestic life. She will surely be punished. The Yanomami are not always gentle with their wives.

Although not as powerful as the Orinoco, the Ocamo is a great river. The landscape is as tedious as ever, a continuous forest, but navigating makes it less so: one must look out for sand banks, rocks just beneath the water's surface, enormous trees that block the current. Here we are en route to the Upper Ocamo, territory of the Shiitari, as the southern Yanomami call them. Three Indians are with us, including Hebewe and the leader of the Bichaansiteri of the right bank. Just as we were leaving, he showed up dressed from head to toe in a shirt whose tails reached his calves, pants, and, most surprising, tennis shoes. Usually, he is naked, as is almost everyone else, his penis attached by the foreskin to a small cord knotted around his waist. He explains: "The Shiitari are great sorcerers. They will probably cast spells on all the paths. With these, my feet will be protected." He wanted to come with us because his older brother whom he hasn't seen in at least twenty years lives there. As for us, we want to visit new tribes and do business with them. Since the whole trip is by water, we can bring a lot of objects with us; there is no weight limit as there is when on foot.

The topography has gradually changed. A chain of hills dominates the right bank, the forest gives way to a kind of savanna with sparse vegetation. We can clearly see a waterfall, sparkling in the sun's rays. On this evening's menu: a duck Lizot killed earlier today. I demand that it be grilled and not boiled as usual. The Indians consent reluctantly. While waiting for it to cook,

I wander off. Scarcely two hundred meters away, I come upon a temporary campsite. This forest, for a white man surrounded by all of nature's hostilities, teems with secret human life; it is traveled, crossed, inhabited by the Yanomami from top to bottom. It is rare to walk an hour or two without coming across a trace of their passage: campsites of hunters on expeditions, visiting tribes, groups of people collecting wild fruit.

The duck is soon cooked, overcooked even. We eat it. Even without salt, it is good. But only ten minutes later, our three companions begin to whimper:

"We're sick! We're so sick!"

"What's wrong?"

"You made us eat raw meat!"

Their bad faith is cynical, but there is something comic in watching these sturdy men rub their bellies and look as though they will burst into tears. Surprised perhaps by our teasing, they decide that to cure themselves they will have to eat a little more. One goes off to fish, another (who knows how to shoot) takes the rifle and tries to retrieve the forest partridge we heard singing in the vicinity... One gunshot goes off, and a partridge is killed. The fisherman soon returns with two big piranhas. These waters are swarming with the cannibal-fish. If the partridge flesh is delicious, the fish on the other hand is tasteless. This does not prevent the Indians from boiling everything all at once in a stew... Soon, all that is left are the bones.

The next day, we come across four canoes. The Yanomami go down the river to trade with the downstream tribes. The boats are filled with packages of drugs. All the Indians (at least the men) are great users of *ebena*, and the shamans would not be able to function without consuming (snorting) it in very strong dosages. But the trees that produce these hallucinogenic seeds do not grow everywhere, so that certain tribes, such as those of Sierra Parima, hardly have any at all. On the other hand, the Shiitari maintain a quasi-monopoly on production of the drug; they do not even need to cultivate the trees, which grow naturally on the savanna of their region. They harvest much of it, and through successive trade agreements from tribe to tribe, *ebena* eventually reaches those who are deprived of it.

We stop for a few moments to chat with the Indians. Upon learning that we've planned a visit to their home, three of them — two young men and one older man — jump into our canoe and go back up with us. Shortly before noon, we arrive at a small cove. These are the Aratapora rapids. According to our passengers, the *chabuno* is still far away. We have, therefore, to unload the canoe, carry the baggage five hundred meters up the river, then pull the canoe through foaming waters. The current is strong, but there are a lot of us. Almost two hours of effort nonetheless. We rest for a moment at the edge of the cove. The area is pretty, the forest less suffocating, revealing a beach of fine sand from which emerge enormous boulders. Dozens of grooves, some more than two centimeters deep, are etched in the surface: these are blade polishers. Everything one might need for the manufacture of polished stone hatchets is here: the sand, the water, the stone. But it is not the Yanomami who desecrate the boulders this way; they do not know how to work with rock. From time to time, they will find a polished hatchet in the forest or at the river's edge, and think it the work of the spirits of the sky. They will use it to crush *ebena* seeds against the bottom of a clay pot. Who were these patient polishers? We do not know. In any case, they were former occupants of current Yanomami territory and have disappeared, probably centuries ago. All that remain are the traces of their labor, scattered throughout the region.

We reload the canoe, head off and arrive fifteen minutes later: the *chabuno* is actually quite close to the rapids, whose rushing we can still hear. The Indians have lied to us. What they wanted was to show up at their home with White Men in a motor boat. They allowed us to struggle for two hours, when we could have easily finished the trip on foot. Now, they are beside themselves with pride and are acting cocky. The inhabitants (about fifty) are calling from the bank. Among them, a man with a goatee, our Bichaansiteri companion's brother. They recognize each other immediately. The older brother is very excited, gesticulates and talks a lot as he takes us to his house. The younger brother is no less happy, but doesn't let it show, as is fitting for a visitor. Stretched out in his hammock, one hand over his mouth, an expression of feigned displeasure on his face, he lets some time go by. Then we have some banana puree, and we can relax. Such are the rules of etiquette.

To celebrate the event, the older brother organizes a drug session and prepares the *ebena*. Several men run under their tents and reappear more or less dressed up. Two robust fellows have donned long dresses: they are not aware of the difference between men and women's clothing. Our companions, more accustomed to the business of white men, have no reservations about poking fun at these bumpkins. The missionaries have an imbecilic mania to distribute clothing to the Indians for which they have absolutely no use, as opposed to metallic tools, fishing line, etc., undeniably more useful in that they facilitate their work. These second-hand clothes, soon filthy, are pure prestige items for their new owners. The critique continues when the food is offered: "These people are savages! They serve their guests ungutted fish!"

Crushed, then dried and mixed with another vegetable substance, *ebena*, a fine, green powder, is ready to be consumed: a reed tube is filled and your neighbor blows it up your nose by exhaling powerfully into your nostrils. All the men, crouched in a circle, take some. They sneeze, cough, grimace, spit, drool: the drug is good, pleasingly strong, everyone is happy. A good start to a shamanic session. The visiting brother, who holds a position of leadership in his tribe, is also a mid-level shaman. Lower level shamans treat their families or dogs. These animals, recently acquired from whites, occupy a place in the hierarchy of beings approaching human: like people, they are burned when they die. But the Indians have little respect for them: they scarcely feed them. As a result, dogs have taken over garbage collection at the *chabunos*.

The most esteemed shamans exceed others in experience, skill, the number of chants they know, and spirits they can invoke. Among the Bichaan-siteri, there is one of this caliber. He officiates almost daily, even when no one is sick (and so he needs a lot of drugs). This is because the community must be constantly protected from the illnesses and evil spirits that shamans from enemy tribes mobilize against it. He himself makes sure to expel all the diseases capable of annihilating the others. Among the Indians, a nation of ghosts haunts the world of men. The chants, an obsessive repetition of the same melodic line, nevertheless allow for certain vocal variations: they sometimes oscillate between a Gregorian chant and pop music. Beautiful to hear, they match exactly the slow movement of the dance, the to and fro of arms crossed or raised up along the tent awnings. Shamed be anyone who doubts the seriousness of these rites (it is, after all, a matter of life and death). And yet, the shaman will stop from time to time to tell his wife: "Hurry and bring some bananas to relative so-and-so! We forgot to give him some!" Or else, approaching us: "Listen, Lizot! I need some fishing line!" And, quite simply, he continues his service.

We have gone up the Ocamo a bit once again to do some night hunting, which has brought us an unexpected encounter. A small Yanomami tribe has just set itself up at the river's edge, and their *chabuno* is not quite finished. We are their first whites, we are the exotic ones this time. For us, they are hardly different from the others, there are no surprises. All the tribes now possess metallic instruments, even those with whom contact will not be established for years. As a result, differences between groups at the edge of the Orinoco and those of the interior are slight: among the former, there is a look of beggarliness (due to the clothes) but that is not deeply ingrained, since social and religious life has not at all been affected by the missionaries' vain attempts (at least not up until now). In short, there are no "civilized" Yanomami (with all the repugnant degradation which that state signifies) to contrast with still "savage" Yanomami: they are all, equally, proud and warlike pagans.

Four young men gesticulate on the bank. We dock. They are blessedly euphoric and do not hide it. Their excitement before the *Nabe* is so great that they have difficulty expressing themselves; a torrent of words is halted by the clicking of their tongues, while they hop in place and mark the rhythm by slapping their thighs. It is a true pleasure to see and hear them rejoice like this. The Shiitari are likable. Upon leaving, a few hours later, we offer them three crocodiles that Lizot has killed.

On the day of departure, we exchange our goods for drugs. Not for personal use, but to exchange with the Parima tribes, which are sorely deprived of them. This will be an excellent passport for us. The leader is happy, he did good business with his brother's people, who promise to visit him again. In exchange for all his clothes (which he knows the missionaries will easily replace), he has obtained a lot of *ebena*. As we push off from the shore, an incident: one of the two boys we took up river with us (he must have been about thirteen or fourteen years old) suddenly jumps into the canoe. He wants to go with us, see the country. A woman — his mother — throws herself into the water to hold him back. He then seizes a heavy paddle and tries to hit her. Other women come to the rescue and manage to extract him, raging madly, from the canoe. He bites his mother. Yanomami society is very liberal with respect to boys. They are allowed to do just about anything they want. They are even encouraged from early childhood to demonstrate their violence and aggression. Children play games that are often brutal, a rare thing among the Indians, and parents avoid consoling them when, having received a hit on the head with a stick, they come running and bawl:

"Mother! He hit me!"

"Hit him harder!"

The (desired) result of this pedagogy is that it forms warriors.

We pass over the rapids easily. It is a reverse procession of the same space. It is just as dull. We spend the night camping in the open. We have already slept a few hours when suddenly there is a downpour. As quickly as possible, we take down the hammocks and somehow take shelter beneath large leaves. It passes, we go back to bed, go back to sleep. One hour later, it starts all over again: rain, waking up with a start, running for cover, etc. A terrible New Year's Eve.

Returning to Mavaca, we learn the outcome of the combat two weeks earlier, which had set the Patanawateri against the Hasubueteri. The results are grave: four deaths, it seems, (out of a unit of forty to fifty men) amont the latter, three by firearm. What happened? For this raid, the Patanawateri allied with another tribe, the Mahekodoteri, a very bellicose people, permanently at war with almost all the tribes in the region. (They would gladly do Lizot in; he is a friend of their enemies.) One of the three Salesian missions was established near their *chabuno*. That says a lot about the failure of the priests who, after close to fifteen years, have not been able to temper the Indians' warlike ardor one iota. Just as well. This resistance is a sign of health.

Still the fact remains that the Mahekodoteri possess three or four rifles, a gift from the missionaries with the promise that they be used only for hunting and not for war. But try to convince warriors to renounce an easy victory. These are not saints. This time they fought like whites, but against the arrows of other Yanomami. This was not unforeseeable. The attackers — there must have been about twenty-four — let a volley of arrows fly over the *chabuno* at dawn, then retreated into the forest. But instead of running back to the path leading to their territory, they waited for the counterattack. When a group is attacked, the warriors must launch a counter-offensive, lest they be considered cowards. This would soon be known, and their *chabuno* would become a target for other tribes (to carry off their women, steal their goods, and, quite simply, for the pleasure of war). The Hasubueteri, thus, fell in ambush. The rifles, which they were not expecting at all, exploded, a man fell. The others finished him off with arrows. Stunned, his companions fled in confusion. They threw themselves into the Orinoco to swim across it. And there, three of them perished, two from bullet wounds, one from an arrow. One of the wounded, fished out, received a final blow: a bow thrust into his stomach.... The hatred for the enemy is strong.... Now, the Hasubueteri are preparing their revenge. Passions are passed on from father to son.

Somewhat panicked by these events, the missionaries, strongly urged by Lizot, decide to no longer furnish munitions to the Indians. A wise decision, for the Mahekodoteri, exalted by this initial success, would from now on use their rifles in every combat, and assured of their superiority, would multiply the raids. There could be large-scale slaughters that would have been practically impossible with arrows. (Except in the very rare cases where a group invites another to a party with the deliberate intention of massacring them upon arrival. It was in this way that several years ago thirty Bichaansiteri lost their lives, responding to an invitation from southern tribes: they were treacherously shot by arrows in the *chabuno*.)

We have spent the first three weeks of January peacefully traveling back and forth between Mavaca and the tribes of the Manaviche riverside, another tributary of the Orinoco. We are famished and have been eating at the Indians' in short visits of two to three days. Even if there is no meat or fish, there are always bananas (more than six kinds are cultivated). Staying with the Karohiteri, Lizot's best friends, is very pleasant. We relax there, the people are friendly, not very demanding, even given to kindness. The shaman offers me tapir meat and urges me to remain among them. This is a change from the other tribes where, having just arrived, one is immediately accosted: "Give me this, give me that. I've run out of fishhooks, I need a machete.

What do you have in your bag? Your knife is nice!" And this goes on constantly. They are tireless, and were it not for the strong impression Lizot has made on them, they would quite simply try to steal our things. The few sentences I have learned and remember, having said them hundreds of times, are: "I don't have enough. There isn't any. We don't have any more. Wait! Later!" The tiresome Yanomami.

They do have a sense of humor and are quite prone to jokes. To start with, they avoid telling the truth on principle (even among themselves). They are incredible liars. As a result, a long process of verification and inspection is required to validate a piece of information. When we were in the Parima we crossed a road. When asked about its destination, the young man who was guiding us said he didn't know (he had traveled this path maybe fifty times).

"Why are you lying?"

"I don't know."

When I asked the name of a bird one day, they gave me the term that signifies penis, another time, tapir. The young men are particularly droll:

"Come with us into the garden. We'll sodomize you!"

During our visit with the Patanawateri, Hebewe calls over a boy around twelve years old:

"If you let yourself be sodomized, I'll give you my rifle."

Everyone bursts into laughter. It is a very good joke. Young men are merciless with visitors their age. They are dragged into the gardens under some pretext and there, held down while the others uncap their penis, the supreme humiliation. A running joke: You're slumbering innocently in your hammock when an explosion plunges you into a nauseating cloud. An Indian has just farted two or three centimeters from your face...

Life in the *chabunos* is generally monotonous. As everywhere else, ruptures in the customary order — wars, festivals, brawls, etc. — do not occur every day. The most evident activity is the preparation of food and the processes by which it is obtained (bows, arrows, rope, cotton). Let us not think for a minute that the Indians are undernourished. Between basic farming, hunting (game is relatively abundant), fishing and harvesting, the Yanomami get along very well. An affluent society, then, from a certain perspective, in that all people's needs are met, even more than met, since there is surplus production, consumed during celebrations. But the order of needs are ascetically determined (in this sense, the missionaries create an artificial need for unnecessary clothing among certain tribes). Furthermore, fertility, infanticide and natural selection assure tribes of a demographic optimum, we might say, as much in quantity as in quality. The bulk of infant mortality occurs in the first two years: the most resistant survive. Hence, the flourish-

THE ARCHEOLOGY OF VIOLENCE

ing, vigorous appearance of almost everyone, men and women, young and old. All of these bodies are worthy of going naked.

It is uniformly said in South America that Indians are lazy. Indeed, they are not Christians and do not deem it necessary to earn their bread by the sweat of their brow. And since, in general, they are most concerned with taking other people's bread (only then do their brows sweat), we see that for them joy and work fall outside of one another. That said, we should note that among the Yanomami, all the needs of society are covered by an average of three hours of work per person, per day (for adults). Lizot calculated this with chronometric rigor. This is nothing new, we already know that this is how it is in most primitive societies. Let us remember this at sixty when demanding our retirement funds.

It is a civilization of leisure since they spend twenty-one hours doing nothing. They keep themselves amused. Siestas, practical jokes, arguments, drugs, eating, taking a dip, they manage to kill time. Not to mention sex. Which is not to say that that is all they think about, but it definitely counts. *Ya peshi!* This is often heard: I feel like having sex!... One day, at Mavaca, a man and a woman struggle on the floor of a house. There are cries, screams, protests, laughter. The woman, who seems to know what she wants, has slipped a hand between the man's legs and grabbed a testicle. At his slightest move to flee, a slight squeeze. This must hurt, but she doesn't let go: "She wants to copulate! She feels like copulating!" And this, it seems, is indeed what happens.

As if relations between people were not enough to nourish community life, natural phenomena become social events. This is because, in a certain way, there is no nature: a climatic disorder, for example, immediately translates into cultural terms. One late afternoon among the Karohiteri, a storm breaks out, preceded by violent whirlwinds which threaten to carry away the roofs. Immediately, all the shamans (six or seven of them, the great one and the lesser ones) position themselves along the tents, standing, attempting to push back the tornado with great cries and grand gestures. Lizot and I are recruited to contribute our arms and voices. For this wind, these gusts, are in fact evil spirits, surely sent by shamans from an enemy tribe.

Sharp cries, at once urgent and plaintive, suddenly burst forth all over Mavaca. About twenty women have spread all around the *chabuno*. Each is armed with a fistful of twigs with which she beats the ground. It looks as though they are trying to extract something. This turns out to be the case. A child is gravely ill, his soul has left him; the women are looking for it, summoning it to reenter the body and restore health to the little one. They find it, and, forming a line, push it in front of them in the direction of the *chabuno*, waving their bouquets. They are both graceful and fervent.... The shaman stands beside us. Spontaneously, he starts telling the myth that is the basis and foundation of this female ritual. Lizot takes furious notes. The man then asks whether women do the same thing in our country: "Yes, but that was long ago. We've forgotten everything." We feel poor.

I have seen the rites of death as well. This was among the Karohiteri.... Around midnight, the low chant of the shaman awakens us; he is trying to cure someone. This lasts for a while, then he is quiet. A great lament then rises into the night, a tragic chorus of women before the irremediable: a child dies. The parents and grandparents chant around the small cadaver curled in its mother's arms. All night, all morning, without a moment of interruption. The next day, the broken, hoarse voices are heartrending. The other women of the tribe participate in the mourning in shifts, the men do not leave their hammocks. It is oppressive. Beneath the sun, the father, still chanting, prepares the pyre. Meanwhile, the grandmother dances around it, her dead grandson in a kind of sling: five or six steps forward, two or three back. All the women are united beneath the funeral tent, the men surround the pyre, bows and arrows in their hands.

When the father places the body onto the pyre, the women burst into low sobs, all the men cry, a similar pain goes through us. We cannot resist the contagion. The father breaks his bow and arrows and throws them into the fire. Smoke rises and the shaman rushes forward to make it to go straight up to the sky, for it contains evils spirits. About five hours later, when the ashes are cold, a close relative takes a basket and meticulously collects any fragments of bone that were not burned. Reduced to powder and preserved in a calabash, they will give rise to a funeral festival later on. The following day at dawn, everyone has gone down to the river — the women and children in order to purify themselves carefully, the men to wash their arrows, soiled by the baleful emanations of smoke.

Around the twentieth of January, we are on the road for an expedition into the Sierra Parima. We first have to go up the Orinoco for almost two days. As we pass the Mahekodoteri *chabuno,* several Indians threaten us with words and gestures. Lizot is careful to stay exactly in the middle of the river; they would be quite capable of lancing a few arrows at us. Easy passage of the first rapid. A huge otter dozes on a rock, then plunges in, hardly disturbing the water's surface. Before we know it, our companions have set up camp for the night, cutting vines with their teeth. It is clear that were the supply of metal tools suddenly to run out, it would not have much bearing on the Indians: they would go back to their old methods (fire replacing metal). Lizot kills a large capybara, but we lose it, and the current carries it off. Hoping that a trunk might have stopped it, we look for it for an hour, in vain. It's a shame, since this was at least fifty kilos of good meat. We find a polisher here as well. The next day another rapid stops us, but we do not cross it, for, from here on in, we will continue on foot. Upriver, the Orinoco is practically unnavigable. Losing its majestic proportions, it is transformed little by little into a torrent. We are very close to its source, discovered not too long ago.

Our day ends, and we spend the night in the Shuimiweiteri *chabuno,* which dominates a high, rocky impasse. The normal rites of welcome take place, we give the chief drugs, which are rare here, and which are immediately prepared and consumed. "Stay with us," he insists. "Do not go to see the others. They are bad!" These good apostles are hardly thinking of our welfare. What is bothering them are the presents that will be distributed to the other tribes: they would gladly be the recipients of this manna. They give us a guide nonetheless. Quite often, a group will invite another to engage in trade, then at the last minute decide that it has given more than it has received. Without another thought, they will catch up to the others, who have left, and use threat to demand that the gifts be returned, although they themselves will not return what they have received from their partners. The idea of a contract would no doubt be laughable to them. Their word is one thing they would never dream of giving. We will have to deal with it as best we can.

In the course of the night, the increasingly loud cries of a sick young woman wake everyone up. The diagnosis is immediate: a ghost has seized the woman's animal double, an otter. The other women make the patient walk up and down, imitating all the cries of the animal in order to make it come back. The treatment is effective, for at dawn, she wakes up cured.... Societies, one might say, only allow themselves those illnesses they know how to treat; the field of pathology has more or less been mastered. It is no doubt because of this that our own civilization, able to discover so many new remedies through science and technology, is so besieged by illness. The way to a middle ground between the two is not evident. Too bad for us.

The Parima is not really a chain of mountains with valleys below. It is rather a disorderly herd of conical and pyramid-shaped mountains, pressed up against each other, often more than a thousand meters high and separated at their base by swampy lowlands. Between the *chabunos* of the region, the paths follow crests: we climb, descend, climb again, etc. It is an effort, but all things considered, less tiring (if one is in good health) than wallowing through stagnating water or slipping on the rotten tree trunks that serve as bridges. After four hours, we reach the Ihirubiteri. We hardly stop there (just long enough to drop off some *ebena* so that we will be welcome on our way back) despite their insistence that we stay (again, a matter of the gifts to be distributed to the others). We forge ahead, and it is long. Happily, everything has an end, and toward evening, we come to the Matowateri.

There are compensations. It was worth coming all this way.

We penetrate the *chabuno* and immediately there is an incredible ovation. They recognize Lizot. We are surrounded by dozens of men brandishing bows and arrows, shouting and dancing around us: "*Shori! Shori!* Brother-in-law! Brother-in-law! Take these bananas, and these! We are friends! *Nohi!* Friends!" When there are too many bunches in our outstretched arms, they remove them and replace them with others. This is pure joy. Hallelujah! *Hei! Hei!* They allow us to rest a bit, but not long enough. For I am soon snapped up, seized and transported by a bunch of fanatics yelling incomprehensible things in unison. What is this?

First of all, there is a visiting tribe in the (therefore overcrowded) *chabuno* that has never seen whites. The men, intimidated at first, stay behind the others, barely daring to look at us (the women remain beneath the awnings). But they soon lose their reservations; they approach us, touch us, and from that moment on, there is no stopping them. Second, they are much more interested in me than in Lizot. Why? I cannot explain this without describing myself a bit. During our walks, we wear shorts and tennis shoes and, of course, go bare-chested. Our bodies are exposed, and consequently, so is the body hair adorning my pectorals (nothing extreme, let me assure you). And this fascinates the Indians who have nothing more to show than Lizot in this regard. I am the first featherless biped they've met. They do not hide their enthusiasm: "*A koï!* He is so hairy! *Wa koï!* You are a strange hairy man! Just like a big anteater! He is a veritable anteater! Have you seen this hairy man?" They cannot get over it, raving and insisting that I take a complete tour of the *chabuno* so that the women, lounging in their hammocks, might witness the spectacle from the comfort of their own homes. What to do? No one asks my opinion, and there I am, a strange animal paraded from awning to awning amidst a deafening chorus of exclamations (see above). Meanwhile, I am hardly in a state to rejoice, since I feel rather like Jesus in the Passion. For the women are not content to look or touch: they pull, they grab to see if it is well-attached, and I have a very hard time protecting my *guillery*. Moments like this stay with you. In the process, I've collected quite a few bananas. Which is better than nothing.... During all of this, the charitable Lizot has been doubled over with laughter.

During our stay, there was a beautiful shamanism session. Our drugs were welcome. The shaman danced and chanted and waged a tough battle against an evil spirit, which he finally succeeded in imprisoning in a basket. He then killed it with a hatchet and, completely exhausted by the struggle, fell to the floor, panting. The spectators warmly encouraged him.

Instead of plunging deeper into the Parima, we have turned back. This is no loss. We have stopped at the Ihirubiteri *chabuno* where we briefly rested on the way. And here we were able to attend the Yanomami's most solemn festival, the *reahu*, the ritual consumption of the ashes of the dead. Some distance from the chabuno, we crossed a provisional campsite, occupied by guests of the Ihirubiteri. They were getting ready for the afternoon's festivities, but they still found time to force our hand: a few cans of hooks, a few spools of fishing line; it's always the same.

The leader settles us next door to him in the *chabuno* and offers us banana and sweet potato puree. He is in possession of an enormous pair of testicles which swing gracefully. They make a strong impression on us. Their owner seems to think he is normal. While the visitors are getting ready, things are just as busy here. Every man carefully tidies the front of his dwelling with little sweeps of his hand or a small broom. Soon the area is cleared of droppings, bits of animal and fish bones, broken baskets, fruit pits, and scraps of wood. When everything is clean, everyone goes to bed and there is a brief resting period.

Then the festival begins. As though propelled, two boys about twelve years old burst into the *chabuno,* and run, bows and arrows raised, dancing around its entire circumference in opposite directions of each other. They inaugurate the visitors' dance of introduction. They exit at the same time and are immediately followed by two adolescents, and then by the men, two by two, singing. Every five or six steps, they stop and dance in place, sometimes flinging their weapons to the floor. Some brandish machetes or metallic hatchets. Lizot points out that they usually exhibit the objects that they intend to trade during the dance. This way the others know what to expect ahead of time and can begin their calculations.

Shouts and whistles stream from all the awnings: the spectators approve, applaud, cheer, yell out their admiration at the top of their lungs. Are they being sincere? In getting to know the Yanomami, I am suspicious, and imagine that secretly they must be saying to themselves, "These people are not even capable of dancing properly." I myself cannot hold back my praise. All of them are magnificently painted, and circles and lines of *urucu* and black *genipa* undulate and stir on their naked bodies. Others are painted white. Some display sumptuous feather ornaments on their ears and arms. The hard afternoon light sparks the richest hues of the forest.

Once the men have paraded out in pairs (this time the women do not dance), they come together to do a sort of honorary walk to the same rhythm and to the sound of the same chants. The point simply is: it is beautiful.

As soon as the visitors have gone back into the *chabuno,* the rite that is the reason for this festival is celebrated. Men from both tribes who are related to the dead person will eat his ashes. The women and children are excluded from the meal. An enormous leaf tied at both ends — it looks like a rowboat — has been filled to the brim with banana puree. I am not sure how much there is exactly, but it must be dozens of kilos. The ashes are blended into the puree, whose taste is probably not even altered. It is cannibalism, to be sure, since the dead are being eaten, but in a very attenuated form compared to what exists elsewhere in South America. The participants crouch around the vessel and dip their calabashes into it. The women's chants of mourning set the atmosphere for the men's funereal banquet. All of this is carried out without ostentation; non-participants go on with their activities, or their passivity. And yet, the festival of the *reahu* is a crucial moment in tribal life. Sacredness is in the air. They would take a dim view of us were we to approach this Holy Communion. As for taking pictures, that would be unthinkable.... Things involving death must be handled with care.

It is then the hosts' turn to be polite to the visitors. Painted, feathered and adorned, the men dance. But it is obvious that they put less conviction into it than the others, no doubt thinking it is not worth the effort. Then the people proceed to the trade. The *chabuno* is buzzing. They display their riches, admire the size of arrowheads, the straightness of rods, the solidity of rope, the beauty of ornaments. Things come, go, all in relative silence and in great mutual distrust. The point is not to get a bad deal.

Night has fallen long ago, but the festivities continue. The adolescents of both tribes (there are about twenty or twenty-five) now celebrate a hunting ritual. Singing and dancing all together, bows and arrows raised, they make the night echo, hammering it with their steps. Their singing is full of glorious life.

We have scarcely had a moment's rest. After the young hunters dance, the ritual of separation lasts until dawn, the two tribes saying their good-byes. This consists of an oratorical duel. A man from one tribe, seated, shouts a series of sentences very loudly and very quickly, like a psalmody. From the other end of the *chabuno* his partner responds — he simply has to repeat what the other has said without making a mistake, without omitting a single word, at the same speed. They don't say anything of particular significance to each other, they exchange news, repeated a thousand times, the only pretext an attempt to make the adversary stumble and to ridicule him. When the two men have finished, two others replace them, and so on.

At the first light of day, everything stops. The celebration is over.

The guests receive two enormous packages of food, meat and bananas pre-pared in advance by the *reahu's* organizers and well-packed in leaves (the Yanomami are experts in packaging). This is the signal for departure. Silent and swift, they disappear into the forest....

As we walked toward the Orinoco, we stopped a moment to relieve our-selves. The Indians are always interested in the way we pee. They crouch. The vulgarity of our way consists in letting the stream splash onto the ground and make noise. One of them observed me carefully.

"You pee like an old man. It's all yellow."

This was not a triumphant return, but, something much more subtle. And when Lizot, who was walking ahead, shouted: "Listen! The rapids!" I did not play coy, I did not say: "Already?" I said let's go.

A thousand years of wars, a thousand years of celebrations! That is my wish for the Yanomami. Is this pious? I'm afraid so. They are the last of the besieged. A mortal shadow is being cast on all sides.... And afterwards? Perhaps we will feel better once the final frontier of this ultimate freedom has been broken. Perhaps we will sleep without waking a single time.... Some day, then, oil derricks around the *chabunos,* diamond mines in the hillsides, police on the paths, boutiques on the riverbanks.... Harmony everywhere.

2
SAVAGE ETHNOGRAPHY
(ON *YANOAMA*)

Let us first say that no petty quibbling can alter the respect and fondness this book[1] deserves, which, without hesitation, we can call great. And let us also bear witness to the admiration that the quasi-anonymous author of this startling book, Elena Valero, whose story was tape-recorded by the fortunate Italian doctor, Ettore Biocca, will rouse in the souls of all innocent readers. Having given everybody their due, let us proceed.

This book is, we might say, an autobiography, recounting twenty-two years in a woman's life, which is nevertheless not its central theme, fascinating as it might be. For through the personal experience of Elena Valero, the social life of a primitive society, captured in its most absolute otherness and its most sophisticated wealth, is braced, embraced, described in deft and nuanced strokes: the Indian tribe of the Yanoama who live at the Venezuelan–Brazilian border in the mountains of the Parima. The encounter between Elena Valero and the Indians took place in 1939, when she was eleven years old; a poisoned arrow in her stomach established her first con-

---

First published in *l'Homme*, cahier 1, vol. ix, 1969, pp. 58-65.

[1] Ettore Biocca, *Yanoama. Récit d'une femme brésilienne enleveé par les Indiens*, Paris, Plon, Terre humaine, 1968.

tact with them. A band of warriors attacked her family, poor whites of Brazil in search of precious wood in an area as yet unexplored. The parents and the two brothers fled, leaving Elena in the hands of her assailants, an unwitting spectator to the most brutal and unexpected rupture that one can imagine in the life of a young girl (who could read and write and had had her First Communion). The Indians kidnapped her and adopted her; she became a woman among them, then became the wife of two successive husbands, the mother of four boys. In 1961, after twenty-two years, she abandoned the tribe and the forest to reenter the world of the whites. Thus, Elena Valero spent twenty-two years — scarcely believable for us — in an apprenticeship, undergone at first in pain and tears, which then lessened and was even experienced as happiness, in the savage life of the Yanoama Indians. One might say that through the voice of this woman, whom fate threw into a world beyond our world, forcing her to integrate, assimilate and interiorize the very *substance* of a cultural universe light-years away from her own as the most intimate part of herself, one might say, then, that through Elena Valero's voice, the Indians are actually speaking; that thanks to her, the face of their world and their being-in-this-world are gradually outlined through a free, unconstrained discourse, having come out of her own world, and not ours, juxtaposed with the other without touching it.

In short, for the first time, miraculously, a primitive culture is being recounted by itself; the Neolithic directly exhibits its marvels, an Indian society describes itself *from within*. For the first time, we can slip into the egg without breaking the shell, without breaking and entering: a rare occasion that merits celebration. How was this possible? The answer is obvious: because one day Elena Valero decided to interrupt her great journey, the story of which would otherwise never have been told. Thus, in a way, the Indian world rejected Elena from its breast, despite her long association with it, allowing us to penetrate it through the bias of her book. The woman's departure invites us to consider the child's arrival, this "acculturation" against the grain, which raises the question: how was Elena Valero able to become so profoundly Indian and yet cease to be so? The case is interesting in two ways, first in that it concerns an exceptional personality, secondly in that, through a repercussion, it sheds light on the opposite movement of Indians toward the white world, on this repugnant degradation that the cynical or the naive do not hesitate to christen "acculturation." The young girl's age should command our attention. Her entrance into the Indian world occurred violently, through a kidnapping. But she was, it seems to us, at the perfect age both to deal with the trauma and eventually adapt to her new life, and to maintain a distance from it, to take a step back, however small, which would prevent her from becoming *completely* Indian and would later incite her to decide to return to her first world, one she never totally forgot.[2] Had she been a few years younger, that is, had she not yet perfectly integrated her own original civilization, she would have certainly made a radical leap, would have become a Yanoama, and would never have dreamt of leaving.

Elena Valero is not the only case of a white child abducted by Indians. But they almost always disappear forever. The reason for this is simple: these very young children soon die, or more likely, lose all memory of their place of origin. Elena's difference, luckily for us, is that she was already irreversibly white at eleven years of age, a person from the western world. In her story, we clearly see that after twenty-two years, she had not completely forgotten her native Portuguese, which she still understood well. And let us note that for many years after her capture, she could still recite a few "Our Fathers" and a few "Hail Marys" if she found herself in a critical situation. On the other hand, had she been older, that is, almost fully grown (for a girl), she might not have been able to withstand the shock as well, and would not have manifested the surprising will to live which allowed her to emerge safe and sound from difficulties we can only imagine. While still preadolescent, she had to flee her hosts' *chabuno* and live in the forest alone for seven months without fire (her attempts, by the way, to make a fire through friction, the Indian method, were in vain). Consequently, her age and her personality surely made the task easier. And let us not forget that this was a woman, that is, an individual much less vulnerable than a man. In other words, for a boy taken at the same age as she was, the work of learning the Indian world might not have been as easily accomplished. A short time after her capture, the young girl met a Brazilian boy her age who had also been kidnapped. Suddenly, he was no longer spoken of. An abducted woman is an extra commodity for the community, a free gift, a bonanza, while a man is a taker of women giving nothing in exchange; the tribe would, in principle, have nothing to gain by letting him live.

Throughout the book, one notices that Elena Valero was as much *faced* with the Indian world as *in* it: one can see her obvious pleasure in observation, a capacity for wonder, a tendency to question and compare. Elena was

---

[2] This to us establishes the difference between a document such as *Yanoama* and the autobiographies of indigenous peoples collected in other parts of the world, in North America in particular. An informant, no matter how great his talent and how good his memory, remains too entrenched in his own world, too close to it, or else, on the contrary, too detached, for his world has been destroyed by contact with our civilization. Ultimately then, there is either the impossibility of speaking, or fatal discourse. This is why an Indian could never have written *Yanoama* and why this book is singular.

able to use these clearly ethnographic talents precisely because she did not allow herself to be engulfed by Indian life, because she had always maintained a bit of a distance, because she was always Napagnouma, Daughter of Whites, not only to her Yanoama companions, but to herself. The savage ethnology that our heroine practices goes as far as contestation; for example, for a long time, she remained skeptical of the Indians' religious beliefs and of the existence of the *Hekoura,* the spirits of plants, animals and nature that inspire the shamans and protect the people. "The women asked me: 'Don't you believe in it?' I replied: 'No, I don't believe in it. I don't see anything and I've never seen a *Hekoura.*'" Certain practices inspired a repulsion in her that she rather imprudently neglected to conceal from the Indians, especially the endocannibal ritual during which the ashes of dead relatives' bones are consumed. There, in its most naked dimension, appears a trace of our culture, namely the horror provoked by anthropophagy. Elena relates the argument (for it is truly an argued *disputatio*) that she had about this with her husband, who said to her: "You, you put your relatives underground where worms eat them; you don't love your people." To which she vehemently replied: "'What I say is true. You burn the body, then you gather the remains and crush them. Even after they are dead, you make them suffer. Then you put the ashes in a stew of bananas and you eat them. Finally, after having eaten them, you go into the forest and you shit them out; the remains still have to go through that.' The *touchawa* looked at me seriously and said: 'Never let anyone ever hear you say that.'" These facts and a thousand others clearly show that Elena preserved a certain freedom in her relationship with the Indians, that she always made an effort to maintain her difference while among them. This signifies that the idea of a return to her people never totally left her, except, we should stress, during the time she was married to her first husband, Fusiwe. In the second part of her narrative, she draws a portrait of him filled with warmth and affection, and ultimately with bitterness as well, from which the crushing figure of a classic hero emerges. Without a doubt, Thévet, whose *Pourtraicts des hommes illustres* includes a portrait of the great chief Tupinamba Coniambec, could have added this one of Fusiwe. Elena's very Indian modesty and discretion when speaking of her husband only further emphasizes the depth of the bond that united her to this man, despite the occasional outbursts of rage, as when he broke her arm with a bludgeon. "I was staying with the Namotri," she recounts, when Fusiwe took her for his wife. "After that day, I no longer tried to escape. Fusiwe was big, he was strong."

So much for Elena Valero. What of the horizon against which this life's quasi-legendary trajectory is outlined? Legendary, indeed, in that this Eurydice returns from the beyond: a beyond in two senses, we would say, since primitive societies such as those of the Yanoama constitute the limit, the beyond of our own civilization, and perhaps, for this reason, the mirror of its own truth, and that, moreover, these very cultures are, from here on in, dead or dying. Thus, in two senses, Napagnouma is a ghost.

What of the Yanoama? The ethnographic richness of the book that describes them is such that one has difficulty fully understanding the swarm of details, the depth and variety of observations mentioned in passing, the precision and the abundance in the description of multiple facets of these tribes' lives. Abandoning, then, the idea of retaining the wealth of material that saturates the narrative, we shall limit ourselves to pointing out a few salient traits. Not without taking a moment, however, to suggest a project which might be of interest. It would consist of ordering and analyzing all the raw material collected here and extracting from it — limiting our reading to *Yanoama* — a sort of monographic study, the results of which would then be measured against those in the four volumes that Biocca has dedicated to these Indians. The comparison would perhaps be fruitful.

The description of endocannibalism is particularly noteworthy. The fact in itself has been recognized for a long time, and we know that the Amazonian Northwest is a bastion of ritual anthropophagy, albeit in a more attenuated form than in other regions. When a person dies, the body is enclosed in a basket and hung on a tree until the flesh disappears, or else the body is burned immediately. But in both cases, the bones are gathered, ground, reduced to powder and preserved in a calabash. Little by little, based on ceremonial needs, they are consumed in a puree of bananas. It is striking to come across the same theory of endocannibalism from the mouths of the Yanoama as that formulated by the Guayaki. And yet Guayaki anthropophagy — unattenuated — is the exact opposite of that of the Yanoama, since they grill the flesh and eat it and throw away the charred bones. But, in both cases, indigenous thought holds this ritual to be a means of reconciling the living and the dead. One can also note that in both tribes, dead relatives are eaten collectively in lavish celebrations to which even faraway friends are invited and that, whether bone powder or grilled flesh, man is never eaten alone, but always blended into a vegetable substance (here, banana puree, among the Guayaki, *pindo* pith). Endocannibalism inscribes itself in a homogeneous space which surely stems from a single system despite its various forms. Yet can such a theory be elaborated without also including exocannibalism, such as that which the Tupi-Guarani practice? And would not the two forms of anthropophagy fall within a field which a single analysis would unite? Volhard and Boglar's hypothesis, in any case, which articulates Northern Amazonian endocannibalism as "beginning agriculture," is not wholly convincing. Ongoing research will perhaps shed more light on this matter. (The chapter of the book entitled "Endocannibalism and the Elimination of Widows" remains a mystery to us, since it is a question neither of one nor the other nor of a relationship between the two.)

Equally invaluable are the very numerous indications that *Yanoama* offers on the topic of shamanism. One can find complete and detailed descriptions of cures carried out by Yanoama doctors, literal transcriptions of chants through which the shamans invoke their *Hekoura,* "spirits" that protect men. To be a shaman, one must know the chants to call all the *Hekoura.* One chapter shows us precisely how a young man learns this trade, under the strict guidance of elder doctors. His studies are not easy: abstinence, fasting, repeated snorting of *ebena,* the hallucinogenic drug which the Yanoama put to such great use, the constant intellectual effort of remembering the chants that the masters teach; all of this drives the neophyte to a state of physical exhaustion and quasi-despair, necessary for winning the *Hekouras'* good grace and becoming worthy of their benevolence: "Father, here come the *Hekouras;* there are many of them. They are dancing toward me, Father. Now, yes, now I, too, will be a *Hekoura!...*" We would be mistaken to think of the *Hekouras* as an instrumental vision: far from existing as neutral tools exterior to the shaman, content to invoke them and use them according to professional need, they become for him the very substance of his self, the root of his existence, the very vital force that keeps him at once in the circle of men and in the realm of the gods. An indication of the shamans' ontic status is one of the names that designates them: *Hekoura,* precisely. And the sober and tragic end of a young shaman, fatally wounded by an arrow, indeed demonstrates this: "Turning toward his father, he murmured: Father, the last *Hekoura* near me, the one that made me live until your arrival, Pachoriwe [the monkey *Hekoura*] now abandons me. [...] He pressed himself against the trunk, stiffened and died." What do current conceptions of shamanistic phenomena have to say about this? And what "possesses" this young man, allowing him to put off his death for several hours until he can gaze upon his father one last time and then, this final wish fulfilled, die? In reality, the meager categories of ethnological thought hardly appear capable of measuring the depth and density, or even the difference, of indigenous thought. Anthropology uncovers, in the name of who knows what pallid certainties, a field to which it remains blind (like the ostrich, perhaps?), one that fails to limit concepts such as mind, soul, body, and ecstasy but at the center of which Death mockingly poses its question.

Fate, which is perhaps not fate, would have Napagnouma become the wife of a chief, Fusiwe, who already had four wives. Though she was the fifth, she was not the last. She was visibly the favorite, and her husband encouraged her to give orders to the others, at which she balked. But that is not the question. What is of inestimable interest to us is that, in speaking of her husband, she paints the very portrait of an Indian chief such as it appears in recurring fashion throughout the entire South American continent. We find once again the traits that ordinarily describe the model of political authority, of chieftainship among the Indians: oratorical talent, the gift of song, generosity, polygyny, valor. This loose enumeration does not signify that any system organizes these properties or that any logic assembles them into a significant whole. Quite the contrary. Let us simply say that the person of Fusiwe perfectly illustrates the Indian conception of power, radically different from our own, in that all efforts of the tribe tend precisely to separate chieftainship and coercion and thus to render power powerless in a sense. Concretely, a chief — it would perhaps be more apt to call him a director or guide — holds absolutely no power over his people, outside of that which is quite different — of his prestige among them and of the respect that he is able to inspire. Hence the subtle game between the chief and his tribe, readable between the lines of Elena's narrative, which consists of the former knowing how to appreciate and measure at every moment the intentions of the latter, in order to then make himself their spokesperson. A delicate task, with many fine points, to be accomplished under the tribe's discreet but vigilant control. Should the tribe locate the slightest abuse of power (that is, the use of power), the chief's prestige ends: he is abandoned for another more aware of his duties. For having attempted to drag his tribe into a war expedition that it refused, for having confused his *desire* and the tribe's intentions, Fusiwe ruined himself. Forsaken by almost everyone, he nevertheless persisted in waging *his* war to finally die in it. For his death, almost solitary, was in fact a suicide: the suicide of a chief who could not bear the repudiation inflicted by his companions, one who, unable to survive as chief in the eyes of his people and his white wife, preferred to die as a warrior. The question of power in this kind of society, posed properly, breaks with the academicism of simple description (a perspective close to and complicitous with the most tiresome exoticism) and points familiarly to men of our society: the dividing line between archaic societies and "western" societies is perhaps less a matter of technical development than of the transformation of political authority. Here, as well, is an area that would be essential for the sciences of man to learn to inhabit, if only to better occupy its own place in Western thought.

There is a circumstance, however, in which Indian societies tolerate the provisional encounter between chieftainship and authority: war, perhaps the only moment where a chief agrees to give orders and his men to execute them (and this still has to be examined more closely). Since war is almost constantly present in the text that we are dealing with, it leads us to ask: what impressions will the reader, even the slightly forewarned reader, have afterwards? There is reason to fear that these impressions will be unfavorable. What to think, indeed, of people who ceaselessly kill each other with relentless intensity, who do not hesitate to riddle with arrows today those who only yesterday were their best friends? And from then on, the illusions of the Noble Savage's peaceful habits collapse, since we only see war of literally everyone against everyone, the presocial state of man according to Hobbes. We should be clear: Hobbes' *bellum omnium contra omnes* does not correspond to an historic moment in human evolution any more than Rousseau's state of nature does, although the abundance of warlike episodes might suggest the contrary with regard to the Yanoama. First, Elena Valero's narrative spans twenty-two years; secondly, she probably gave priority to reporting that which impressed her most, namely, combat. Finally, let us not forget, without trying to reduce the sociological importance of war in these cultures, that the arrival of whites everywhere in America — North as well as South — led almost automatically to a doubling of hostility and war between tribes. These points made, it seems to us that even the term war does not appropriately describe the facts. For which entities are opposed? These are local *allied* tribes, that is, tribes that trade their women, and who, as a result, are related to each other. We may have a hard time understanding how brothers-in-law can think of massacring each other, but it seems clear that "war" among the Indians must first be thought of in terms of the circulation of women, who are never killed. In any case, the Yanoama know this very well, and when possible, substitute the bloody confrontations using arrows with ritual combat using clubs, thanks to which vengeance can be played out. The result is that the boundaries between peace and violence, between marriage and war, become very blurred and that one of the merits of this book is to infuse this problem with incomparably lively material.

A final word in conclusion: what of the reader of such a work if he is an ethnologist? It leaves him overwhelmed, but not satisfied. Indeed, compared to the teeming life of a primitive society, the scholar's discourse seems the hesitant mumbling of a one-eyed stutterer. A somewhat bitter book, then, leaving us with the certainty that we travel on the surface of meaning which slides a little further away with each step we take to approach it. But this is no longer a matter of ethnology. Things remaining what they are, the language of science (which is not being put into question in any way here) seems to remain, by destiny perhaps, a discourse on Savages and not a discourse of Savages. We cannot conquer the freedom, any more easily than they, to be one and the other at once, to be here and there at the same time, without losing everything altogether and no longer residing anywhere. And so each is refused the ruse of knowledge, which in becoming absolute, abolishes itself in silence.

3

THE HIGHPOINT OF THE CRUISE

The boat travels the last meters and washes smoothly onto the beach. The guide jumps on land and shouts: "Women and children first!", a joke met with joyous laughter. He gallantly offers his arm to the women, and they disembark in lively commotion. They are all there, the Browns and the Murdocks, the Foxes and the Poages, the MacCurdys and the Cooks. Before departure, they were advised to cover themselves well, but several of the men have opted for shorts. They slap themselves on the calves and scratch their large, pink knees which the mosquitoes have immediately spotted. We aren't going to live our lives in air-conditioned hotels! You have to rough it from time to time, get in touch with nature.

"We leave again in two hours... watch your scalps!"

This is perhaps the tenth contingent of tourists he has led to the Indian village. Routine for him. Why change his repartee? It is met with favor every time. But for these people, it is very different. They have paid a pretty penny

First published in *les Temps Modernes,* No. 299–300, June–July, 1971, pp. 2345–2350.

to come here and see the savages. And for their money they get the merciless sun, the blended odors of river and forest, the insects, all of this strange world which they will bravely conquer.

"With this light, I'm going to set the aperture at..."

Some distance away, we see the domes of four or five great collective living quarters. Cameras purring and clicking, the siege begins.

"It was so interesting to see those Negroes! What a curious thing those rituals are!"

"...no more than ten dollars, I told him. In the end, it worked..."

"The're very backward. But much more likable than our own, don't you think?"

"...Then when I saw we could do the Bahamas as well for the same price, I said to my wife: that's it, we're going..."

The little group advances slowly on the path lined with urucu trees. Mr. Brown explains that the Indians paint themselves with the red juice of the fruit when they go to war.

"I read this book, I don't remember what tribe it was on. But it doesn't matter, they're all the same."

Such erudition inspires respect.

"The Prescotts? They're just fools. They said they were tired. The truth is, they were scared! Yes, scared of the Indians."

The path goes through a large garden. Mr. Murdock looks at the banana trees. He would very much like to eat a fruit, but it is a little high, he would have to jump. Hesitating, he pulls off his hat for a moment and wipes his bald head.

"At least you don't have to worry about getting scalped!"

He gives up on the banana. Everyone is in a good mood. Here they are at the end of the path, between two of the enormous huts. They stop a moment, as though at a threshold. The oval place is deserted, clean, unsettling. It seems like a dead city.

"This is where they do their dances at night."

At the center is a pole decorated with black and white diamond shapes. A very skinny dog sprinkles the base of it, barks weakly and trots away.

"And I bet that's where they torture people at the stake!"

Mr. Brown is not completely sure, but he is the expert. Whispers, pictures, delicious shudders.

"Do you think they know how to speak?"

Yellow and green, red and blue parrots and great macaws are taking a nap, perched on rooftops.

"They could at least say something, come out, greet us, I don't know."

This is becoming disconcerting, this heavy silence, the weight of the light. Fortunately, the inhabitants begin to emerge from tiny openings, bare-breasted women, children clinging to their skirts, men, too, looking out from under their brows at the strangers and lazily throwing bits of wood to the dogs. Confused conversations begin, the ladies want to caress the heads of small children who run away, a young man with a wide grin tirelessly repeats: "O.K.! Good Morning! O.K.!" Mr. Poage is delighted.

"Well, old chap, how goes it?"

He slaps the back of the polyglot. In short, the ice has been broken, we are at home with the savages, not everyone could say as much. Of course, it is not exactly what we expected, but just the same. There they are, the Indians. Bows and arrows lean against the houses' palm-leaf walls.

Everyone goes off on their own. There is clearly nothing to fear, and it is better not to crowd, for the photos and all, not to look ready for war.

Determined, Mr. Brown, followed by his wife, makes his way toward the nearest Indian. He will methodically take a complete tour of the village. Two hours to get the tribe on film is not very much. Off to work. The man is sitting in the shade of a small wooden bench in the shape of an animal. From time to time, he brings a baked clay tube to his mouth; he smokes his pipe without displacing his gaze, which seems to see nothing. He doesn't even flinch when Mr. Brown plants himself in front of him. His black locks tumble over his shoulders, revealing the large empty holes in his pierced ears.

As Mr. Brown is about to act, something stops him. What am I going to say to him? I'm not going to call him Mister, after all. And if I address him casually, he might get mad and throw a wrench into the works.

"What do you think? How would you address this... this man?"

"Just don't say anything. In any case, he surely wouldn't understand."

He approaches and utters, somewhere between injunction and request: "Photo."

The Indian's eyes travel from Mr. Brown's feet to his knees.

"One peso."

Good. At least he knows what money is. We should have known... Anyway, that's not expensive.

"Yes, but you have to take off all that! Photo, but not with that!"

Mr. Brown mimes the sliding of pants down legs, demonstrates the unbuttoning of a shirt. He undresses the savage, he frees him of his filthy, second-hand clothes.

"Me, take off clothes, five pesos."

Good God, how profit-minded can you be? He is getting carried away for a picture or two. Mrs. Brown is starting to lose her patience.

"Well, are you going to take this picture?"

"You see how difficult he's being!"

"Get a new Indian."

"It'd be the same thing with the others."

The man is still seated, indifferent and smoking peacefully.

"Very well. Five pesos."

He goes inside for several moments and reappears entirely naked, athletic, relaxed and comfortable with his body. Mr. Brown daydreams wistfully, and Mrs. Brown lets her gaze wander over his sex.

"Do you really think..."

"Oh, don't complicate things. This one is enough."

Click, click, click, click... Five pictures at different angles. Ready for the sixth.

"Finished."

Without raising his voice, the man has given an order. Mr. Brown does not dare disobey. He disdains himself, loathes himself... I, a civilized white man convinced of racial equality, consumed by fraternal feelings toward those who did not have the good fortune to be white, I comply with the first word from a miserable wretch who lives in the nude, when he's not dressed up in stinking rags. He demands five pesos, and I could give him five thousand. He has nothing, he is less than nothing, and when he says "finished," I stop. Why?

"Why the devil does he act this way? What difference does it make to him, one or two more pictures?"

"You've come across an expensive starlet."

Mr. Brown is in no mood for humor.

"Look! What does he want to do with that money anyway? These men live on nothing, like animals!"

"Maybe he wants to buy a camera."

The Indian examines the old five peso bill for a long time, then puts it in the house. He sits down and takes up his pipe again. This is really annoying, he isn't paying us the slightest attention, we're here and it's as if we weren't... Hatred: this is what Mr. Brown begins to feel before this block of inertia. Coming all this way, the expense on top of it. It is impossible to retain a dignified attitude, to humble this savage by telling him to go to hell. Mr. Brown does not want to have come for nothing.

"What about the feathers? Aren't there any feathers?"

With grand gestures he adorns the Indian with finery, covers his head in ornaments, equips him with long wings.

"You taking pictures me wearing feathers, fifteen pesos."

The offer is not discussed. Mrs. Brown smiles approvingly. Her husband chooses martyrdom.

"O.K. Fifteen pesos."

The five peso bill, the ten peso bill are subjected to the same careful scrutiny. And a demigod emerges from the dark lair. A large headdress, a pink and black sun, has been fastened to his hair, now tied in a ponytail. In the dark orifices of his ears, two wooden disks. Two bunches of white feathers at his ankles; the vast torso is divided by two necklaces of small shells slung diagonally across his chest. His hand rests on a heavy club.

"Anyway, this was worth it. He's beautiful!"

Mrs. Brown admires him unabashedly. Click, click, click, click... The demigod only intervenes after the tenth photo in which Mr. Brown, modest and paternal, poses next to the Red Skin.

And it starts all over again when he wants to buy the small clay statuettes, the headdresses, the arrows, a bow. Once the price is indicated, the man doesn't say another word. Brown has to knuckle under. The proffered weapons are finely made, embellished with the down of a white bird. Much different from the large bow and the handful of long arrows that rest against the hut, sober, unadorned, serious.

"How much?"

"A hundred pesos."

"And those?"

For the first time the Indian expresses an emotion; his icy face is momentarily unsettled by mild surprise.

"That? My bow. For animals."

Scowling, he points to the mass of the forest and mimes the gesture of shooting an arrow.

"Me not selling."

This one is not getting past me. We'll see who's stronger, if he can hold out.

"But I want this one, with the arrows."

"Look, what do you want with this one? The others are really much prettier!"

The man looks first at his own weapons, then at those he carefully made for potential customers. He takes an arrow and admires its straightness, he feels the bone tip with his finger.

"A thousand pesos."

Mr. Brown was not expecting this at all.

"What! He's crazy! That's much too expensive!"

"That, my bow. Me killing animals."

"You're making a fool of yourself. Pay it. Too bad for you!"

The husband holds out a thousand peso bill. But the other refuses, he wants ten hundred peso bills. Mr. Poage is asked to break the large bill. Mr. Brown, exhausted, leaves, his bow and hunting arrows in hand. He finishes off his roll of film discreetly, like a thief, taking advantage of the fact that no one can see him.

"What a bunch of thieves these people are! Completely corrupted by money!"

Mr. MacCurdy more or less sums up the tourists' general feelings as they come back to the boat.

"Two hundred pesos! Can you believe it? To film three minutes of these girls dancing naked! I'm sure they'd sleep with anyone for twenty!"

"What about me! This is the first time I've seen my husband get taken. And by whom!"

"And bargaining is out of the question. They really are crude. Lazy. It's easy to make a living that way!"

"The Prescotts were right!"

4

OF ETHNOCIDE

A few years ago, the term ethnocide did not exist. Profiting from the ephemeral favors of fashion, and more certainly, from its ability to respond to a demand, to satisfy a certain need for terminological precision, the use of the word has largely and rapidly extended beyond its place of origin, ethnology, to enter somewhat into the public domain. But does the accelerated distribution of a word insure the coherence and rigor of the idea it has set out to convey? It is not clear that the meaning of the word benefits from the extension and that ultimately we know exactly what we are talking about when we refer to ethnocide. In the minds of its inventors, the word was surely destined to translate a reality that no other term expressed. If the need was felt to create a new word, it was because there was something new to think about, or else something old that had yet to be thought. In other words, we felt it inadequate or inappropriate to use the much more widely used "genocide" to satisfy this new demand. We cannot, consequently, begin serious reflection on the idea of ethnocide without first attempting to determine that which distinguishes the aforementioned phenomenon from the reality that "genocide" represents.

Created in 1946 at the Nuremberg trials, the legal conception of genocide is a recognition of a type of criminality heretofore unknown. More precisely,

First published in *Encyclopedia Universalis*, Paris, Éd. Universalis, 1974, pp. 2826–2869 it refers to the first manifestation, duly recorded by the law, of this criminality: the systematic extermination of European Jews by German Nazis. The legal definition of the crime of genocide is rooted, thus, in racism; it is its logical and, finally, necessary product: a racism that develops freely, as was the case in Nazi Germany, can only lead to genocide. The successive colonial wars throughout the Third World since 1945 have also given rise to specific accusations of genocide against colonial powers. But the game of international relations and the relative indifference of public opinion prevented the institution of a consensus analogous to that of Nuremberg; the cases were never pursued.

If the Nazis' anti-Semitic genocide was the first to be tried in the name of the law, it was not, on the other hand, the first to be perpetrated. The history of western expansion in the 19th century, the history of the establishment of colonial empires by the great European powers is punctuated by methodical massacres of native populations. Nevertheless, by its continental expansion, by the vastness of the demographic drop that it provoked, it is the genocide of the indigenous Americans that retains the most attention. Since 1492, a machine of destruction of Indians was put into gear. This machine continues to function where the last "savage" tribes subsist along the great Amazonian forest. Throughout these past years, the massacres of Indians have been denounced in Brazil, Colombia, and Paraguay. Always in vain.

It is primarily from their American experience that ethnologists, in particular Robert Jaulin, were led to formulate the concept of ethnocide. The concept was first used to refer to the Indians of South America. Thus we have at hand a favorable terrain, we might say, for research on the distinction between genocide and ethnocide, since the last indigenous populations of the continent are simultaneously victims of these two types of criminality. If the term genocide refers to the idea of "race" and to the will to exterminate a racial minority, ethnocide signals not the physical destruction of men (in which case we remain within a genocidal situation), but the destruction of their culture. Ethnocide is then the systematic destruction of ways of living and thinking of people different from those who lead this venture of destruction. In sum, genocide assassinates people in their bodies, ethnocide kills them in their minds. In either case, it is still a question of death, but of a different death: physical and immediate elimination is not cultural oppression with deferred effects, depending on the ability of resistance of the oppressed minority. The question here is not to choose the lesser of two evils: the answer is too obvious, less barbarity is better than more barbarity. That said, it is ethnocide's true significance upon which we shall reflect here.

Ethnocide shares with genocide an identical vision of the Other; the Other is difference, certainly, but it is especially wrong difference. These two attitudes are divided on the kind of treatment that should be reserved for difference. The genocidal mind, if we can call it that, simply and purely wants to deny difference. Others are exterminated because they are absolutely evil. Ethnocide, on the other hand, admits the relativity of evil in difference: others are evil, but we can improve them by making them transform themselves until they are identical, preferably, to the model we propose and impose. The ethnocidal negation of the Other leads to self-identification. One could oppose genocide and ethnocide as two perverse forms of pessimism and optimism. In South America, the killers of Indians push the position of Other as difference to its limit: the savage Indian is not a human being, but a mere animal. The murder of an Indian is not a criminal act; racism is even totally absent from it, since the practice of racism would imply the recognition of a minimum of humanity in the Other. Monotonous repetition of a very old insult: in discussing ethnocide, before it was called that, Claude Lévi-Strauss reminds us in *Race et Histoire* how the Indians of the Isles wondered whether the newly arrived Spaniards were gods or men, while the whites wondered whether the indigenous peoples were human or animal.

Who, moreover, are the practitioners of ethnocide? Who attacks people's souls? First in rank are the missionaries, in South America but also in other regions. Militant propagators of Christian faith, they strove to substitute the pagans' barbarous beliefs with the religion of the western world. The evangelical process implies two certainties: first, that difference — paganism — is unacceptable and must be refused; secondly, that the evil of this wrong difference can be attenuated, indeed, abolished. It is in this way that the ethnocidal attitude is rather optimistic: the Other, bad to start with, is considered perfectible; we recognize in him the means to elevate himself, by identification, to the perfection that Christianity represents. To crush the strength of pagan belief is to destroy the very substance of the society. The sought-after result is to lead the indigenous peoples, by way of true faith, from savagery to civilization. Ethnocide is practiced for the good of the Savage. Secular discourse says the same thing when it announces, for example, the official doctrine of the Brazilian government regarding indigenous policies. "Our Indians," proclaim the administrators, "are human beings like anyone else. But the savage life they lead in the forests condemns them to poverty and misery. It is our duty to help them emancipate themselves from servitude. They have the right to raise themselves to the dignity of Brazilian citizens, in order to participate fully in the development of national society and enjoy its benefits." The spirituality of ethnocide is the ethics of humanism.

The horizon upon which the ethnocidal mind and practice take shape is determined according to two axioms. The first proclaims the hierarchy of cultures: there are inferior cultures, and superior cultures. The second axiom affirms the absolute superiority of western culture. Thus, it can only maintain a relationship of negation with other cultures, and in particular with primitive ones. But it is a matter of positive negation, in that it wants to suppress the inferior culture, insofar as it is inferior, to hoist it to the level of the superior culture. The Indianness of the Indian is suppressed in order to make him a Brazilian citizen. From its agents' perspective, consequently, ethnocide would not be an undertaking of destruction: it is, on the contrary, a necessary task, demanded by the humanism inscribed at the heart of western culture.

We call this vocation to measure differences according to the yardstick of one's own culture ethnocentrism. The West would be ethnocidal because it is ethnocentric, because it believes itself to be *the* civilization. One question, nevertheless, is raised: does our culture hold the monopoly on ethnocentrism? Ethnological experience suggests an answer. Let us consider the manner in which primitive societies name themselves. We can see that, in fact, there is no auto-denomination to the extent that societies, in recurring fashion, almost always attribute to themselves a single name: Men. Illustrating this cultural trait with several examples, we may recall that the Guarani Indians call themselves Ava, which signifies men; that the Guayaki say they are Aché, "Persons"; that the Waika of Venezuela proclaim themselves Yanomami, "People"; that the Eskimos are the Inuit, "Men." We could expand the list of these proper names indefinitely, composing a dictionary in which all the words have the same meaning: men. Inversely, each society systematically designates its neighbors by names that are pejorative, disdainful, insulting.

All cultures thus create a division of humanity between themselves on the one hand, a representation par excellence of the human, and the others, which only participate in humanity to a lesser degree. The discourse that primitive societies use for themselves, a discourse condensed in the names they confer upon themselves, is thus ethnocentric through and through: an affirmation of the superiority of its cultural self, a refusal to recognize others as equals. Ethnocentrism appears, then, to be the most shared thing in the world, and in this perspective, at least, western culture does not distinguish itself from the others. It would even be possible, pushing the analysis a bit further, to think of ethnocentrism as a formal property of all cultural formations, as inherent to culture itself. It is part of a culture's essence to be ethnocentric, precisely to the degree to which every culture considers itself the culture par excellence. In other words, cultural alterity is never thought of as positive difference, but always as inferiority on a hierarchical axis.

The fact remains, nevertheless, that if every culture is ethnocentric, only western culture is ethnocidal. Thus, it follows that ethnocidal practice is not necessarily linked to ethnocentric conviction. Otherwise, all cultures would have to be ethnocidal, and this is not the case. It is on this level, it seems to us, that a certain insufficiency can be located in the research that scholars, rightly concerned with the problem of ethnocide, have conducted for some time now. Indeed, it is not enough to recognize and affirm the ethnocidal nature and function of western civilization. As long as we are content to establish the white world as the ethnocidal world, we remain at the surface of things, repeating a discourse — certainly legitimate, for nothing has changed — that has already been pronounced, since even Bishop Las Casas, for example, at the dawn of the 16th century, denounced in very clear terms the genocide and ethnocide to which the Spanish subjected Indians of the Isles and of Mexico. From reading works devoted to ethnocide, we come away with the impression that, to their authors, western civilization is a sort of abstraction without sociohistoric roots, a vague essence which has always enveloped within it an ethnocidal spirit. Now, our culture is in no way an abstraction; it is the slowly constituted product of history, a matter of genealogical research. What is it that makes western civilization ethnocidal? This is the true question. The analysis of ethnocide implies an interrogation, beyond the denunciation of facts, of the historically determined nature of our cultural world. It is thus toward history that we must turn.

Western Civilization is no more an extratemporal abstraction than it is a homogeneous reality, an undifferentiated mass of identical parts. This, however, is the image the aforementioned authors seem to give of it. But if the west is ethnocidal as the sun is luminous, then this fatalism makes the denunciation of crimes and the appeal to protect the victims useless and even absurd. Is it not, rather, because western civilization is ethnocidal *first within itself* that it can then be ethnocidal abroad, that is, against other cultural formations? We cannot think of western society's ethnocidal inclinations without linking it to this characteristic of our own world, a characteristic that is the classic criterion of distinction between the Savage and the Civilized, between the primitive world and the western world: the former includes all societies without a State, the latter is composed of societies with a State. And it is upon this that we must attempt to reflect: can we legitimately put into perspective these two properties of the West, as ethnocidal culture, as society with a State? If this is the case, we would understand why primitive societies can be ethnocentric without necessarily being ethnocidal, since they are precisely societies without a State.

Ethnocide, it is said, is the suppression of cultural differences deemed inferior and bad; it is the putting into effect of principles of identification, a project of reducing the Other to the Same (the Amazonian Indian suppressed as Other and reduced to the Same as the Brazilian citizen). In other words, ethnocide results in the dissolution of the multiple into One. Now what about the State? It is, in essence, a putting into play of centripetal force, which, when circumstances demand it, tends toward crushing the opposite centrifugal forces. The State considers itself and proclaims itself the center of society, the whole of the social body, the absolute master of this body's various organs. Thus we discover at the very heart of the State's substance the active power of One, the inclination to refuse the multiple, the fear and horror of difference. At this formal level we see that ethnocidal practice and the State machine function in the same way and produce the same effects: the will to reduce difference and alterity, a sense and taste for the identical and the One can still be detected in the forms of western civilization and the State.

Leaving this formal and in some ways structuralist axis to tackle the diachronic axis of concrete history, let us consider French culture as a particular case of western civilization, as an exemplary illustration of the spirit and the destiny of the West. Its formation, rooted in a secular past, appears strictly coextensible to expansion and to reinforcement of the State apparatus, first under its monarchic form, then under its republican form. To each development of central power corresponds an increased deployment of the cultural world. French culture is a national culture, a culture of the Frenchman. The extension of the State's authority translates into the expansionism of the State's language, French. The nation may consider itself constituted, and the State may proclaim itself the exclusive holder of power when the people upon whom its authority is exercised speak the same language as it does. This process of integration obviously involves the suppression of differences. It is thus that at the dawn of the French nation, when France was only Franchimanie and its king a pale lord of the Northern Loire, the Albigeois crusade swept down on the South in order to abolish its civilization. The extirpation of the Albigensian heresy, a pretext and means for expansion for the Capetian monarchy, establishing France's borders almost definitively, appears to be a case of pure ethnocide: the culture of the South of France — religion, literature, poetry — was irreversibly condemned and the people of the Languedoc became loyal subjects of the king of France.

The Revolution of 1789, in allowing the triumph of the Jacobins' centralist thought over the Girondins' federalist tendencies, brought the political ascendancy of Parisian administration to an end. The provinces, as territorial units, had each relied on an ancient, culturally homogeneous reality: language, political traditions, etc. Provinces were replaced by abstract division into departments, intended to break all references to local particularisms, and thus facilitate the penetration of state authority everywhere. The final stage of this movement through which differences would vanish before State power was the Third Republic, which definitively transformed the inhabitants of the hexagon into citizens, due to the institution of free and obligatory secular schools and obligatory military service. Whatever remained of autonomous existence in the provincial and rural world succumbed. Francification had been accomplished, ethnocide consummated: traditional languages were attacked as backwards patois, village life reduced to the level of folkloric spectacle destined for the consumption of tourists, etc.

This brief glance at our country's history suffices to show that ethnocide, as a more or less authoritarian suppression of sociocultural differences, is already inscribed in the nature and functioning of the state machine, which standardizes its rapport with individuals: to the State, all citizens are equal before the law.

To affirm that ethnocide, starting with the French example, is part of the State's unifying essence, logically leads to the conclusion that all state formations are ethnocidal. Let us briefly examine the case of States quite different from European States. The Incas built a governmental machine in the Andes that the Spanish admired as much for its vast territorial extension as for the precision and detail of administrative techniques that permitted the emperor and his numerous bureaucrats to exercise almost total and permanent control over the empire's inhabitants. The properly ethnocidal aspect of this state machine becomes apparent in its tendency to Incaize the newly conquered populations: not only obliging them to pay tribute to the new masters, but forcing them to celebrate the ritual of the conquerors, the worship of the Sun, that is, Inca himself. The State religion was imposed by force, regardless of the detriment to local cults. It is also true that the pressure exerted by the Incas on the subjugated tribes never reached the violence of the maniacal zeal with which the Spanish would later annihilate indigenous idolatry. Though skillful diplomats, the Incas knew to use force when necessary, and their organization reacted with the greatest brutality, as do all State apparatuses when their power is put into question. The frequent uprisings against the central authority of Cuzco, first pitilessly repressed, were then punished by massive deportation of the vanquished to regions very far from their native territory, that is, territory marked by a network of places of worship (springs, hillsides, grottoes): uprooting, deterritorialization, ethnocide...

Ethnocidal violence, like the negation of difference, is clearly a part of the essence of the State in barbarous empires as well as in the civilized societies of the West: all state organizations are ethnocidal, ethnocide is the normal mode of existence of the State. There is thus a certain universality to ethnocide, in that it is the characteristic not only of a vague, indeterminate "white world," but of a whole ensemble of societies which are societies with a State. Reflection on ethnocide involves an analysis of the State, but must it stop there? Must it limit itself to the observation that ethnocide is the State and that, from this point of view, all States are equal? This would be to fall back into the sin of abstraction with which we have just reproached the "school of ethnocide"; this would be once again to disregard the concrete history of our own cultural world.

Where do we locate the difference that prevents us from putting the barbarous States (the Incas, the Pharaohs, oriental despotism, etc.) and the civilized States (the western world) on the same level or in the same bag? We detect this difference first at the level of the ethnocidal capacity of state apparatuses. In the first case, this capacity is limited not by the State's weakness but on the contrary by its strength: ethnocidal practice — to abolish difference when it becomes opposition — ceases once the State's strength no longer runs any risk. The Incas tolerated the relative autonomy of Andean communities once the latter recognized the political and religious authority of the Emperor. We notice, on the other hand, that in the second case — western States — the ethnocidal capacity is limitless, unbridled. It is for this very reason that it can lead to genocide, that one can in fact speak of the western world as absolutely ethnocidal. But where does this come from? What does western civilization contain that makes it infinitely more ethnocidal than all other forms of society? It is its *system of economic production*, precisely a space of the unlimited, a space without a locus in that it constantly pushes back boundaries, an infinite space of permanent forging ahead. What differentiates the West is capitalism, as the impossibility of remaining within a frontier, as the passing beyond of all frontiers; it is capitalism as a system of production for which nothing is impossible, unless it is not being an end in itself: whether liberal, private, as in Western Europe, or planned, of the State, as in Eastern Europe. Industrial society, the most formidable machine of production, is for that very reason the most terrifying machine of destruction. Races, societies, individuals; space, nature, seas, forests, subsoils: everything is useful, everything must be used, everything must be productive, with productivity pushed to its maximum rate of intensity.

This is why no respite could be given to societies that left the world to its original, tranquil unproductivity. This is why in the eyes of the West, the waste represented by the non-exploitation of immense resources was intolerable. The choice left to these societies raised a dilemma: either give in to production or disappear; either ethnocide or genocide. At the end of the last century, the Indians of the Argentinean pampas were completely exterminated in order to permit the extensive breeding of sheep or cows which founded the wealth of Argentinean capitalism. At the beginning of this century, hundreds of thousands of Amazonian Indians perished beneath the blows of rubber-seekers. Presently, in all of South America, the last free Indians are succumbing beneath the enormous thrust of economic growth, Brazilian growth in particular. The transcontinental roads, construction of which is accelerating, constitute the axes of colonization of the territories traversed: woe to the Indians caught in the path!

What weight do several thousand unproductive Savages have compared to the wealth of gold, rare minerals, petroleum, cattle ranches, coffee plantations, etc.? Produce or die, this is the motto of the West. The North American Indians learned this in the flesh, killed almost to the last to allow for production. One of their executioners, General Sherman, ingenuously declared it in a letter addressed to a famous killer of Indians, Buffalo Bill: "As far as I can estimate, in 1862, there were around nine and a half million buffalo in the plains between Missouri and the Rocky Mountains. All of them have disappeared, hunted for their meat, skins, and bones. [...] At this same date, there were around 165,00 Pawnee, Sioux, Cheyenne, Kiowa, and Apache, whose annual food supply depended on these buffalo. They also disappeared and were replaced by double and triple the number of men and women of the white race, who have made this land a garden and who can be counted, taxed and governed according to the laws of nature and civilization. This was a wholesome change and will be carried out to the end."[1]

The general was right. The change will be carried out to the end; it will end when there is no longer anything left to change.

---

[1] Quoted in R. Thévenin and P. Coze, *Moeurs et Histoire des Indiens Peaux-Rouges*, Paris: Payot, 1952.

5

MYTHS AND RITES
OF SOUTH AMERICAN INDIANS

One cannot seriously attempt an exposition of Indian religions of South America without first mentioning, if only schematically, a few general facts. Though obvious to the specialist, they must nevertheless precede the exposition itself in order to facilitate the examination of the problem of religion for the less familiarized reader: indeed can one approach the field of the practices and beliefs of South American Indians without first knowing how these peoples lived, how their societies functioned? Let us thus be reminded of what is only a truism in appearance: South America is a continent whose immense surface, with a few rare exceptions (such as the Atacama desert in northernmost Chile), was entirely occupied when America was discovered at the end of the 15th century. As the work of prehistorians will attest, this occupation was quite ancient, close to thirty millenniums old. We should

The following texts first appeared in *Le Dictionnaire des mythologies et des religions*, Paris, Éditions Flammarion, 1981, under the direction of Yves Bonnefoy. [Published in English as *Mythologies*, Chicago, University of Chicago Press, 1991.]

note, furthermore, that contrary to current widespread conviction, the density of the indigenous population was relatively high. Demographic research, notably that conducted at the University of California at Berkeley in the United States, constitutes a radical reexamination of the "classic" belief that South America, except in its Andean parts, was a quasi-desert. Through the size of the population (several tens of millions), the continental vastness of its territory, South America offered the conditions for extensive cultural and therefore religious diversity.

What are the principal sociocultural characteristics, the essential ethnological determinants of South American peoples? The territorial extension and resulting climatic variation make for a succession of ecological environments and landscapes that lead from the humid, equatorial forest of the North (the Amazonian basin) to the savannas of Patagonia and the harsh climates of Tierra del Fuego. Differences in the natural surroundings, through the specific adaptations they demand in man, have fashioned very contrasting cultural models: the sedentary farmers of the Andes, the itinerant slash-and-burn farmers of the forest, nomadic hunters and collectors. But one must immediately note that hunting cultures in South America are absolutely in the minority. Its area of expansion essentially corresponds to zones where agriculture was impossible either because of the climate (Tierra del Fuego) or because of the nature of the vegetation (the Argentinean pampas with their absence of forest). Everywhere else, if agriculture is possible in terms of indigenous technology (the use of fire, the stone ax, the hoe, etc.), then it exists, and has for several millenniums, as the discoveries of archeologists and ethnobotanists show. This concerns the largest part of the South American continent. And it has been established that for the few isolated hunting societies that bizarrely break up the monotony of this cultural landscape, the absence of agriculture is the result not of the persistence of a pre-agricultural way of life, but of a loss: the Guayaki of Paraguay, the Siriono of Bolivia practiced slash-and-burn agriculture, as did their neighbors. But as a result of various historical circumstances, the practice was lost long ago, and they became hunters and collectors once again. In other words, instead of an infinite variety of cultures, we find an enormous, homogeneous mass of societies with similar modes of production.

In order to locate an ordering principle in the diversity of peoples who inhabit a given region, to submit the multiplicity of cultures to primary classification, we prefer to call upon linguistic criteria. And from then on, we see the image of almost perfect cultural unity vanish, an image suggested by the recurrence of almost identical material resources. What, in effect, is South America's linguistic makeup, drawn in broad strokes? In no other region of the world, perhaps, is the breakdown of languages pushed to such an extreme. There are dozens of large linguistic families, each comprising a number of dialects sometimes so distanced from the mother tongue that those who speak them cannot understand each other. Moreover, a considerable number of so-called isolated languages have to be taken into consideration, for they are impossible to integrate into the principal linguistic stock. This extraordinary crumbling of language results in a sort of cultural dispersion. The unity of language, in fact, often provides the foundation for the cultural unity of a people, the "style" of its civilization, the spirit of its culture. Of course, there are some exceptions to this "rule." Thus from the point of view of their language, the Guayaki, nomad hunters, belong to the great Tupi-Guarani stock, which comprises agricultural tribes. Such aberrant cases are very rare and stem from historical conjunctures that are relatively easy to establish. One essential point should be noted here: the Tupi-Guarani, for example, occupied an immense territory by the millions and spoke the same language, with the exception of dialectical variations that were not substantial enough to prevent communication. Now, despite the distances that separate the most far-off tribes, the cultural homogeneity is remarkable, as much in terms of socioeconomic life as in their ritual activities or the structure of their myths. It goes without saying that cultural unity does not in any way signify political unity: the Tupi-Guarani tribes participated in the same cultural model without ever constituting a "nation," since they remained in a permanent state of war.

But in recognizing this affinity between language and culture and discovering in the former the principle of unity of the latter, we immediately find ourselves forced to accept the most immediate consequence of this relationship: there will be as many cultural configurations and thus, systems of belief, as there are languages. To each ethnic group corresponds a specific assortment of beliefs, rites and myths. The problem from now on is methodological: we obviously cannot adopt the illusory solution of a "dictionary" that would offer an endless list of known tribes and the teeming variety of their beliefs and practices. The difficulty in choosing a method for the presentation of religious facts stems in large part from the contradiction between the cultural homogeneity observed on a socioeconomic level and the irreducible heterogeneity on a strictly cultural level, so that each ethnic group possesses and cultivates its particular personality between material resources and "point of honor." Yet could one not discover lines of force capable of dividing an abstract identity, transversals able to regroup specific differences? It is indeed such a division among the Amerindian peoples that the first Europeans approaching the New World put into effect: on the one hand, societies of the Andes subjected to the imperial power of the strong Incan state machine, on the other, tribes that populated the rest of the continent, Indians of the forest, savanna and pampas, people "without faith, law, or king," as the chroniclers of the 16th century said. And it is not too surprising to learn that this European point of view, based largely on the ethnocentrism of those who formulated it, was echoed exactly by the opinion that the Incas professed regarding the populations that crowded the steps of the Empire: they were nothing but pathetic savages to them, only good enough, if they could be so reduced, to paying tribute to the king. It would not be any more surprising to learn that the Incas' repugnance toward the people of the forest had a lot to do with the customs of the latter, considered barbarous: it was often a question of ritual practices.

It is indeed along these lines that the indigenous peoples of South America are divided and separated: the Andeans and the Others, the Civilized and the Savages, or, in the terms of traditional classification, high cultures on the one hand and forest civilizations on the other. Cultural (as well as religious) difference is rooted as much in political modes of functioning as in economic modes of production. In other words, there is no substantial difference — in terms of rites and myths — between hunting peoples and farming peoples who, instead, form a homogeneous cultural whole in the face of the Andean world: an opposition otherwise stated as that of societies without a State (or primitive societies) and societies with a State. This at least allows for the structuring of the religious space of pre-Columbian America, and at the same time the economy of an exposition of it. This is why the first part of this essay will be dedicated to the religious world of primitive societies, farmers and hunters combined. The second part will be a presentation of Andean religion: the issue will be to distinguish two autonomous levels, one inscribed in the very ancient tradition of peasant communities of this region, the other, much more recent, resulting from the formation and expansion of the Incan state. We will thus be sure to "cover" the two domains in which the spirituality of South American Indians unfolds. Though consistent with the general sociocultural dimensions of these societies, the bipartition of the religious field would not offer a sufficiently precise image of its object. Indeed, a certain number of ethnic groups that stem from the classic "primitive" model as much by their modes of production as by their political institutions nevertheless break away from this model precisely through the inhabitual, indeed, enigmatic forms that their religious thought and practice take: a break pushed to its extreme by the Tupi-Guarani tribes whose religious ethnography demands special development, which shall make up the third part of this essay.

We must consider every document concerning Indian America as an ethnographic resource. The information at our disposal is therefore very abundant, since it begins with the discovery of America. But at the same time, this information is incomplete: of the numerous tribes that have disappeared, only the names remain. This lack is nevertheless largely compensated for by the results of two decades of field work among the populations that have not been wiped out. The documents on primitive societies at our disposal, then, range from 16th-century chronicles to the most recent research. As for the Andean religions, more or less extirpated by the Spanish since the mid-seventeenth century, they are known only thanks to descriptions left by Pizzaro's companions and the first colonizers, not including the testimonies gathered directly from the survivors of the Incan aristocracy immediately after the conquest.

1. SOCIETIES OF THE FOREST

Travelers, missionaries, or ethnologists have constantly noted, either to rejoice in it or to deplore it, the strong attachment of primitive peoples to their customs and traditions, that is, their profound religiosity. Any amount of time spent among an Amazonian society, for example, allows one to observe not only the piety of the Savages but the investment of religious concerns into social life to a point that seems to dissolve the distinction between the secular and the religious, to blur the boundaries between the domain of the profane and the sphere of the sacred: nature, in short, like society, is traversed through and through with the supernatural. Animals or plants can thus at once be natural beings and supernatural agents: if a falling tree injures someone, or a wild beast attacks someone, or a shooting star crosses the sky, they will be interpreted not as accidents, but as effects of the deliberate aggression of supernatural powers, such as spirits of the forest, souls of the dead, indeed, enemy shamans. The decided refusal of chance and of the discontinuity between the profane and the sacred would logically lead to abolishing the autonomy of the religious sphere, which would then be located in all the individual and collective events of the tribe's daily life. In reality, though, never completely absent from the multiple aspects of a primitive culture, the religious dimension manages to assert itself as such in certain specific ritual circumstances. They are therefore more easily determined if we first isolate the place and function of divine figures.

THE GODS

In keeping with the European idea of religion such as it describes the relation between the human and the divine, and more specifically, between men and God, evangelists and researchers have been haunted, sometimes unknowingly, by the conviction that there is no authentic religious fact except in the form of monotheism. They have attempted to discover among South American Indians either local versions of the single great god or the embryonic seed of the oneness of the divine. Ethnography shows us the futility of such an undertaking. Almost always, as a matter of fact, the cultural practices of these peoples develop without implicit reference to a single or central figure of the divine, as we shall see. In other words, religious life, seized in its ritual reality, unfolds in a space outside that which western thought is accustomed to calling the sphere of the divine: the "gods" are absent from the cults and rites that men celebrate, because they are not intended for them. But does the absence of worship necessarily signify the absence of the divine? We have believed it possible to detect, here and there, dominant divine figures in the myths of various tribes. But who decides on this dominance, who evaluates the hierarchy of these representations of the divine? It is sometimes precisely ethnographers and more often missionaries who, immersed in the monotheistic fantasy, imagine their expectations fulfilled by the discovery of such and such particular divinity. Who are these "gods" that are not worshiped? Their names, in fact, designate visible celestial bodies: Sun, Moon, stars, constellations, whose metamorphoses from human to astral are recounted in numerous myths; they also name "violent" natural phenomena such as thunder, storms, lightning. Very often the names of the "gods" also refer not to the order of nature, but to that of culture: mythical founders of civilization, inventors of agriculture, cultural heroes who in fact sometimes become celestial bodies or animals once their terrestrial task has been completed – the Twins, the Tupi-Guarani tribes' mythical heroes, abandon Earth to transform themselves into Sun and Moon. Although Sun, the older brother, plays a very important role in the religious thought of the contemporary Guarani, he is not the object of a particular cult. In other words, all these "gods" are most often nothing but names, names more common than personal, and as such, indications and designations of the society's "beyond," of the culture's Other: the cosmic alterity of the heavens and celestial bodies, the earthly alterity of the nature at hand. Alterity that originates above all from the culture itself: the order of Law as an institution of the social (or the cultural) is contemporaneous not to men, but to a time before men; it originates in mythical, prehuman time. The society finds its foundations outside itself in the ensemble of rules and instructions bequeathed by the great ancestors or cultural heroes, both often signified by the name of Father, Grandfather or Our True Father. The name of this distant and abstract god indifferent to men's destiny, this god without a cult, that is, deprived of the general relationship that unites humans with the divine, is the name of Law which, inscribed at the heart of the social, guarantees the maintenance of its order and asks men only to respect tradition. This is indeed what we learn from the tribes of Tierra del Fuego, among whom scholars of the American continents have sometimes been tempted to locate the most advanced forms of "savage" monotheism: the Temaukel of the Ona or the Watauinewa of the Yahgan comprise under their names the intangible norms of the social life left to men by these "gods" and taught to adolescents during initiatory rites. One may note, by the way, that unlike the Andean societies, other South American peoples never depict the "gods." The only notable exception: the *zemi*, or idols of the Tano-Arawak of the Antilles, and the divine images that certain Colombian and Venezuelan tribes house in their temples. In both cases, historians of religion invoke influences from Central America for the former, from the Andes for the latter, that is, from what we call high culture.

A strange religion without gods, that of the South American Indians: an absence so irritating that more than one missionary has proclaimed these people true atheists. People of extreme religiosity nonetheless: a social and collective religiosity more than individual and private, in that it concerns the relation of society, as a world of the living, to this Other, the world of its dead.

THE RITUALS OF DEATH

We must first of all avoid confusion between worship of ancestors and worship of the dead. Indigenous thought, in fact, clearly distinguishes the old dead from the recent dead, and each of these categories of the non-living require different treatment. What is established between the community of the living and that of the ancestors is a diachronic relationship, marked by the rupture of temporal continuity, and a synchronic relationship, marked by the will for cultural continuity. In other words, Indian thought situates the ancestors in a time before time, in a time where the events that occur are what myths recount: a primordial time of various moments in the foundation of culture and the institution of society, a veritable time of the ancestors with whom the souls of the old dead, anonymous and separated from the living by a great genealogical depth, merge. In addition, society, instituted as such in the mythical ancestors' founding act, constantly reaffirms its will, through the voices of leaders and shamans or through the means of ritual practices, to persevere in its cultural being, that is, to conform to the norms and rules bequeathed them by the ancestors and transmitted through myths. To this end, the ancestors are often honored with rituals whose consequences we shall examine. It becomes clear that the ancestors and their mythical gestures, far from being assimilated with the dead, are considered the very life of society.

Relation with the dead is something else entirely. First, they are the contemporaries of the living, those whom age or sickness tears from the community, the relatives and kin of the survivors. If death abolishes the body, it also brings into being, into autonomous existence, that which we call the soul, for lack of a better term. According to the particular beliefs of each culture, the number of souls a person has can vary: sometimes just one, sometimes two, sometimes more. But even if there are more than one, one of them becomes the ghost of the deceased, a sort of living dead. In fact, the actual funeral rites, insofar as they concern the dead body, are essentially intended to ward off definitively the souls of the dead from the living: death lets loose a flood of evil, aggressive powers against which the living must protect themselves. Since the souls do not want to leave the surroundings of the village or encampment, they wander, especially at night, near their relatives and friends for whom they are a source of danger, illness, death. Just as the ancestors, as the mythical founders of society, are marked with a positive sign and are therefore close to the community of their "descendants," so the dead, as potential destroyers of this same society, are marked with a negative sign to such an extent that the living ask: how can we get rid of them?

It follows consequently that one cannot speak of a cult of the dead among the South American peoples: far from entertaining thoughts of celebrating them, they are much more concerned with erasing them from their memory. This is why ceremonies such as the Shipaya's "feast of dead souls," or even the rites at which the Bororo summon the dead (*aroe*), seem to stem more from the will to win the benevolence of the ancient dead than from a desire to celebrate the recent dead: with the ancestors, the community of the living seek to conclude and strengthen the alliance that guarantees its survival; against the dead, defense mechanisms are put into effect to protect society from their attacks.

What do they do with the dead? Generally, they are buried. Almost everywhere, in the area being considered, the tomb is a cylindric hole sometimes covered with a little roof of palm leaves. The body is most often placed there in the fetal position, the face turned in the direction of the soul's supposed resting place. The almost total absence of cemeteries is due not to the periodic upheavals of villages when the gardens become unproductive, but rather to the relation of exclusion that separates the living from the dead. A cemetery is in fact an established space reserved for the dead whom one can later visit and who are maintained, in this manner, in permanence and proximity to the space of the living. The Indians' major concern is to abolish everything including the memory of the dead: how, then, can a privileged space be reserved for them? This will to rupture thus leads many of these societies quite simply to leave the village when a death occurs in order to put the most distance possible between the dead person's grave and the space of the living. All the deceased's goods are burned or destroyed, a taboo is cast upon his name which from now on is no longer spoken. In short, the dead person is completely annihilated.

That the dead can haunt the living to the point of anguish in no way implies a lack of emotion in the latter: the manifestations of mourning (a shaved head for the women, for example, black paint, sexual or alimentary restrictions, etc.) are not merely social, for the sorrow expressed is not feigned. The dead person's burial furthermore is not "slapdash," it is not done hastily, but according to rules. Thus, in certain societies the funeral ritual takes place in two stages. Among the Bororo, a very complex ceremonial cycle follows the burial of the deceased: a ritual hunt, dances (among which, the so-called dance of the *mariddo*, which the men perform with huge rolls of leaves on their heads), and chants go on for about two weeks. The skeleton, rid of its flesh, is then exhumed, painted with *urucu* and decorated with feathers. Placed in a basket, it is finally taken in a procession to a nearby river where it will be thrown. The ancient Tupi-Guarani generally inhumed their dead in great funerary urns buried in the earth. Like the Bororo, in the case of famous chiefs or shamans, they proceeded to exhume the skeleton, which among the Guarani became the object of a cult if the shaman was great. The Guarani in Paraguay still maintain the custom of sometimes preserving a child's skeleton: invoked under certain circumstances, it assures mediation with the gods and thus allows communication between humans and the divinities.

CANNIBALISM

Some societies, however, do not bury their dead: they eat them. This type of anthropophagy must be distinguished from the much more widespread treatment reserved by several tribes for their prisoners of war, such as the Tupi-Guarani or the Carib, who ritually executed and consumed their captives. We call the act of eating the body of one's own dead (and not that of the enemy) endocannibalism. It can take many forms. The Yanomami of the Venezuelan Amazon burn the cadaver on a pyre; they collect the fragments of bone that have escaped combustion and grind them to a powder. This is later to blended into banana puree and consumed by a relative of the deceased. Inversely, the Guayaki of Paraguay grill the cut up cadaver on a wooden grill. The flesh, accompanied by the pith of the *pindo* palm tree, is consumed by the whole tribe, with the exception of the deceased's family. The bones are broken and burned or abandoned. The apparent effect of endocannibalism is the total integration of the dead into the living, since one absorbs the other. One could thus think of this funerary ritual as the absolute opposite of the customary attitude of the Indians, to create as large a gap as possible between themselves and the dead. But this is only an appearance. In reality, endocannibalism pushes the separation of the living and the dead to its extreme in that the former, by eating the latter, deprives them of this final anchorage in the space that the grave would constitute. There is no longer any possibility for contact between them, and endocannibalism accomplishes the mission assigned to funeral rites in the most radical manner.

One can see, then, the extent to which the confusion between the cult of the ancestors and the cult of the dead is false. Not only does the cult of the dead not exist in South American tribes since the dead are destined to complete oblivion, but moreover, indigenous thought tends to mark its relationship to the world of mythical ancestors as positively as it marks negatively its relationship to the world of the real dead. Society seeks conjunction, alliance, inclusion with the ancestors-founders, while the community of the living maintains that of the dead in disjunction, rupture, exclusion. It follows that all events capable of altering a living person logically refer to the supreme alteration, death as division of the person into a cadaver and a hostile phantom. Illness, as potential death, concerns not only the person's individual destiny, but also the future of the community. That is why the therapeutic undertaking aims, beyond curing the sick, at protecting the society, and this is also why the medical act, by the theory of illness that it implies and puts into effect, is an essentially religious practice.

SHAMANISM AND ILLNESS

As doctor, the shaman occupies a central place in the religious life of the tribe which expects him to assure the good health of its members. How does one fall sick? What is illness? The cause is not attached to a natural agent but to a supernatural origin: the aggression of a certain spirit of nature, or the soul of someone recently deceased, an attack by a shaman from an enemy tribe, a (voluntary or involuntary) transgression of an alimentary or sexual taboo, etc. Indian etiology closely associates illness, as bodily unrest, with the world of invisible powers: the mission entrusted to the shaman is determining which of these powers is responsible. But whatever the cause of the pain, whatever the perceptible symptoms, the form of the illness is almost always the same: it consists of a provisional anticipation of that which death produces in a definitive manner, namely the separation between the body and soul. Good health is maintained by the coexistence of the body and the soul united in the person; illness is the loss of this unity by the soul's departure. To cure the illness, to restore good health, is to reconstitute the person's body-soul unity: As doctor, the shaman must discover the place where the soul is held prisoner, liberate it from captivity, and finally lead it back into the patient's body.

THE SHAMAN

We must eliminate the widespread conviction — spread, unfortunately by certain ethnologists — that the shaman, this personage essential to life in all primitive societies, is a sort of lunatic whom his society would take care of and tear away from illness and marginality by charging him with assuring communication between earth and the beyond, between the community and the supernatural. By transforming the psychopath into a doctor, society would integrate him while profiting from his "gifts" and in this way would block the probable development of his psychosis: the shaman would no longer be his tribe's doctor, but in short, a madman cared for by society. The absurdity of such a discourse is due to a single thing: those who utter it have never seen a shaman.

The shaman, indeed, is no different from his patients except that he possesses a knowledge put to their service. Obtaining this knowledge does not depend on the shaman's personality but on hard work, on a thorough initiation. In other words, one is rarely predisposed to becoming a shaman, so that anybody, essentially, could become a shaman should he so desire. Some feel this desire, others do not. Why might one want to be shaman? An incident (a dream, a vision, a strange encounter, etc.) might be interpreted as a sign that such is the path to follow, and the shaman's vocation is under way. The desire for prestige might also determine this "professional" choice: the reputation of a "successful" shaman can easily extend beyond the boundaries of the tribe where he practices his talent. Much more decisive, however, seems the warlike component of shamanic activity, the shaman's will for power, a power that he wants to exert not over men but over the enemies of men, the innumerable people of invisible powers, spirits, souls, demons. It is as a warrior that the shaman confronts them, and as such, he wishes to win a victory over them as much as he wants to restore health to the sick.

Some tribes (in the Chaco, for example) remunerate the shaman's medical acts by gifts of food, fabrics, feathers, ornaments, etc. If the shaman enjoys considerable status in all South American societies, the practice of his trade is nevertheless not without risks. He is a master of life (his powers can restore the sick), but he is also a master of death: these same powers are thought to confer upon him the ability to bring death upon others; he is reputed to be able to kill as well as to cure. It is not a matter of malevolence or personal perversity. The figure of the evil sorcerer is rare in South

America. But if a shaman fails consecutively in his treatments, or if he produces incomprehensible, tragic events in society, the guilty party is soon discovered: it is the shaman himself. Should he fail to cure his patients, it will be said that he did not want to cure them. Should an epidemic occur or a strange death take place: the shaman has without a doubt united with evil spirits to harm the community. He is thus a personage of uncertain destiny: a holder of immense prestige, certainly, but at the same time, someone responsible in advance for the tribe's sorrows, an appointed scapegoat. Lest anyone underestimate the penalty the shaman incurs: it is most often death.

As a general rule, shamans are men. We know of some exceptions however: in the tribes of the Chaco, for example (Abipone, Mocovi, Toba), or among the Mapuche of Chile or the Goajiro of Venezuela, this function is often fulfilled by women who are themselves no less distinguished than the men in this regard. When assured of his shamanic calling, the young man undergoes his professional training. Of varying duration (from several weeks to several years), it is generally acquired under the direction of another shaman long since confirmed. Sometimes it is quite simply the soul of a dead shaman who is in charge of the novice's instruction (as among the Campa of Peru). There are, among the Carib of Guyana (Surinam), veritable shaman schools. The apprentice shaman's instruction takes the form of an initiation: since the illnesses they intend to treat are the effects of an action of supernatural powers on the body, it is a matter of acquiring the means of acting upon these powers in order to control them, manipulate them, neutralize them. The shaman's preparation thus aims at garnering the protection and collaboration of one or several of the guardian-spirits to assist him in his therapeutic tasks. To put the novice's soul in direct contact with the world of the spirits: this is the goal of the apprenticeship. It very often leads to what we call trance, that is, to the moment in which the young man knows the invisible powers recognize him as shaman, learns the identity of his guardian-spirit, and obtains the revelation of the chant, which, henceforth, will accompany all his cures. To permit the soul's initiatory access to the supernatural world, the body must in some way be abolished. This is why the shaman's training entails an asceticism of the body: through a process of prolonged fasting, continual deprivation of sleep, isolation in the forest or bush, massive absorption of smoke or tobacco juice (Tupi-Guarani, tribes of the Chaco) or hallucinogenic drugs (the Amazonian northwest), the apprentice arrives at such a state of physical exhaustion and bodily dilapidation that it is almost a death experience. And it is then that the soul, liberated from its earthly heaviness, alleviated from the weight of the body, finally finds itself on an equal footing with the supernatural: the ultimate moment of the "trance," where, in the vision that is offered him of the invisible, the young man is initiated to the knowledge that henceforth makes him a shaman.

THERAPEUTICS, TRIPS, DRUGS

Indigenous thought, we have seen, determines illness (with the exclusion of all pathology introduced in America by the Europeans) as the rupture of the personal soul-body unity, and recovery as a restoration of this unity. It follows that the shaman, as doctor, is a traveler: he must leave in search of the soul held captive by evil spirits, he must, assisted by his auxiliary spirit, begin a voyage of exploration of an invisible world, combat the keepers of the soul and the body of the patient. Each cure, a repetition of the initiatory voyage that permitted the shaman to acquire his powers, demands that he place himself in a state of trance, of exaltation of the spirit and lightness of the body. And so, a cure, that is, the preparation for a trip, almost never takes place without heavy consumption of tobacco (smoked or drunk as a juice in large quantities) or of various drugs, cultivated especially in the Amazonian west or northwest where the Indians use them extensively. For certain populations such as the Guarani, the soul, as a principle of individuation that makes a person of the living body, merges with the proper name: the soul is the name. Therefore, a particularly serious illness can be diagnosed as the name's unsuitability for the sick person: the error in naming him is the cause of the illness, the sick person does not possess a soul-name that suits him. And so, the shaman leaves on a voyage of discovery for the true name. When the gods have communicated it to him, he tells the sick person and his relatives what it is. Recovery proves that he has in fact found the patient's real name.

While his spirit is in search of the lost soul (sometimes very faraway, as far as the Sun), the shaman dances and chants around the patient who is seated or stretched out on the ground. In many societies, the shaman marks the rhythm of his dance with a musical instrument (*maraca*), but also with the voices of the spirits with which he converses. Depending on the nature of the diagnosis, the shaman may need to effect metamorphosis for the treatment to be a success: and so, he transforms himself into a jaguar, a snake, a bird. From time to time, he interrupts his movement to blow on the patient (often tobacco smoke), to massage him, to suck the parts of the body that are ailing him. Everywhere, the shaman's breath and saliva are reputed to contain great strength. When the stray soul is reintegrated into the sick body, the latter is considered cured, the treatment is over. Very often the shaman proves his success at the end of the treatment by exhibiting a foreign substance that he has succeeded in extracting from the sick person's body: a thorn, a little pebble, bird's down, etc., which he has been keeping in his mouth. The absence of the soul, the presence of a foreign body are not, in reality, two different causes of the illness: rather, it seems, in the place left vacant by the capture of the soul, the evil spirit places an object that by its presence attests to the absence of the soul. Therefore, the reinsertion of the soul is publicly signified, according to the same logic, by the extraction of the object which, perceptible and palpable, guarantees the patient the reality of his cure and proves the doctor's competence.

The therapeutic function, though essential, is not the only one the shaman fills. We have already underlined the difficulty of tracing a clear line of demarcation in Indian cultures between the social and the religious, the profane and the sacred, the mundane and the supernatural. That is to say that the shaman's mediation is constantly solicited for events that punctuate peoples' individual lives or the social life of the tribe. Thus, he will be called to interpret a dream or a vision, to decide whether a certain sign is favorable or ominous when, for example, a war expedition is being prepared against an enemy tribe. In this last circumstance, in fact, the shaman may act as a sorcerer or a spell-caster: he is capable of sending diseases to the enemies that will weaken or even kill them. In short, there is no ritual activity of any importance in which the shaman does not play a decisive role.

RITES AND CEREMONIES

Clearly, the religious life of the societies considered cannot be reduced to a ritualization of their relationship to the dead or to disease. Of equally great bearing is the celebration of life, not only in its natural manifestations (the birth of a child) but also in its more properly social aspects (rites of passage). In conformance with the great religiosity of these peoples, we thus see the religious sphere take into account and pervade the great stages of individual destiny so as to deploy them in socio-ritual events.

Birth

The birth of a child extends far beyond its biological dimension. It concerns not only the mother and the father of the newborn but the entire community, precisely because of its implications and effects on the religious level. The arrival of an additional tribe member involves a disturbance of the cosmic order; this surplus of life, by the imbalance that it establishes, provokes the awakening of all sorts of powers from which the tribe must protect the infant, for they are powers of death hostile to all new life. This undertaking of protection translates into multiple rites of purification, alimentary taboos, sexual restrictions, hunting rituals, chants, dances, etc. (before and after the birth) which find their justification in the certainty that, if they are not completed, the child will be threatened by death. The couvade, practiced by all the Tupi-Guarani tribes, has especially caught the attention of observers: as soon as childbirth begins, the father of the child lies in his hammock and fasts there until the umbilical cord is cut, otherwise the mother and the child run serious risks. Among the Guayaki, a birth, through the cosmic agitation that it unleashes, threatens the child but also the father: under penalty of being devoured by a jaguar, the father must go into the forest and kill a wild animal. The death of the child is of course ascribed to the man's defeat before evil powers.

Initiation

It will not be surprising to discover a structural analogy between the rites that surround a birth and those that sanction the passage of boys and girls into adulthood, a passage immediately read on two levels: first it marks social recognition of the biological maturity of individuals who can no longer be considered children; it then translates the group's acceptance of the new adults and their entry into its bosom, the full and entire appurtenance of the young people to society. The rupture with the world of childhood is perceived in indigenous thought and expressed in the rite as death and rebirth: to become adult is to die in childhood and to be born to social life, since from then on, girls and boys can freely allow their sexuality to bloom. We thus understand that the rites of passage take place, as do the rites of birth, in an extremely dramatic atmosphere. The adult community feigns the refusal to recognize its new equals, the resistance to accept them as such; it pretends to see them as competitors, as enemies. But it also wants to show the young people, by means of ritual practice, that if they feel pride in acceding to adulthood, it is at the price of an irremediable loss, the loss of the carefree and happy world of childhood. And this is certainly why, in many South American societies, the rites of passage comprise a component of very painful physical trials, a dimension of cruelty and pain that makes the passage an unforgettable event: tattooing, scarification, flagellation, wasp stings or ant bites, etc., which the young initiates must endure in the greatest silence: they faint, but without moaning. And in this pseudo-death, in this temporary death (a fainting deliberately provoked by the masters of the rite), the identity of the structure which Indian thought establishes between birth and passage clearly appears: the passage is a rebirth, a repetition of the first birth which must thus be preceded by a symbolic death.

MYTH AND SOCIETY

But we know, moreover, that the rites of passage are also identified as rituals of initiation. Now, all initiatory procedures aim at making the postulant pass from a state of ignorance to a state of knowledge; their goal is to lead to the revelation of a truth, to the communication of knowledge: what knowledge do the South American Indians communicate to young people, what truth do they reveal to them, to what consciousness do they initiate them? The pedagogy inherent in initiatory rites does not, of course, concern the interpersonal relationship that unites the master and disciple; it is not an individual adventure. What is at stake here is society itself, on the one hand, and on the other, young people insofar as they want to belong fully to this society. In other words, the rites of passage, as rites of initiation, have as their mission to communicate to young people a knowledge of the society preparing to welcome them. Still this says little: this knowledge, acquired through an initiatory path, is not, in fact, knowing about society, thus a knowledge exterior to it. It is, necessarily, the knowledge of society itself, a knowledge that is immanent to it, and that constitutes the very substance of society, its substantial self, what it is in itself. In the initiatory rite, young people receive from society — represented by the organizers of the ritual — the knowledge of what society is in its being, what constitutes it, institutes it: the universe of its rules and its norms, the ethical-political universe of its law. Teaching the law and consequently prescribing fidelity to this law assures the continuity and permanence of the being of society.

MYTH AND FOUNDATION

What is the origin of law as the basis of society, who promulgated it, who legislated it? Indigenous thought, we have already noted, envisions the relationship between society and its foundation (that is, between society and itself) as a relationship of exteriority. Or, in other words, if it reproduces itself, it does not necessarily found itself. Initiatory rites, in particular, have the function of assuring the auto-reproduction of society, the repetition of its self, in conformance with traditional rules and norms. But the founding act of the institution of society refers back to the pre-social, to the meta-social: it is the work of those who preceded men in a time prior to human time; it is the work of the ancestors. Myth, as narrative of the founding gesture of society by the ancestors, constitutes the foundation of society, the collection of its maxims, norms and laws, the very ensemble of knowledge transmitted to young people in the ritual of initiation.

In short, then, the initiatory dimension of the rites of passage refers back to the truth toward which the initiates are led; this truth signals the founding of society, under the auspices of its organic law, and society's self-knowledge affirms its own origin in the founding act of the ancestors, whose myth constitutes the chronicle. This is why, on the level of the actual unfolding of the moments of the ritual, the ancestors are, implicitly and explicitly, necessarily implicated and present. Are they not the ones from whom the young people are, in fact, preparing to receive instruction? The ancestors, major figures of all rites of initiation, are in truth the real objects of worship in the rites of passage: the true cults of mythical ancestors or of cultural heroes are the rites of initiation that have a central importance in the religious life of the Amerindian peoples.

Among the Yahgan of Tierra del Fuego, the privileged moment in religious life was the rite of initiation of girls and boys: it essentially consisted of teaching the initiates the traditional rules of society instituted in mythical times by Watauinewa, the cultural hero, the great ancestor. Among the Bororo, the souls of the ancestors (aroe) are invited by a specific group of shamans (aroettaware) to participate in certain ceremonies, including the initiation of the young, whose passage into adulthood and entrance into the social world thus takes place under the aegis of the founding ancestors. The Cubeo of Brazil similarly articulate the initiation of boys with an invocation of the ancestors, represented in this case by great trumpets, as they are elsewhere by calabash-maracas. It is equally very probable among the tribes of the Amazonian Northwest (Tucano, Witoto, Yagua, Tucuna) or of the Upper Xingu (Kamayura, Awet, Bacari) or of the Araquaia (Karaja, Javae), which represent their "gods" in the form of masks worn by male dancers, that these masks, like the musical instruments, symbolize not only spirits of the forest or the rivers, but also the ancestors.

The primitive societies of South America invest themselves totally in their religious and ritual life, which unfolds as a continuously repeated affirmation of the communal Self. Each ceremony is a new opportunity to remember that if society is good, livable, it is due to the respect of norms previously bequeathed by the ancestors. We can then see that the reference to the ancestors is logically implicated in the initiatory rites: only the mythical discourse and the word of the ancestors guarantee the permanence of society and its eternal repetition.

2. THE ANDEAN WORLD

In penetrating the Andean world, we come upon a cultural horizon, a religious space very different from that of the Savages. For the latter, though the great majority are farmers, the importance of natural alimentary resources remains considerable: hunting, fishing, collecting. Nature as such is not abolished by the gardens, and the forest tribes rely as much on fauna and wild plants as on cultivated plants. Not because of a technical deficiency — all they would have to do is increase the surface of plantation — but because predatory exploitation in an ecologically generous environment (game, fish, roots, berries, and fruit) requires less effort. The techno-ecological relationship that the Andean people maintain with their natural environment follows a completely different line of reasoning: they are all, of course, farmers and almost exclusively farmers in the sense that wild resources count very little for them. That is to say the Indians of the Andes form an infinitely more intense relationship with the earth than the Indians of the Amazons: it is truly the nurturing mother for them and this, naturally, has a profound influence on religious life and ritual practices. In terms of real and symbolic occupation of space, the forest Indians are people of the territory, while those of the Andes are people of the earth: they are, in other words, peasants.

Rootedness in the earth is extremely old in the Andes. Agriculture started with the third millennium before our era and underwent exceptional development as attested by the very advanced specialization of cultural techniques, the vastness of the irrigation system, and the surprising variety of plant species obtained by selection and adapted to the different ecological levels from sea level to the high central plateau. Andean societies stand out on the South American horizon by a stratification absent elsewhere: they are hierarchicalized, or divided along the vertical axis of political power. Aristocracies or religious and military castes reign over a mass of peasants who must pay them tribute. This division of the social body into the dominating and the dominated is very ancient in the Andes, as archeological research has established. The civilization of Chavin, dating from the beginning of the first millennium before our era, already shows that the habitat was becoming urban and that social life was being organized around the temples, places of worship and pilgrimage, under the aegis of priests. The history of the Andes by this period seems a succession of emerging and crumbling empires strongly tinted with theocracy, the last and best known of which is that of the Incas. Only fragments of information are available about pre-Incan Andean religions, through the funerary furniture of the tombs, the monuments that have subsisted, the fabrics, the ceramics, etc. The Incan period, which extends from the 13th century to the arrival of the Spanish, is naturally better known through the great abundance of archeological documents, chroniclers' descriptions, and the inquests of the missionaries who systematically undertook to extirpate idolatries in order to Christianize the Indians.

The foundation and expansion of the Incan empire changed the religious face of the Andes, as one might expect, but without altering it profoundly. Indeed, the Incas' political imperialism was at once cultural and religious since the subjected peoples not only had to recognize the emperor's authority, but had to accept the religion of the victors. On the other hand, the Incas had hardly attempted to substitute their own collection of beliefs for those of the populations integrated into the empire: they did not undertake any extirpation of the local cults and rites. This is why we find two great religious systems in the Andes of this period: that of the Incas proper, whose diffusion went hand in hand with political expansion, and that of the local religions, in effect well before the appearance of the Incan state.

POPULAR RELIGION

Popular religion clearly expresses the Andean Indian's relationship to the world: it is essentially a religion of peasants, an agrarian religion, for both the coastal people and inhabitants of the plateau. The Andean Indian's primary concern was to gain the favor of powers that presided over the seasonal cycle and that assured the abundance of the harvest and fecundity of the llama herds. This is no doubt why, beyond local particularities, we can speak of pan-Andean cults and beliefs encompassing the coast and the plateau, or the Quechua and the Aymara and the Mochica.

The gods
The natural elements that ordered the daily life of these peasant peoples were exalted to the status of divine powers: Sun and Moon, often thought of as brother and sister as well as husband and wife; the evening and morning stars; the rainbow; the Pacha-Mama, Mother Earth, etc. All these divine figures were the object of cults and impressive ceremonies, as we shall see later. The essential plant of Andean agriculture, maize, was represented by numerous images of ears of corn in gold, silver or stone; these were the *sara-mama*, mothers of corn from which abundant harvest was expected. These divinities were honored with offerings, libations (drinks made of fermented corn), or sacrifices: llama immolation, in particular, the blood of which was sprinkled over the corn fields and used to anoint the faces of participants in the ritual.

The cult of ancestors and of the dead

These cults show the difference between the savage tribes and the Andean peoples. Among the former, as we have seen, the ancestors are not dead contemporaries of the living, but mythical founders of society. In the Andes, on the contrary, the socio-religious life of the community depended largely on the cult of both the ancestors and the dead; the latter were the descendants of the former, and Andean thought, in contrast to Amazonian thought, made an effort to emphasize the continuity between the world of the living and the world of the dead: a continuity of the peasant community that occupied the same soil under the protection of its gods and its dead. The mythical founding ancestor was frequently represented by a rock, *markayok*, venerated no less than the place, *pakarina*, from which the ancestor emerged from the subterranean world. Each community, or *ayllu*, thus had his ancestor and rendered him a cult: *markayok* and *pakarina*, testified to the permanence and identity throughout time of the *ayllu* and founded the solidarity of families that comprised the community.

While the funerary rites of the Indians of the forest tend to annihilate the dead in order to cast them into oblivion, the Andean Indians, on the contrary, placed them in veritable cemeteries: tombs were grouped in the shelter of caves or in sorts of crypts built in the shape of towers, or in holes bored into cliffs. They continued to participate in collective life, for relatives came to visit and consult them; regular offerings maintained their benevolence, and they were offered sacrifices. Far from forgetting their dead, the Indians of the Andes did everything possible so that the dead would not forget the living and would look out for their prosperity: a relationship of alliance and inclusion, and not one of exclusion and hostility, as in the forest. This is why, according to the Spanish priests in charge of extirpating the idolatries, the real dead — in the form of skeletons or mummies (*malqui*) — like the mythical dead, were objects of cult and veneration: in certain ceremonial circumstances, they were decorated with feathers and precious materials.

The huaca

This was the name given by the Indians to all beings or natural objects thought to contain a supernatural power. Sacred stones representing the ancestors were *huaca*, as were the mummified dead. But *huaca* also were idols and the places they could be found, a mountain or a plant, a spring or a grotto, a child born with a deformity, a temple, a constellation, or a tomb. On a trip, privileged places such as a mountain pass or a resting place in a path were marked by a heap of stones, *apachita*, which the travelers also considered *huaca:* they added their own stone to this pile and offered up a quid of coca leaves. The space thus intersected with the supernatural, and the system of the *huaca* constituted a sort of sacred encoding of the world.

The ensemble of the *huaca* included not only the connections between spatial landscapes and the sacred sphere, but also objects, figurines, and amulets that represented each family's powers of tutelage. These were the *conopa*: sometimes stones of unusual shape or color, sometimes statuettes sculpted or molded into the shape of a llama or an ear of corn. Familial *conopa* were kept in homes to protect the inhabitants from illness, or even buried in the fields to guarantee fertility. Communal *conopa* (those of the *ayllu*) were extracted at certain moments of the year from the hiding places where they were concealed: they were given homage, offered sacrifices of llamas or coca, and prayed to.

There was at least one doctor or shaman in each community. He was often appointed by the God of Thunder who who would strike him with lightning. Outside of his therapeutic functions, the shaman also served as a fortuneteller. But unlike the forest tribes, shamanism in the Andes was not the center of religious life. It developed into an ensemble of ritual practices, all of which tended to ask the gods, the ancestors, the dead, all the powers called *huaca*, to assure the well-being of the *ayllu* by guaranteeing Mother Earth's prosperity. This distinctly agrarian religion translates the peasant's profound devotion to his soil over which the divine must watch.

THE RELIGION OF THE INCAS

In origin and substance, Incan religion does not differ profoundly from so-called popular religion. Toward the 13th century of our era, the Incas were a small tribe of the Cuzco region. The religious and ritual life of these farmers and shepherds was rooted, like all peasant communities of the coast or of the plateau, in a desire for the repetition of the cosmic order, the eternal return of the same, and in the hope that, through celebratory rites and sacrificial offerings, the divine powers, the ancestors, and the dead would guarantee the fertility of the earth and the permanence of society. For reasons still unknown, the tribe of the Incas began a march of conquest in the 13th century which ended only with the arrival of the Spanish. But during this relatively brief period, the Incas pushed back the borders of their empire immeasurably (which counted between twelve and fifteen million inhabitants in 1530), and built up an astonishing machine of power, a state apparatus which is still surprising in the "modernity" of its institutions.

Imperial society, inscribed in a rigorously hierarchical pyramid, expressed the radical division between the Incas' triumphant aristocracy and the mass of peoples, ethnic groups, and tribes integrated into the empire, whose power they recognized by paying it tribute. At the top of the hierarchy reigned the monarch, the Inca, at once chief of his ethnic group, master of his empire, and earthly representative of the principal divine power. It would be a mistake to think that the Incas' political-military expansionism was accompanied by religious proselytizing which imposed their own system on the subjected peoples by eliminating the traditional rites and beliefs of the vanquished. It is a mistake, because, in essence, the Incas' religion hardly differed from that of its dependents; secondly, because the Incas' domination tended to gain only the obedience of the subjects and not, as the Spanish had done, to extirpate their idolatries. In reality, they allowed the traditional religious "encoding" to subsist, and imposed upon it a "supercoding" constituted by their own religion: freedom of worship was allowed the Incan vassals under the condition that they recognize and honor the gods of the conquerors as well.

As their power gradually increased, the conquerors proceeded to rework their ancient system of beliefs by exalting certain figures in their pantheon, by making feasts and ceremonies grandiose, by giving considerable sociopolitical weight to religion through the institution of a large, extremely hierarchical clergy, by constructing multiple temples and places of worship, by allocating to this clergy a large part of the tribute paid to the Incas by their subjects.

The cult of the Sun

The solar star, Inti, emerged as a major figure in the Incan pantheon as the result of two things: tradition, which for quite some time had made the sun a pan-Peruvian divinity; and sociopolitical innovation, which through the institution of an imperial system, would traverse practically all the archaic despotisms and lead to the identification of the master of the empire with the sun. This is why the latter became the principal Incan god, as the great founding ancestor of royal lineage: emperors were children of the Sun. And so the cult that was rendered took on a value both of dynastic ancestor cult worship and of official religion imposed on all: it was through sun-worship that Incan religion became a religion of the State.

When the Incas obtained the submission of an ethnic group, they immediately took a certain number of administrative measures (a population census, resource count, etc.) and religious measures: the vanquished had to integrate the cult of Inti into their religious system. This involved the implementation of a cult-oriented infrastructure, the erection of temples, the establishment of a clergy to officiate there, and of course, providing this clergy with important resources which assured its subsistence and allowed it to accomplish the sacrifices necessary to celebrate the Sun. We know that the Incas initiated a tripartition of land for all the subjected communities: one part remained at the disposition of the *ayllu,* another was allocated to the State, and the third devoted to the Sun. The construction of numerous Sun temples erected in the provinces followed the model of the most famous among them, that of the imperial capital, the Coricancha, the true religious and political center of the empire, a place of worship and pilgrimage where the mummies of past emperors could also be found. Coricancha's surrounding walls, rectangular in shape, measured four hundred meters in length. All along the meticulously constructed masonry ran a band of fine gold, thirty to forty centimeters wide. The Coricancha housed various sanctuaries filled with offerings of gold or silver as well as the numerous personnel assigned to serve in the temple. There was also a garden where stalks of corn made of gold were stuck in the ground. By working ritually in this garden, Inca himself opened the season of sowing in the empire.

Outside of the hierarchical ensemble of priests, fortunetellers, and servants, the personnel of each Sun temple included a group of women chosen from throughout the empire by royal administrators for their grace and beauty — virgins of the Sun, the *Aclla.* They were assembled and educated in sorts of cloisters (*aclla-huasi*), where they learned to manufacture luxurious fabrics of vicuna and alpaca, which were offered in enormous quantities at the sacrifices. They prepared *chicha,* a drink made of fermented corn, required at every ceremony. Like the vestals, they were vowed to absolute chastity, yet it was among these women that Inca chose his concubines as well as the women he gave as rewards to great men of the empire. Some of the *aclla* were sacrificed at crucial moments: the accession of a new emperor, the serious illness or death of the Inca, earthquakes, etc. Four thousand people, it is said, composed Coricancha's personnel, of which fifteen hundred were virgins of the Sun. In each temple, the virgins were subjected to the authority of a matron, *Mama-Cuna,* considered the wife of the Sun: At the summit of the hierarchy was the high priest of the Sun, the Vilca-Oma, the emperor's uncle or brother, who lived ascetically in the Coricancha where he directed the religious life of the empire.

The cult of Viracocha

Viracocha was a divine anthropomorphic figure at once very ancient and pan-Peruvian, since he was known and honored as much by the Aymara as by the Quechua. Throughout the often obscure myths devoted to Viracocha, we can see the image of an eternal god-creator of all things (sky and earth, Sun and Moon, day and night) and a hero-civilizer who, after having created and destroyed several successive civilizations, engendered the men of the present to whom he assigned their respective territories, taught the arts which would allow them to live, and prescribed the norms, which would assure the proper social and cosmic order. His task completed, Viracocha, having reached the seaside, transformed his cloak into a boat and disappeared forever toward the West. In the first encounters with the Spanish, the Indians called them viracocha.

The Incas imposed the cult of their ethnic god, the Sun, on the entire empire. In a reverse process, they transformed Viracocha, a pan-Andean figure, into a tribal god. It was under the reign of the great emperor Pachacuti (he ruled from 1438 to 1471) that this reworking of the Incan pantheon's hierarchy took shape, after which Inti ceded the central place to Viracocha, though the emperor remained a descendant of the Sun. This preeminence accorded to Viracocha may be the cumulative effect of several things: the purely theological work of priests seeking a more fundamental religious presence than that of the visible, be it solar; the personal belief of Pacachuti himself that, in a dream, Viracocha helped to win an essential military victory over the Chanca; and finally the logic inherent perhaps in all despotic systems that their theocratic vocation can be realized in the affirmation and institution of monotheism.

It is, in any case, along this path that Pacachuti continued. He had a temple dedicated to Viracocha built at Cuzco where the god was depicted in the form of a solid gold statue the size of a ten-year-old child. Sanctuaries of Viracocha were also built in each provincial capital, equipped with clergy devoted to his exclusive service and resources intended to assure the maintenance of the temple and the priests. The cult of Viracocha — ancient Lord, distant Lord, very excellent Lord — never became a popular cult as did that of the Sun. Perhaps the Incas did not care, since they wanted to institute a cult that was more abstract, more esoteric, and less rooted in the sensual world than the popular cults, and thereby mark their specificity as dominant caste even on the religious level. This is why the cult of Viracocha, as opposed to the popular cults, did not survive for an instant at the end of the empire.

The cult of Thunder and the huaca

Illapa, Thunder, was also a pan-Andean figure in the Incan pantheon. Master of storm, hail, lightning and rain, he produced tumult in the skies by snapping a slingshot. As farmers, the Andean people were very attentive to Illapa's activities. They implored him to send enough rain and offered him great sacrifices in periods of drought. The Andean societies' agrarian character explains the superior position of Illapa, after Viracocha and Inti, in the Incan pantheon.

For the caste of the Incas, as for the peasant masses, the *huaca* constituted a sacred grid of space. The Incas added their own system to the popular *huaca* network, defined in sanctified places by a real or imaginary link between the person of the emperor and the places he went or dreamt of. Whatever their form, the *huaca* were venerated and honored with sacrifices (beers made of corn, coca, llamas, children or women whose hearts would be offered to the divinity). The town of Cuzco alone was said to have five hundred *huaca*. The *huaca* of the empire were positioned on imaginary axes, *zekes*, which started at Coricancha and, like rays, reached the borders of the empire. The proliferation of inferior as well as superior divinities in the Andes was a sign of the infiltration of space and time by the sacred. The marking of space by the *huaca* echoed the punctuation of time by ritual practices.

Feasts and ceremonies

Rare or unforeseeable events offered an opportunity for important ceremonial manifestations: eclipses of the sun or moon, earthquakes, droughts gave rise to solemn sacrifices which attempted to appease the anger of the deities. Everything, furthermore, that affected the person of the emperor had repercussions on the well-being of the empire: as the son of the Sun, he occupied the point of contact between the world of the gods and the world of men, so that the collective destiny of the people narrowly depended on the personal destiny of the Inca. Inversely, to transgress the norms of social life was to offend the emperor and thus to incite the wrath of the gods. This is why the enthronement of a new Inca, the death of the emperor, his illnesses, his military defeats put into question the very salvation of the empire and the survival of the people: numerous human sacrifices (children, prisoners of war, virgins of the Sun) were used to reestablish the altered socio-cosmic order in men's favor.

These exceptional circumstances in which evil difference distorted the "prose of the world" called for a somewhat improvised ritual response. But there was also an annual cycle of religious ceremonies that closely followed the movement of social life, a movement articulated primarily in the agrarian cycle: sowing, harvesting, solstices, paying tribute. Although the year was divided into twelve lunar months, it was the Sun's movement in the sky that preoccupied the Indians of the Andes. Each month was marked by a particular feast that determined the moment of planting, harvesting, distributing the fields, preparing them for sowing, etc. These feasts took place in the temples, and more often, in public squares reserved for this purpose, notably, in the great square in Cuzco where all the figures of the Incan pantheon were displayed, including the mummies of former emperors. In this regular ceremonial cycle, three feasts distinguished themselves by their size and importance: two correspond to the solstices, the third was originally a festival of the Moon.

Austral winter solstice (June 21st) was devoted to the Inti Raymi, the celebration of the Sun, and at the same time the glorification of his son on earth, the Inca himself. This is why all the high-ranking officials and local chiefs of the country were called to Cuzco for this occasion. The emperor, surrounded by all his relatives and court, waited in the great square of his capitol for the first glow of the star to appear. Everyone then knelt and the Inca offered the Sun a drink of *chicha* in a silver vase. As with all great festivals, the Inti Raymi was accompanied by libations, sacrifices, chants and dances. During the period of summer solstice (December 21st), the Capac Raymi took place, a solar festival as well, but devoted besides to the completion of the rites of initiation, marking the passage of young nobles into adulthood. While in the peasant masses this passage was not ritually marked, in the dominant class it gave rise to great ceremonies: entry into adulthood, entry into the aristocracy of the lords. As in all initiatory rituals, the *huarachicoy* (the *huara* is the loincloth given to the young people at the end of the ritual) included, in addition to the sacrifices to the gods, physical trials (flagellations, wrestling, fasting, races), exhortations to follow the example of the ancestors, etc. Along with the loincloth, they were given back their weapons, and their ears were pierced and adorned with disks. In the huarachicoy, the emphasis was placed less on the passage into adulthood than on entry with full privileges into the aristocracy and on the need for absolute loyalty in the service of the Inca.

The third large Incan ceremony took place in September. The *sitowa* was the process of general purification of the capitol, from which all evils would be expelled. At the appearance of the new moon, the crowd, gathered in the great square, would shout: Disease, disaster, misfortune, leave this country! Four groups of a hundred armed warriors rushed forth onto the four main roads — leading to the four regions into which the empire was divided — to drive away the evils. In the city, the inhabitants shook their clothes out upon entering their homes. Chants, dances and processions went on all night. At dawn, everyone took a purifying bath in the rivers. The gods and emperors participated in the sitowa for their statues and mummies were exhibited in the square. White llamas were offered to them in sacrifice, and *sanku* a paste of corn flour prepared for the occasion was dipped into the animals blood; the gods and mummies were anointed with it, and all the Cuzco inhabitants ate a piece.

In this society so infused with religiosity, every undertaking, whether individual or collective, humble or imperial, had to be preceded by an inquiry with the supernatural powers: hence the very important role of the fortunetellers. They observed the arrangement of coca leaves thrown onto the ground, saliva trickling through fingers, innards of sacrificed animals, llamas' lungs blown up so that the blood vessels could be interpreted. Any disorder in such a world could only stem from the (voluntary or involuntary) transgression of some prohibition; uncovering the guilty party and purifying him also fell upon the fortunetellers. When circumstances demanded it, a collective and public session of confession took place, intended to reestablish the socio-cosmic order upset by the infractions committed. The temples of Pachacamac and Lima, places of traditional pilgrimage, sheltered oracles famous throughout the empire; the emperors themselves did not hesitate to consult them. Let us add in conclusion that despite the efforts of the Church, several indigenous rites, syncretically blended into Christian worship, still exist today among the Aymara of Bolivia and the Quechua of Peru.

3. THE TUPI-GUARANI WORLD

Though brief, the preceding account nevertheless allows us to draw a faithful portrait of the religious beliefs and practices of the South American peoples by noting their essential characteristics. The religiosity of forest societies appears at once extroverted and collective: it is chanted, danced, and acted. If the sacred, as we have said, traverses the social through and through, inversely, the social totally permeates the religious. To say that religious "sentiment" exists primarily in its public expression in no way questions the intensity of individual adherence. Like all primitive peoples, the Indians of South America have shown, and still show, exemplary fidelity to their myths and rites. Nevertheless, the "personal element of the religious fact" is largely erased in favor of its collective component, which explains the enormous importance of ritual practice. The exceptions to this general situation stand out all the more. Various researchers in the second half of the 19th century collected an ensemble of texts among the populations (now extinct) along the lower and middle sections of the Amazon that is very different from the classic body of myths. The religious, indeed, mystical uneasiness that is manifested there suggests the existence in these societies not of narrators of myth but of philosophers or thinkers devoted to the work of personal reflection, a striking contrast to the ritual exuberance of other forest societies. This particularity, rare in South America, was developed to an extreme among the Tupi-Guarani.

The term Tupi-Guarani comprises a considerable number of tribes which belong to the same linguistic family and which are culturally homogeneous. These populations occupied a vast territory: in the South, the Guarani extended from the Paraguay river in the West to the Atlantic coast in the East; the Tupi populated this same coast as far as the mouth of the Amazon in the North and penetrated the back country to an unknown depth. These Indians numbered in the millions. The economic life and social organization of the Tupi-Guarani conformed to the model in force in the entire forest area: slash-and-burn agriculture, hunting, fishing, villages made up of several large collective houses. A notable fact about the Indians: their demographic density was clearly higher than that of neighboring populations, and the communities could assemble up to two thousand individuals or more. Although all these tribes have long since disappeared, with the exception of some five thousand Guarani who survive in Paraguay, they are nevertheless among the best known of the South American continent. It is in fact the Tupi of the coast who established the first contact between Europeans and the Indians at the dawn of the 16th century. Travelers and missionaries of various nationalities have left abundant literature about these peoples, rich in observations of all sorts, particularly in those regarding beliefs and customs.

As in all primitive societies of the continent, the Tupi-Guarani's religious life centered around shamanism. The *paje*, doctor-shamans, fulfilled the same tasks as elsewhere; ritual life, whatever the circumstances (initiation, execution of a prisoner of war, burial) was always accomplished in reference to the norms that had always assured social cohesion, the norms and rules of life imposed on men by the cultural heroes (Maira, Monan, Sun, Moon, etc.) or by the mythical ancestors. In this, the Tupi-Guarani did not differ in any way from other forest societies. And yet the chronicles of French, Portuguese, and Spanish travelers bear witness to a difference so considerable that it confers upon the Tupi-Guarani an absolutely unique place on the horizon of South America. The newcomers found themselves confronted with religious phenomena of such vastness and of such a nature that they were rigorously incomprehensible to the Europeans.

What was this? Besides the constant wars that pitted various tribes against each other, this society was deeply wrought by a powerful movement, religious in origin and intention. The Europeans, of course, could only see in this a pagan manifestation of the devil led by the henchmen of Satan. This strange phenomenon was Tupi-Guarani prophecy, which has constantly been misinterpreted. Until recently, it was considered messianism, the response, current among numerous primitive peoples, to a serious crisis resulting from contact with western civilization. Messianism is thus a reaction to culture shock. To reduce the radically different nature of Tupi-Guarani prophecy to messianism would be to underestimate it, for the simple and irrevocable reason that it came into being among the Indians well before the arrival of the whites, perhaps toward the middle of the 15th century. It is a matter, then, of a native phenomenon which owes nothing to contact with the West, and which, for this very reason, was in no way directed against the whites; it is indeed a matter of native prophecy, for which ethnology has not found a single equivalent anywhere else.

THE PROPHETS

Though hardly in a position to understand this phenomenon, the first chroniclers did not confuse the *karai*, enigmatic personages who had emerged from society, with the shamans. The *karai* were not in any way concerned with therapeutic practices, reserved only for the paje, nor did they fulfill a specialized ritual function; they were neither ministers of a traditional cult nor the founders of a new cult, neither shamans nor priests. What then were the *karai*? These men were situated totally and exclusively in the realm of the spoken word, speaking was their only activity: they were men of discourse (the content of which will be examined later) which they were committed to voicing in all places, and not only in the heart of their own community. The *karai* moved about constantly, going from village to village to harangue attentive Indians. These prophets' nomadic vocation is even more surprising given that local tribes, sometimes gathered in federations of several villages, were waging a merciless war. Yet the *karai* could travel from camp to camp with impunity: they ran no risk at all, and in fact, were received fervently everywhere; people went so far as to strew the paths leading to their village with leaves, to run to meet them and lead them back in procession: no matter where they came from, the *karai* were never considered enemies.

How was this possible? In primitive society, the individual is defined first by his appurtenance to a kinship group and a local community. A person thus finds himself inscribed from the outset in a genealogical chain of relatives and in a network of kin. Among the Tupi-Guarani, one's lineage depended on the father, descent being patrilinear. And yet the *karai* said that they did not have a father, but were the sons of a woman and a divinity. Here we must look not at the megalomaniacal fantasy which caused these prophets to auto-deify themselves, but at the denial and the refusal of the father. To state, in effect, the absence of the father affirmed their disjuncture from a lineage of relatives, and consequently, from society itself. In this type of society, such a discourse was invested with an incomparably subversive charge: it denied, in effect, the very framework of primitive society, that which has recently been termed blood ties.

We can easily see that the nomadism of the *karai* was a result neither of their fantasy nor an excessive taste for travel, but indeed of their disjuncture from any community at all. They were literally from nowhere, and, by definition, could not establish residence anywhere, since they were not members of any lineage. And it is for this very reason that upon arriving at any village, they could not be considered representatives of an enemy tribe. To be an enemy is to be inscribed in a social structure, which was precisely not the case of the *karai*. And this is also why, not being from anywhere, they were in a sense from everywhere. In other words, their semi-divinity, their partial non-humanness forced them, by tearing them from human society, to live according to their nature of "beings from the beyond." But it assured them, at the same time, of total security in the course of their travels from tribe to tribe: the hostility shown toward all foreigners was not felt toward the *karai*, for the Indians considered them gods and not men: which amounts to saying that the Indians, far from thinking the *karai* mad, did not doubt the coherence of their discourse and were ready to welcome their word.

THE DISCOURSE OF THE PROPHETS

What did the *karai* say? The nature of their discourse was similar to their status in relation to society. It was discourse beyond discourse, in the same way that they themselves were beyond the social. Or to put it another way, what they articulated before fascinated and enchanted Indian crowds was a discourse of rupture with traditional discourse, a discourse that developed outside of the system of norms, rules and antique values bequeathed and imposed by the gods and mythical ancestors. It is here that the prophetic phenomenon that shook this society implicates us in an unsettling way. Here, in effect, is a primitive society which, as such, tends to persevere in its being by the resolute, conservative maintenance of norms in operation since the dawn of human time, and from this society mysteriously emerge men who proclaim the end of these norms, and the end of the world (dependent on these norms).

The prophetic discourse of the *karai* can be summed up in an observation and a promise: on the one hand, they constantly affirmed the fundamentally evil character of the world, on the other, they insisted that conquest of a good world was possible. "The world is evil! The earth is ugly!" they said. "Let us abandon it," they concluded. And their absolutely pessimistic description of the world was met with the general acceptance of the Indians who listened to them. It follows that, despite its total difference from every primitive society's discourse – a discourse of repetition and not of difference, a discourse of fidelity to tradition and not of an opening to innovation – it follows, thus, that the discourse of the *karai* did not seem unhealthy to the Indians, a lunatic's delirium, since it reverberated in them as the expression of a truth for which they were waiting, new prose describing the new face – the evil face – of the world. In short, it was not the discourse of the prophets that was unhealthy, but indeed, the world of which they spoke, the society in which they lived. The misfortune of living in this world had rooted itself in them in the evil that was destroying society, and the newness of their discourse was due exclusively to the change that had gradually emerged in social life in order to alter it and disfigure it.

Where did this change come from and how did it take place? We are not attempting to construct here a genealogy of difference in this society, but only to elucidate its principal effect: the appearance of the prophets and their discourse that warned of the immanence of evil. The radicalness of the discourse is measured by the depth of evil it unveiled: it so happened that Tupi-Guarani society, under the pressure of various forces, was in the process of ceasing to be a primitive society, that is, a society refusing change, a society refusing difference. The discourse of the *karai* announced the death of society. What illness, then, had corrupted the Tupi-Guarani tribes to this extent? The combined effect of demographic factors (a strong increase in population), sociological factors (the tendency of the population to concentrate in large villages, rather than to disperse, as is the usual process), political factors (the emergence of powerful chieftains) brought the deadliest of innovations to light in this primitive society: that of social division, that of inequality. Profound malaise, the sign of a serious crisis, stirred these tribes, and it is this malaise that the *karai* became conscious of. They recognized and declared it as the presence of evil and sorrow in society, as the world's ugliness and deception. One might say the prophets, more sensitive than others to the slow transformations taking place around them, were the first to become aware of and to articulate what everyone was feeling more or less confusedly but strongly enough so that the discourse of the *karai* hardly seemed the aberrations of madmen. There was thus profound agreement between the Indians and the prophets who told them: we must find another world.

LAND WITHOUT EVIL

The emergence of the prophets and their discourse identifying the world as a place of evil and a space of sorrow resulted from historical circumstances specific to this society: the reaction to a profound crisis, the symptom of a serious illness in the social body, the foreboding of the death of society. What remedy did the *karai* propose in the face of this threat? They urged the Indians to abandon *ywy mba'emegua*, the evil earth, to reach *ywy mara eÿ*, Land without Evil. The latter was the resting place of the gods, the place where arrows hunted by themselves, where corn grew without being tended, territory of the divines where there was no alienation; territory that, before the destruction of the first humanity by the universal flood, was a place common to both humans and the divine. It is thus the return to the mythical past that furnished the prophets with the means to escape the present world. But the radicalness of their desire for rupture with evil was not limited to the promise of a carefree world; their discourse was infused with the destructive charge of all norms and all rules, a charge of total subversion of the ancient order. Their call to abandon the rules did not leave aside a single one; it explicitly encompassed the ultimate foundation of human society, the rule of the exchange of women, the law prohibiting incest: henceforth, they said, give your women to whomever you want!

Where was the Land without Evil? Here, too, the prophets' limitless mystique appeared in all its significance. The myth of earthly paradise is common to almost all cultures, and it is only after death that men can gain access to it. For the *karai,* the Land without Evil was a real place, concrete, accessible here and now, that is, without going through the ordeal of death. In conformance with the myths, it was generally situated in the East, where the sun rises. The great Tupi-Guarani religious migrations at the end of the 15th century were devoted to finding it again. Under the leadership of the prophets, thousands of Indians abandoned villages and gardens, fasted and danced without respite, began the march toward the East in search of the land of the gods. Having come to the edge of the ocean, they discovered a major obstacle, the sea, beyond which surely the Land without Evil was to be found. Certain tribes, however, thought they would find it in the West, in the direction of the setting sun. Thus, more than ten thousand Indians migrated from the mouth of the Amazon at the beginning of the 16th century. Ten years later, about three hundred of them reached Peru, already occupied by the Spanish: all the others had died of privation, hunger, fatigue. The prophecy of the *karai* affirmed the danger of death that society was running, but it also translated in its practical effect — the religious migration — a will for subversion that went as far as the desire for death, as far as collective suicide.

To all this we should add that prophecy has not disappeared with the Tupi of the coastal region. It has in fact been maintained among the Guarani of Paraguay whose last migration in search of the Land without Evil took place in 1947: it led a few dozen Mbya Indians into the Santos region of Brazil. If the migratory flow has run dry with the last Guarani, their mystical vocation, on the other hand, continues to inspire their *karai.* The latter, henceforth unable to guide people to the Land without Evil, have not ceased the interior journeys that start them on a path of the search for thought, the task of reflection on their own myths, the path of properly metaphysical speculation, as the texts and sacred chants, which we can still hear from their mouths, attest. Like their ancestors five centuries ago, they know that the world is evil and they await its end, no longer through impossible access to the Land without Evil, but through its destruction by fire and by the great celestial jaguar, which will let nothing of contemporary humanity survive except the Guarani. Their immense, pathetic pride maintains them in the certainty that they are the Chosen Ones and that, sooner or later, the gods will call them to unite with them. In the eschatalogical wait for the end of the world, the Guarani Indians know that their kingdom will come, and the Land without Evil will be their true dwelling place.

BIBLIOGRAPHY

1. SOCIETIES OF THE FOREST

Biocca, E., *Yanoama*, Paris: Plon, 1968 (French translation).

Butt, A., "Réalité et idéal dans la pratique chamanique," *l'Homme*, vol. II, No. 3, Paris, 1962.

Clastres, P., *Chronique des Indiens Guayaki*, Paris: Plon, 1972.

Colbacchini, A. and Albisetti, C., *Os Bororos orientais*, São Paulo, 1942.

Dobrizhoffer, M., *Historia de los Abipone*, Facultad de Humanidades, Universidad Nacional del Nordeste (Argentina), 1967-1970, Vol. 3 (Spanish translation from the original Latin).

Girard, R., *Les Indiens de l'Amazonie péruvienne*, Paris: Payot, 1963 (French translation).

Gumilla, J., *El Orinoco ilustrado y defendido*, Caracas, 1963.

Gusinde, M., Die Feuerland-Indianer, Vol. 3, 1931-1939, Vienna.

Handbook of South American Indians, Smithsonian Institute, Vol. I, III, IV, Washington, 1946.

Huxley, F., *Aimables Sauvages*, Paris: Plon, 1960 (French translation).

Lévi-Strauss, C., *Mythologiques*, Vol. 4, Plon, 1966-1972.

Lizot, J., *Le Cercle des feux*, Éditions du Seuil, 1976.

Lozano, P., *Descripción corografica del Gran Chaco Gualamba*, Tucuman (Argentina), 1941.

Métraux, A., *Religions et Magies indiennes d'Amérique du Sud*, Gallimard, 1967.

Perrin, M., *Le Chemin des Indiens morts*, Payot, 1976.

Reichel-Dolmatoff, G., *Desana*, Gallimard, 1973 (French translation).

Sebag, L., "Le chamanisme ayoreo," *l'Homme*, vol. V, No. 1 and No. 2.

2. THE ANDEAN WORLD

Baudin, L., *L'Empire socialiste des Inka*, Paris, Institut d'ethnologie, 1928.

Buschnell, G.H.S., *Le Pérou*, Arthaud, 1958 (French translation).

Engel, F.A., *Le Monde précolombien des Andes*, Hachette, 1972.

Garcilaso de la Vega, *Comentarios reales de los Incas*, Buenos Aires, 1943.

Guaman Poma de Ayala, *Nueva Coronica y Buen Gobierno*, Paris, Institut d'ethnologie, 1936.

Métraux, A., *Les Incas*, Éditions du Seuil, 1962.

Murra, J., *Formaciones economicas y politicas del mundo andino*, Lima, 1975.

Pease, F., *Les Derniers Incas du Cuzco*, Mame, 1974 (French translation).

Rowe, J.H., "Inca Culture at the Time of the Spanish Conquest," *Handbook of South American Indians*, Vol. II, Washington, 1946.

Wachtel, N., *La Vision des vaincus*, Gallimard, 1971.

Zuidema, R.T., *The Ceque System in the Social Organization of Cuzco*, Leide, 1962.

3. THE TUPI-GUARANI WORLD

Abbeville, C., *Histoire de la Mission des Pères Capucins en l'Isle de Maragnon...*, Graz, 1963.

Cadogan, L., *Ayvu Rapyta. Textos miticos de los Mbya-Guarani del Guaira*, São Paulo, 1959.

Cardim, F., *Tratados da terra e gente do Brasil*, Rio de Janeiro, 1925.

Cartas dos primeiros jesuitas do Brasil, Vol. 3, ed. by S. Leite, São Paulo, 1954.

Clastres, H., *La Terre sans Mal*, Éditions du Seuil, 1975.

Clastres, P., *Le Grand Parler. Mythes et Chants sacrés des Indiens Guarani*, Éditions du Seuil, 1974.

Evreux, Y. d', *Voyage dans le Nord du Brésil, fait durant les années 1613 et 1614*, Leipzig and Paris, 1864.

Léry, J. de, *Histoire d'un voyage faict en la terre du Brésil*, Vol. 2, Paris, 1880.

Lozano, P., *Historia de la conquista del Paraguay...*, Vol. 5, Buenos Aires, 1873.

Métraux, A., *La Religion des Tupinamba et ses rapports avec celle des autres tribus tupi-guarani*, Paris, 1928.

Montoya, R. de, *Conquista espiritual...*, Bilbao, 1892.

Nimuendaju, C., *Leyenda de la Creación y Juicio final del Mundo...*, São Paulo, 1944 (Spanish translation).

Sepp, A., *Viagem à misses jesuiticas...*, São Paulo, 1972.

Soares de Souza, G., *Tratado descriptivo do Brasil em 1587*, São Paulo, 1971.

Staden, H., *Vera Historia...*, Buenos Aires, 1944 (Spanish translation).

Thévet, A., "La cosmographie universelle. Histoire de deux voyages," in *les Français en Amérique*, Vol. II, PUF, 1953.

6
POWER IN PRIMITIVE SOCIETIES

Ethnology has developed brilliantly in the past two decades, allowing primitive societies to escape, if not their destiny (disappearance) then at least the exile to which an age old tradition of exoticism in Western thought and imagination has condemned them. The naïve conviction that European civilization is absolutely superior to all other systems of society has gradually been substituted by the recognition of a cultural relativism which, in renouncing the imperialist affirmation of a *hierarchy* of values, henceforth admits, and refrains from judging, the coexistence of sociocultural *differences*. In other words, we no longer cast upon primitive societies the curious or amused look of the somewhat enlightened, somewhat humanistic amateur; we take them seriously. The question is how far does taking them seriously go?

What exactly do we mean by primitive society? The answer is furnished by the most classical anthropology when it aims to determine the specific being of these societies, when it aims to indicate what makes them irreducible social formations: primitive societies are societies without a State; they are societies whose bodies do not possess separate organs of political

First published in *Interrogations*, No. 7, June 1976, pp. 3–8.

power. Based on the presence or absence of the State, one can initially classify these societies and divide them into two groups: societies without a State and societies with a State, primitive societies and the others. This does not mean, of course, that all societies with a State are identical to one another: we could not reduce to a single type the diverse historical configurations of the State, and nothing allows us to confuse the archaic despotic State, or the liberal bourgeois State, or the totalitarian fascist or communist States. Being careful, then, to avoid this confusion which would prevent, in particular, an understanding of the radical novelty and specificity of the totalitarian State, we shall note that a common property makes societies with a State as a whole different from primitive societies. The former all have this dimension of division unknown among the others; all societies with a State are divided, in their being, into the dominating and the dominated, while societies without a State are ignorant of this division: to establish primitive societies as societies without a State is to say that they are, in their being, homogeneous, because they are not divided. Here again we find the ethnological definition of these societies: they do not have a separate organ of power, power is not separated from society.

Taking primitive societies seriously comes down to this proposition, which, in fact, defines them perfectly: a distinct political sphere cannot be isolated from the social sphere. From its dawn in Greece, we know that Western political thought has been able to discern the essence of the human and social in the political (man is a political animal), while also seizing the essence of the political in the social division between the dominating and the dominated, between those who know and thus command and those who do not know and thus obey. The social is the political, the political is the exercise of power (legitimate or not, it matters little here) by one or several over the rest of society (for better or worse, it matters little here): for Heraclitus, as for Plato and Aristotle, there is no society except under the aegis of kings; society is unthinkable without its division between those who command and those who obey, and there where the exercise of power is lacking, we find ourselves in the infra-social, in non-society.

It is more or less in these terms that at the dawn of the 16th century the first Europeans judged the Indians of South America. Noting that the chiefs held no power over the tribes, that one neither commanded here nor obeyed, they declared that these people were not policed, that these were not veritable societies. Savages without faith, law, or king.

It is quite true that, more than once, ethnologists themselves have felt a certain perplexity not so much in understanding, but simply in describing a particualrly exotic detail of primitive societies: those called leaders are stripped of all power, chieftainship is located outside the exercise of political power. Functionally, this seems absurd: how can one think of a chieftainship and power separately? What use are chiefs if they lack precisely the essential attribute that would make them chiefs, namely the ability to exercise power over the community? In reality, that the savage chief does not hold the power to command does not necessarily mean that he is useless: on the contrary, he is vested by society with a certain number of tasks, and in this capacity, can be seen as a sort of unpaid civil servant of society. What does a chief without power do? He is responsible, essentially, for assuming society's will to appear as a single totality, that is, for the community's concerted, deliberate effort to affirm its specificity, its autonomy, its independence in relation to other communities. In other words, the primitive leader is primarily the man who speaks in the name of society when circumstances and events put it in contact with others. These others, for primitive societies, are always divided into two classes: friends and enemies. With friends, alliances are formed or reinforced; with enemies, war is waged when the case presents itself. It follows that the concrete empirical functions of the leader are exhibited in the field of international relations and as a result, demand qualities relating to this type of activity: skill, diplomatic talent in order to consolidate the networks of alliance which will insure the community's security; courage, a warlike disposition in order to assure an effective defense against enemy raids or, if possible, victory in the case of an offensive expedition.

But are these not, one might argue, the very tasks of a defense minister? Certainly. With, however, a fundamental difference: the primitive leader never makes a decision on his own authority (if we can call it that) and imposes it on his community. The strategy of alliance that he develops, the military tactics that he envisions are never his own, but ones that respond exactly to the desire or to the explicit will of the tribe. Any deals or negotiations are public, the intention to wage war is proclaimed only if society wants it to be so. And, naturally, it cannot be any other way: were a leader, in fact, to decide on his own whether to carry out a policy of alliance or hostility with his neighbors, he would have no way of imposing his goals on society, since, as we know, he is deprived of all power. He has only one right, or rather, one duty as spokesperson: to tell Others of the society's will and desire.

What, on the other hand, about the chief's functions, not as his group's appointee to external foreign relations, but in his internal relations with the group itself? It goes without saying that if the community recognizes him as leader (as spokesperson) when it affirms its unity in relation to other unities, society endows him with a certain amount of confidence guaranteed by the qualities that he displays precisely in the service of his society. This is what we call prestige, very generally confused, wrongly, of course, with power. We understand quite well, then, that at the heart of his own society, the leader's opinion, propped up by the prestige which he enjoys, should, if necessary, be listened to with more consideration than that of other individuals. But the particular attention with which the chief's word is honored (and this is not always the case, by the way) never goes so far as allowing it to be transformed into a word of command, into a discourse of power: the leader's point of view will only be listened to as long as it expresses society's point of view as a single totality. It follows that not only does the chief not formulate orders, which he knows ahead of time no one will obey, but he cannot even arbitrate (that is, he does not hold the power to) when a conflict arises, for example, between two individuals or two families. He will not attempt to settle the litigation in the name of a nonexistent law of which he would be the organ, but to appease it by appealing to reason, to the opposing parties' good intentions, by referring constantly to the tradition of good relations eternally bequeathed by the ancestors. From the chief's mouth spring not the words that would sanction the relationship of command-obedience, but the discourse of society itself about itself, a discourse through which it proclaims itself an indivisible community and proclaims its will to persevere in this undivided being.

Primitive societies are thus undivided societies (and for this reason, each considers itself a single totality): classless societies — no rich exploiters of the poor; societies not divided into the dominating and the dominated — no separate organ of power. It is time we take this last sociological property of primitive societies completely seriously. Does the separation between chieftainship and power mean that the question of power is not an issue, that these societies are apolitical? Evolutionist thought — and its apparently least reductive variant, Marxism (especially Engelsian) — replies that this is indeed the case, and that this has to do with the primitive, that is, primary, character of these societies: they are the childhood of humanity, the first stage of its evolution, and as such, incomplete. They are destined, consequently, to grow, to become adult, to go from the apolitical to the political. The destiny of every society is to be divided, for power to be separated from society, for the State to be an organ that knows and says what is in everyone's best interest and puts itself in charge of imposing it.

Such is the traditional, quasi-general conception of primitive societies as societies without a State. The absence of a State marks their incompleteness, the embryonic stage of their existence, their ahistoricity. But is this really the case? We can easily see that such a judgment is in fact only an ideological prejudice, implying a view of history as humanity's *necessary* movement across social configurations that are mechanically engendered and connected. But this neo-theology of history and its fanatic continuism should be refused: primitive societies henceforth cease to occupy the degree zero of history, swelling with all of history to come, inscribed in advance in their being. Liberated from this scarcely innocent exoticism, anthropology can then seriously consider the true question of the political: why are primitive societies Stateless? As complete, adult societies and no longer as infra-political embryos, primitive societies do not have a State because they refuse it, because they refuse the division of the social body into the dominating and the dominated. The politics of the Savages is, in fact, to constantly hinder the appearance of a separate organ of power, to prevent the fatal meeting between the institution of chieftainship and the exercise of power. In primitive society, there is no separate organ of power, because power is not separated from society; society, as a single totality, holds power in order to maintain its undivided being, to ward off the appearance in its breast of the inequality between masters and subjects, between chief and tribe. To hold power is to exercise it; to exercise it is to dominate those over whom it is being exercised: this is precisely what primitive societies do not want (did not want); this is why the chiefs here are powerless, why power is not detached from the single body of society. The refusal of inequality and the refusal of separate power are the same, constant concern of primitive societies. They know very well that to renounce this struggle, to cease damming these subterranean forces called desire for power and desire for submission (without liberation from which the eruption of domination and servitude can not be understood) they would lose their freedom.

Chieftainship in primitive society is only the supposed, apparent place of power. Where is its real place? It is the social body itself that holds and exercises power as an undivided unity. This power, unseparated from society, is exercised in a single way; it encourages a single project: to maintain the being of society in non-division, to prevent inequality between men from instilling division in society. It follows that this power is exercised over anything capable of alienating society and introducing inequality: it is exercised, among other things, over the institution from which the insidiousness of power could arise, chieftainship. In the tribe, the chief is under surveillance; society watches to make sure the taste for prestige does not become the desire for power. If the chief's desire for power becomes too obvious, the procedure put into effect is simple: they abandon him, indeed, even kill him. Primitive society may be haunted by the specter of division, but it possesses the means by which to exorcise it.

The example of primitive societies teaches us that division is not inherent in the social being, that in other words, the State is not eternal, that it has, here and there, a date of birth. Why has it emerged? The question of the origin of the State must be shaped in this way: under what conditions does a society cease to be primitive? Why do the encodings that ward off the State fail at such or such moment of history? No doubt only a close examination of the functioning of primitive societies will be able to shed light on the problem of origins. And perhaps the light cast upon the State's moment of birth will also illuminate the conditions of the possibility (realizable or not) of its death.

7

FREEDOM, MISFORTUNE, THE UNNAMEABLE

One does not frequently encounter thought freer than that of Étienne de La Boétie. There is a singular firmness of purpose in this still adolescent young man (why not call him a Rimbaud of thought?), an audacity and seriousness in an apparently accidental question: how ridiculous to attempt to think of it in terms of the century, to reduce the haughty – unbearable – gaze to the closed and always retraced circle of events. There have been nothing but misunderstandings since the *Contr'Un* of the Reformed! It is certainly not the reference to some sort of historical determinism (the political circumstances of the moment, appurtenance to a social class) that will succeed in disarming the ever virulent *Discours*, that will succeed in contradicting the essential affirmation of freedom that is its basis. Local and ephemeral history is hardly an occasion, a pretext, for La Boétie: there is nothing about him of the pamphleteer, the publicist, the militant. His aggression explodes

First published as "La Boétie et la question du politique," in *La Boétie: Le Discours de la servitude voluntaire* (Paris: Payot, 1976) , pp. 229–246. [La Boétie's original text is published in English as *Slaves by Choice*, trans. Malcolm Smith, Surrey England, Runnymede Books, 1988.]

to greater ends: he asks a totally liberating question because it is absolutely free of all social or political territoriality, and it is indeed because his question is trans-historical that we are in a position to understand it. How can it be, La Boétie asks, that the majority obeys a single person, not only obeys him, but serves him, not only serves him, but wants to serve him?

Right off the nature and significance of such a question excludes the possibility of reducing it to this or that concrete historical situation. The very possibility of formulating such a destructive question reflects, simply but heroically, a logic of opposites: if I can be surprised that voluntary servitude is a constant in all societies — in mine, but also in those read about in books (with the perhaps rhetorical exception of Roman Antiquity) — it is, of course, because I imagine the opposite of such a society, because I imagine the logical possibility of a society that would not know voluntary servitude. La Boétie's heroism and freedom: precisely this smooth transition from History to logic, precisely this gap in what is most naturally obvious, precisely this breach of the general conviction that we can not think of society without its division between the dominating and the dominated. The young La Boétie transcends all known history to say: something else is possible. Not at all, of course, as a program to be implemented: La Boétie is not a partisan. As long as they do not revolt, the destiny of the people is, in a sense, of little importance to him; this is why, the author of *Discours de la servitude volontaire* can at the same time be a civil servant of the monarchic State (hence, the ridiculousness of making this work a "classic of the people"). What he discovers, by slipping outside of History, is precisely that the society in which people want to serve the tyrant is historical, that it is not eternal and has not always existed, that it has a date of birth and that something must have happened, necessarily, for men to fall from freedom into servitude: "...what misfortune so denatured man, only born in truth to live freely, to make him lose the memory of his first existence and the desire to retrieve it?"

Misfortune: tragic accident, bad luck, the effects of which grow to the point of abolishing previous memory, to the point of substituting the love of servitude for the desire for freedom. What does La Boétie say? Clairvoyantly, he first affirms that this passage from freedom into servitude was unnecessary; he calls the division of society into those who command and those who obey accidental — how difficult it has been ever since to think about the unthinkable misfortune. What is designated here is indeed this historical moment of the birth of History, this fatal rupture which should never have happened, this irrational event which we moderns call the birth of the State. In society's fall into the voluntary submission of almost all people to a single person, La Boétie deciphers the abject sign of a perhaps irreversible decline: the new man, a product of incomprehensible misfortune, is no longer a man, or even an animal, since "animals... cannot adapt to serving, except with protest of a contrary desire...." This being, which is difficult to name, is denatured. Losing freedom, man loses his humanity. To be human is to be free; man is a being-for-freedom. What misfortune, indeed, was able to bring man to renounce his being and make him desire the perpetuation of this renouncement?

The enigmatic misfortune from which History originates has denatured man by instituting a division in society; freedom, though inseparable from man's first being, is banished from it. The sign and proof of this loss of freedom can be witnessed not only in the resignation to submission, but, much more obviously, in the love of servitude. In other words, La Boétie establishes a radical distinction between societies of freedom which conform to the nature of man — "only born in truth to live freely" — and societies without freedom in which one commands and others obey. One will note that, for the moment, this distinction remains purely logical. We know nothing, in effect, about the historical reality of societies of freedom. We simply know that, by natural necessity, the first configuration of society must have been free, with no division between the tyrant oppressor and the people enamored of serving him. Then the misfortune occurs: everything is turned upside down. The result of this split between free society and slave society is that all divided societies are slave societies. That is to say, La Boétie does not make distinctions within the ensemble constituted by divided societies: there is no good prince with whom to contrast the evil tyrant. La Boétie is scarcely concerned with studies in character. What does it really matter whether the prince is kind or cruel: whatever the case, is it not the prince whom the people serve? La Boétie does his research not as a psychologist but as a mechanic: he is interested in the functioning of social machines. There is no progressive slide from freedom to servitude: no intermediary, no configuration of a social reality equidistant from freedom and from servitude, only the brutal misfortune which drowns the before of freedom in the after of submission. What does this mean? It means that all relationships of power are oppressive, that all divided societies are inhabited by absolute Evil, that society, as anti-nature, is the negation of freedom.

The birth of History, the division between good and bad society are a result of misfortune: a good society is one in which the natural absence of division assures the reign of freedom, a bad society is one whose divided being allows the triumph of tyranny.

Diagnosing the nature of evil that gangrenes the entire divided social body, La Boétie does not state the results of a comparative analysis of undivided and divided societies, but expresses the effects of a pure logical opposition: his *Discours* echoes the implicit but crucial assertion that division is not an ontological structure of society, and that consequently, before the unfortunate appearance of social division, there was necessarily, in conformance to man's nature, a society without oppression and without submission. Unlike Jean-Jacques Rousseau, La Boétie does not say that such a society could never have existed. Even if men have forgotten about it, even if he, La Boétie, has no illusions about the possibility of its return, what he knows is that before the misfortune, this was society's mode of existence.

This understanding, which could only have been *a priori* for La Boétie, is now inscribed in the order of knowledge for those of us who repeat the *Discours'* question. We can now acquire an empirical knowledge of what La Boétie did not know, not from logical deduction, but from direct observation. This is because ethnology inscribes its project on the horizon of the division already recognized by La Boétie; its aim is to gather a body of knowledge that concerns, first and foremost, societies prior to the misfortune. Savages prior to civilization, people prior to writing, societies prior to History: they are certainly well-named, these primitive societies, the first societies to unfold in the ignorance of division, the first to exist before the fatal misfortune. Ethnology's privileged, if not exclusive, object: societies without a State.

The absence of the State, anthropology's internal criterion for determining the existence of primitive societies, implies the non-division of this existence. Not in the sense that division of society preexists the institution of the State, but rather in the sense that the State itself introduces the division, the State as motor and foundation of this division. Primitive societies are egalitarian, it is said somewhat incorrectly. This suggests that the relations between people there are relations between equals. These societies are "egalitarian," because they are unaware of inequality: no one is "worth" more or less than another, no one is superior or inferior. In other words, no one can *do* more than anyone else; no one is the holder of power. The inequality unknown to primitive societies splits people into holders of power and those subject to power, dividing the social body into the dominating and the dominated. This is why the chieftainship cannot be an indication of the division of the tribe: the chief does not command, for he cannot do any more than each member of the community.

The State, as an instituted division of society into high and low, is the actual implementation of power relations. To hold power is to exercise it: power that is not exercised is not power, it is only appearance. And perhaps, from this point of view, certain kingships, African and other,[1] would be classified as that of appearance, more misleading than one might imagine. Whatever the case, power relations produce the capacity for division in society. In this regard they are the very essence of the state institution, the

---

[1] Cf. in particular the very beautiful article by Jacques Dournes, *Sous couvert des maîtres*, in "Archives Européenes de Sociologie," vol. XIV, 1973, No. 2.

configuration of the State. Reciprocally, the State is but an extension of power relations, the ever more marked deepening of the inequality between those who command and those who obey. All social machines that function without power relations will be considered primitive societies. Consequently, all societies whose functioning implies, however minimally it may seem to us, the exercise of power will be considered a so-called State society. In Boétian terms, societies before or after the misfortune. It goes without saying that the universal essence of the State is not realized in a uniform manner in all state formations, the variety of which history shows us. Only in contrast to primitive societies — societies without a State — are all the others revealed to be equivalent. But once the misfortune has come to pass, once the freedom that naturally governed the relations between equals has been lost, absolute Evil is capable of anything: there is a hierarchy of the worst, and the totalitarian State in its various contemporary configurations is there to remind us that however profound the loss of freedom, it is never lost enough, we never stop losing it.

La Boétie cannot call the destruction of the first society, in which the enjoyment of freedom expressed men's natural existence, anything but misfortune. Misfortune, that is, an accidental event that had no reason to produce itself but nevertheless did. *Le Discours de la servitude volontaire* explicitly formulates two questions: why, first of all, did the denaturing of man take place, why did division foist itself upon society, why did the misfortune come to pass? Secondly, how did men persevere in the denatured being, how did inequality constantly reproduce itself, how did the misfortune perpetuate itself to the point of seeming eternal? La Boétie does not answer the first question. It concerns, stated in modern terms, the origin of the State. Where does the State come from? This is asking for reason from the irrational, attempting to reduce chance to necessity, wanting, basically, to abolish the misfortune. A legitimate question, but an impossible answer? Indeed, nothing allows La Boétie to give the reason for the incomprehensible: why do men renounce freedom? He attempts, however, to respond to the second question: how can the renunciation of freedom endure? The principal intention of the *Discours* is to articulate this answer.

If, of all beings, man is the "only [one] born in truth to live freely," if he is, by nature, a being-for-freedom, the loss of freedom must have effects on human nature itself: man is denatured, he changes his nature. He probably does not assume an angelic nature. Denaturing occurs not toward the high but toward the low; it is a regression. But does this imply a fall from humanity into animality? This is not it either, for we observe that animals only submit to their masters when inspired by fear. Neither angel nor animal, neither prior to nor beyond the human, such is the denatured man. Literally, the unnameable. Hence, the necessity for a new idea of man, for a new anthropology. La Boétie is in fact the unsung founder of the anthropology of the modern man, of the man of divided societies. He anticipates Nietzsche's undertaking — even more than Marx's — more than three centuries away to ponder decline and alienation. The denatured man exists in decline because he has lost freedom. He exists in alienation because he must obey. But is this the case? Must not animals themselves obey? The impossibility of determining the denaturing of man as a regressive displacement toward animality resides in this irreducible problem: men obey, not through force or constraint, not under the effect of terror, not because of fear of death, but voluntarily. They obey because they want to obey; they are in servitude because they desire it. What does this mean? Would the denatured man still be a man because he chose to no longer be a man, that is, a free being? Such is, nevertheless, the presentation of man: denatured, yet still free, since he chooses alienation. Strange synthesis, unthinkable conjunction, unnameable reality. The denaturing that results from the misfortune engenders a new man, so that in him the will for freedom yields its place to the will for servitude. The denaturing causes man's will to change directions, toward an opposite goal. It is not that the new man has lost his will, but that he directs it toward servitude: the people, as though victims of fate, of a spell, want to serve the tyrant. And though unintentional, this will suddenly reveals its true identity: it is desire. How does this begin? La Boétie has no idea. How does this continue? It is because men desire that it be this way, answers la Boétie. We have hardly advanced; objecting to this is easy. For the stakes, subtly but clearly fixed by La Boétie, are anthropological. This is a matter of human nature that raises the question: is the desire for submission innate or acquired? Did this desire preexist the misfortune which would then have allowed it to come into being? Or is its emergence due instead, ex nihilo, to the occasion of the misfortune, like a lethal mutation that defies all explanation? These questions are less academic than they seem, as the example of primitive societies suggests.

There is a third question that the author of the *Discours* could not ask, but that contemporary ethnology is in a position to formulate: how do primitive societies function in order to prevent inequality, division, power relations? How do they come to ward off the misfortune? How do they prevent it from beginning? For, let us repeat, if primitive societies are societies without a State, it is hardly because of a congenital inability to attain the adulthood that the presence of the State would signify, but rather because of a refusal of this institution. They are unaware of the State because they do not want one; the tribe maintains a disjunction between chieftanship and power, because it does not want the chief to become the holder of power; it refuses to allow the chief to be a chief. Primitive societies are societies that refuse obedience. And here let us also guard against all references to psychology: the refusal of power relations, the refusal to obey, is not in any way, as the missionaries and travelers thought, a character trait of Savages, but the effect of the functioning of social machines on an individual level, the result of collective action and decision. There is, moreover, no need to invoke prior knowledge of the State by primitive societies in order to become aware of this refusal of power relations: they would have experienced the division, between the dominating and the dominated, would have felt the ominousness and unacceptability of such a division and would have then returned to the situation prior to the division, to the time before the misfortune. A similar hypothesis refers to the affirmation of the eternity of the State and of society's division according to a relation of command-obedience. This conception, scarcely innocent in that it tends to justify society's division by trying to locate in division a structure of society as such, is ultimately invalidated by the teachings of history and ethnology. Indeed, there is no example of a society with a State that once again became a society without a State, a primitive society. It seems, on the contrary, that there is a point of no return as soon as it is crossed, and such a passage can only take place one way: from the non-State toward the State, never in the other direction. Space and time, a particular cultural area or a particular period in our history propose the permanent spectacle of decadence and degradation in which the great state apparatuses engage: the State may well collapse, splinter into feudal lordships here, divide into local chieftainships elsewhere, power relations are never abolished, the essential division of power is never reabsorbed, the return to the pre-State moment is never accomplished. Irresistible, overthrown but not annihilated, the power of the State always ends up reasserting itself, whether it be in the West after the fall of the Roman Empire, or in the South American Andes, millennial site of appearances and disappearances of States whose final expression was the empire of the Incas.

Why is the death of the State always incomplete, why does it not lead to the reinstitution of the undivided being of society? Why, though reduced and weakened, do power relations nevertheless continue to be exercised? Could it be that the new man, engendered in the division of society and reproduced with it, is a definitive, immortal man, irrevocably unfit for any return to predivision? Desire for submission, refusal of obedience: society with a State, society without a State. Primitive societies refuse power relations by preventing *the desire for submission from coming into being*. Indeed, (following La Boétie) we cannot remind ourselves too often of what should only be a truism: the desire for power cannot come into being unless it manages to evoke its necessary complement, the desire for submission. There is no realizable desire to command without the correlative desire to obey. We say that primitive societies, as societies without division, deny all possibility of the realization of the desire for power and the desire for submission. As social machines inhabited by the will to persevere in their non-divided being, primitive societies institute themselves as *places where evil desire is repressed*. This desire has no chance: the Savages want nothing to do with it. They consider this desire evil, for to let it come into being would immediately lead to allowing social innovation through the acceptance of the division between the dominating and the dominated, through the recognition of the inequality between masters of power and subjects of power. So that relations between men remain free and equal, inequality must be prevented; the blossoming of the evil, two-faced desire which perhaps haunts all societies and all individuals of all societies must be prevented. To the immanence of the desire for power and the desire for submission – and not of power itself or submission itself – primitive societies oppose the musts and the must nots of their Law: We must change nothing in our undivided being, we must not let the evil desire be realized. We see clearly now that it is not necessary to have had the experience of the State in order to refuse it, to have known the misfortune in order to ward it off, to have lost freedom in order to insist on it. To its children, the tribe proclaims: you are all equal, no one among you is worth more than another, no one worth less than another, inequality is forbidden, for it is false, it is wrong. And so that the memory of the primitive law is not lost, it is inscribed painfully – branded – on the bodies of the young people initiated into the knowledge of this law. In the initiatory act, the individual body, as surface of inscription of the Law, is the object of a collective investment which the entire society wishes for in order to prevent individual desire from transgressing the statement of the Law and infiltrating the social arena. And if by chance one of the equals that make up the community decided he wanted to realize the desire for power and invest the body of society with it, to this chief desirous of commanding, the tribe, far from obeying, would answer: you, our equal, have wanted to destroy the undivided being of our society by affirming yourself superior to the others, you, who are worth no more than the others. You shall now be worth less than the others. This imaginary discourse has an ethnographically real effect: when a chief wants to act the chief, he is excluded from society, abandoned. If he insists, the others may kill him: total exclusion, radical conjuration.

Misfortune: something is produced that prevents society from maintaining desire for power and desire for submission in immanence. They emerge in the reality of the exercise, in the divided being of a society henceforth composed of unequals. Just as primitive societies are conservative because they want to conserve their being-for-freedom, divided societies do not allow themselves to change; the desire for power and the will for servitude are continuously realized.

Total freedom of La Boétie's thought, we were saying, trans-historicity of his discourse. The strangeness of the question he poses hardly dissolves in recalling the author's appurtenance to the jurist bourgeoisie, nor in only wanting to recognize in it the indignant echo of royal repression which in 1549 crushed the revolt of the Gabelles in the south of France. La Boétie's undertaking escapes all attempts to imprison it in the century; it is not familiar thought in that it develops precisely against what is reassuring in all familiar thought. The *Discours* is solitary and rigorous thought that feeds only on its own movement, on its own logic: if man is born to be free, human society's first mode of existence must have necessarily unfolded in non division, in non-inequality. There is, with La Boétie, a sort of *a priori* deduction of the Stateless society, of primitive society. Now it is perhaps on this point that one could, curiously, detect the century's influence, La Boétie, taking into account what happened in the first half of the 16th century.

We seem, indeed, to neglect too often that if the 16th century is that of the Renaissance, the resurrection of the culture of Greek and Roman Antiquity, it is also witness to an event whose significance will transform the face of the West, namely the discovery and conquest of the New World. The return to the Ancients of Athens and Rome, certainly, but also the irruption of what up until then had not existed, America. We can measure the fascination that the discovery of the unknown continent held over western Europe by the extremely rapid diffusion of all news from beyond the seas. Let us limit ourselves to revealing a few chronological points.[2] Starting in 1493, Christopher Columbus' letters regarding his discovery were published in Paris. One could read in 1503, again in Paris, the Latin translation of the story of the first voyage of Amerigo Vespucci. America, as the proper name of the New World, appeared for the first time in 1507 in another edition of the voyages of Vespucci. From 1515 on, the French translation of the voyages of the Portuguese became best-sellers. In short, one did not have to wait very long in the Europe of the beginning of the century to know what was happening in America. The abundance of news and the speed of its circulation — despite the difficulties of transmission at the time — indicate among the cultivated people of the time as passionate an interest in these new lands and the people who lived there as in the ancient world revealed by books. A double discovery, the same desire to know which invested at once the ancient history of Europe and its new geographical extension.

We should note that this wealth of travel literature is mostly of Spanish and Portuguese origin. The explorers and the Iberian Conquistadors actually

---

[2] Cf. G. Chimard, *L'éxotisme américain dans la littérature française au XVIe siécle,* Paris, 1911.

left for adventure in the name of, and with the financial support of, Madrid and Lisbon. Their expeditions were, in fact, enterprises of the State, and the travelers were, consequently, responsible for regularly informing the very fussy royal bureaucracies. But it does not necessarily follow that the French of the time only possessed documents furnished by neighboring countries to satisfy their curiosity. For if the crown of France was hardly concerned at this time with plans for colonization beyond the Atlantic and only peripherally interested in the efforts of the Spanish and the Portuguese, the private enterprises concerning the New World were, on the other hand, many and ambitious. The shipowners and merchants of the ports of the English Channel and of the entire Atlantic front launched, at the very beginning of the 16th century, perhaps before, expedition upon expedition toward the Isles and toward what André Thevet would later call equinoctial France. The State's silence and inertia were answered by the intense, buzzing activity of vessels and crews from Honfleur to Bordeaux, which very early on established regular commercial relations with the South American Savages. It is thus that in 1503, three years after the Portuguese explorer Cabral discovered Brazil, the Captain of Gonneville touched the Brazilian coast. After countless adventures, he managed to get back to Honfleur in May 1505, in the company of a young Indian, Essomerica, son of a chief of the Tupinamba tribe. The chronicles of the period have only retained a few names, such as that of Gonneville, among the hundreds of hardy sailors who crossed the ocean.[3] But there is no doubt that the quantity of information we have concerning these voyages gives only a weak idea of the regularity and intensity of the relations between the French and the Savages. Nothing surprising in this: these voyages were sponsored by private shipowners who, because of the competition, were certainly concerned about keeping their dealings as secret as possible. And the relative rarity of written documents was probably largely made up for by information supplied firsthand by sailors returning from America, in all the ports of Brittany and Normandy, as far as La Rochelle and Bordeaux. Essentially this means that since the second decade of the 16th century, a gentleman of France was in a position, if he wanted, to keep himself informed about the events and people of the New World. This flow of information, based on the intensification of commercial exchange, would continue to grow and become more detailed at the same time. In 1544, the navigator Jean Alfonse, describing the populations of the Brazilian coast, was able to establish a properly ethnographic distinction between three large tribes, subgroups of the very large Tupi ethnicity. Eleven years later, André Thevet and Jean de Lévy approached these same

---

[3] Cf. Ch. A. Julien, *Les Voyages de découverte et les Premiers Etablissements*, Paris, 1947.

shores to bring back their chronicles, irreplaceable testimonies on the Indians of Brazil. But, with these two master chroniclers, we already find ourselves in the second half of the 16th century.

Discours de la servitude volontaire was written, Montaigne tells us, when La Boétie was 18 years old, that is, in 1548. That Montaigne, in a subsequent edition of the *Essais*, returns to this date to say that his friend was in fact only 16, does not make much difference as far as the problem that concerns us. It would simply make his thought seem all the more precious. That La Boétie, furthermore, was able to revise the text of the *Discours* five years later while a student at Orléans seems to us both possible and without consequence. Either the *Discours* was indeed written in 1548 and its substance, its internal logic could not undergo any alteration, or else it was written later. Montaigne is explicit: it dates from La Boétie's eighteenth year. Thus, all subsequent modification can only be detail, superficial, destined to specify and refine the presentation. Nothing more. And there is also nothing more equivocal than this erudite obstinacy to reduce thought to that which is being proclaimed around it, nothing more obscurantist than this will to destroy the autonomy of a thought by the sad recourse to influences. And the *Discours* is there, its rigorous movement developing firmly, freely, as though indifferent to all the century's discourses.

It is probably for this reason that America, though not entirely absent from the *Discours*, only appears there in the form of a (very clear) allusion to these new people that have just been discovered: "But, in this regard, if, by chance, a new breed of people were born today, neither accustomed to subjugation nor attracted to freedom, and they did not not know what one or the other was, or just barely the names, if they were presented with the choice to be serfs, or to live freely according to laws with which they did not agree: there can be no doubt that they would much rather obey only reason, than to serve a man...." We can, in short, rest assured that in 1548, knowledge in France concerning the New World was varied, already old, and constantly updated by the navigators. And it would be quite surprising that someone like La Boétie would not have been very interested in what was being written on America or in what was being said about it in the ports of Bordeaux, for example, near his hometown of Sarlat. Of course, such knowledge was not necessary for this author to think of and write the *Discours*; he could have articulated it without this. But how could this young man, interrogating himself with such seriousness on voluntary servitude, who dreamt of society before the misfortune, how could he not be struck by the image that travelers traced, for many years already, of this "new breed of people," American Savages living without faith, king or law, these peoples without law, without emperor, each his own lord?

In a society divided along the vertical axis of power between the dominating and the dominated, the relations that unite men cannot unfold freely. Prince, despot or tyrant, the one who exercises power desires only the unanimous obedience of his subjects. The latter respond to his expectation, they bring into being his desire for power, not because of the terror that he would inspire in them, but because, by obeying, they bring into being their own desire for submission. The denaturing process excludes the memory of freedom, and consequently, the desire to reconquer it. All divided societies are thus destined to endure. The denaturing process is expressed at once in the disdain necessarily felt by the one who commands for those who obey, and in the subjects' love for the prince, in the cult that the people devote to the person of the tyrant. Now this flow of love rising ceaselessly from the depths to ever greater heights, this love of the subjects for the master equally denatures the relations between subjects. Excluding all freedom, these relations dictate the new law that governs society: one must love the tyrant. Insufficient love is a transgression of the law. All watch out for the respect of the law, all hold their neighbor in esteem only out of fidelity to the law. The love of the law — the fear of freedom — makes each subject an accomplice of the Prince: obedience to the tyrant excludes friendship between subjects.

What, from now on, will become of the non-divided societies, of societies without a tyrant, of primitive societies? Displaying their being-for-freedom, they cannot justly survive except in the free exercise of free relations between equals. All relations of another nature are essentially impossible because they are deadly for society. Equality engenders friendship, friendship can only be experienced in equality. What the young La Boétie would not have given to hear what the Guarani Indians of today say in their most sacred chants, Indians who are the aged but intractable descendants of the "new breed of people" of yore! Their great god Namandu emerges from the shadows and invents the world. He first creates the Word, the substance common to the divine and the human. He assigns to humanity the destiny of collecting the Word, of existing in it and protecting it. Humans, all equally chosen by the deities, are Protectors of the Word, and protected by it. Society is the enjoyment of the common good that is the Word. Instituted as equal by divine decision — by nature — society assembles as a whole, that is, an undivided whole: then, only *mborayu* can reside there, the life of the tribe and its will to live, the tribal solidarity of equals; *mborayu*: friendship, so that the society it founds is one, so that the men of this society are all one.[4]

---

[4] Cf. P. Clastres, *Le Grand Parler. Mythes et chants sacrés des Indiens Guarani*, Éd. du Seuil, 1974.

8

PRIMITIVE ECONOMY

The age-old infatuation with primitive societies assures the French reader of a regular and abundant supply of ethnological works. They are not of equal interest, however, far from it. From time to time, a book will stand out on the grayish horizon of these works: the occasion is too rare to let it go unnoticed. Iconoclastic and rigorous, salutary as well as scholarly, is the work of Marshall Sahlins, which many will be delighted to see finally published in French.[1]

An American professor of great reputation, Sahlins is an expert on Melanesian societies. But his scientific project can hardly be reduced to the ethnography of a certain cultural area. Extending far beyond monographic pointillism, as the transcontinental variety of his references attests, Sahlins undertakes the systematic exploration of the social dimension long scrutinized by ethnologists; he approaches the field of economics in a radically new way; he archly asks the fundamental question: what of economics in primitive societies?[2] A question of decisive weight, as we shall see. Not that

---

[1] M. Sahlins, *Age de pierre, Age d'abondance. L'conomie des sociétés primitives*, Gallimard, 1976. [*Stone Age Economics*, Chicago, Aldine-Atherton, 1972.] If Sahlins' book is full of knowledge, it is also full of humor. Tina Jolas, who translated it into French, has rendered it perfectly.

[2] Let us clarify a potential misunderstanding right off. The stone-age economics of which Sahlins speaks concerns not prehistoric men but, of course, primitives observed for several centuries by travellers, explorers, missionaires and ethnologists.

others have not asked it before him. Why come back, in that case, to a problem that seemed settled long ago? We quickly see, following Sahlins' method, that not only has the question of the primitive economy not received a response worthy of being called one, but that numerous authors have treated it with incredible lightness when they did not simply surrender it to a veritable distortion of ethnographic facts. We find ourselves confronted here, no longer with the misinterpretation possible in all scientific research, but, lo and behold, with the enterprise of adapting primitive social reality to a preexisting conception of society and of history, still vigorous, as we shall try to demonstrate. In other words, certain representatives of what we call economic anthropology have not always known, to put it mildly, how to separate the duty of objectivity, which at the very least requires a respect for the facts, from the concern of preserving their philosophical or political convictions. And once the analysis is subordinated, whether deliberately or unconsciously, to this or that discourse on society when rigorous science would demand precisely the opposite, we very quickly find ourselves carried off to the frontiers of mystification.

It is to denouncing this that the exemplary work of Marshall Sahlins is devoted. And one would be mistaken to suppose his ethnographic information much more abundant than that of his predecessors: although a field researcher, he does not offer any earth-shattering facts whose novelty would force us to rethink traditional ideas of primitive economy. He contents himself — but with what vigor! — to reestablishing the truth of givens long since collected and known; he has chosen to interrogate directly the available material, pitilessly pushing aside received ideas regarding this material. Which amounts to saying that the task Sahlins assigns himself could have been undertaken before him: the file, in short, was already there, accessible and complete. But Sahlins is the first to have reopened it; we must see him as a pioneer.

What does this concern? Economic ethnologists have continued to insist that the economy of primitive societies is a subsistence economy. Clearly such a statement does not mean to be a truism: namely, that the essential, if not exclusive, function of a given society's production system is to assure the subsistence of the individuals who make up the society in question. To establish archaic economy as a subsistence economy, we designate less the general function of all production systems than the manner in which the primitive economy fulfills this function. We say that a machine functions well when it satisfactorily fulfills the function for which it was conceived. It is using a similar criterion that we shall evaluate the functioning of the machine of production in primitive societies: does this machine function in conformity to the goals that society assigns it? Does this machine adequately insure the satisfaction of the group's material needs? This is the real question one must pose when looking at primitive economy. To this, "classic" economic anthropology responds with the idea of subsistence economy:[3] primitive economy is a subsistence economy in that it just barely manages to assure society's subsistence. Their economic system allows the primitives, at the price of incessant labor, not to freeze or starve to death. The primitive economy is an economy of survival in that its technical underdevelopment irremediably forbids the production of surplus and stockpiling that would at least guarantee the tribe's immediate future. This is the image of primitive man conveyed by "scholars": the Savage crushed by his ecological environment, constantly stalked by famine, haunted by the permanent anxiety of finding something to keep his loved ones from perishing. In short, the primitive economy is a subsistence economy because it is an economy of poverty.

To this conception of primitive economy, Sahlins contrasts not another conception, but quite simply, ethnographic facts. He proceeds with, among other things, a close examination of the work devoted to those primitives most easily imagined as the most deprived of all, fated as they are to occupy an eminently hostile environment with technological inefficiency: the hunters-collectors of the Australian and South African deserts, precisely those who illustrate perfectly, in the eyes of ethnoeconomists such as Herskovits, primitive poverty. Now, what is really the case? Monographs on the Australians of Arnhem Land and the Bochimans of the Kalahari, respectively, offer the new detail of statistics: the time devoted to economic activities is measured. And then one sees that far from spending all their lives in the feverish quest for aleatory nourishment, these so-called wretches spend only five hours a day on it, at most, and more often between three and four hours. Thus, as a result, in a relatively short period of time, the Australians and Bochimans very suitably insure their subsistence. And we must also note that, first, this daily work is only rarely sustained, interspersed as it is with frequent breaks; second, that it never involves the whole tribe: besides the fact that children and young people participate little or not at all in economic activities, not even adults devote themselves all at once to the search for food. And Sahlins notes that these quantified givens, recently gathered, confirm older testimonies of 19th-century travelers on all points.

Thus in spite of serious and well-known information, certain founding fathers of economic anthropology have, out of whole cloth, invented the myth of a savage man condemned to a quasi-animal condition through his inability to exploit the natural environment efficiently. This is wide of the

---

[3] Cf. Chapter 1 of Sahlins' book for numerous quotations of authors who express this point of view.

mark, and it is to Sahlins' credit to have rehabilitated the primitive hunter by reestablishing factual truths against the theoretical (theoretical!) travesty. Indeed, it follows from his analysis that not only is the primitive economy not an economy of poverty, but that primitive society is the original affluent society. A provocative statement, which troubles the dogmatic torpor of pseudo scholars of anthropology, but an accurate one: if the primitive machine of production, in short periods of low intensity, assures the satisfaction of people's material needs, it is, as Sahlins writes, because it functions beyond its objective possibilities, it is because it could, if it wanted to, function longer and more quickly, produce surplus, form a stockpile. Consequently, if primitive society, though able, does nothing about it, it is because it does not want to. The Australians and Bochimans, once they feel they have collected sufficient alimentary resources, stop hunting and collecting. Why should they fatigue themselves harvesting more than they can consume? Why would nomads exhaust themselves, uselessly transporting heavy provisions from one point to another, when, as Sahlins says, the surplus is in nature itself? But the Savages are not as mad as the formalistic economists who, for lack of discovering in primitive man the psychology of an industrial or commercial company head, concerned with ceaselessly increasing his production in order to increase his profit, doltishly infer from this primitive economy's intrinsic inferiority. Sahlins' undertaking, as a result, is salubrious, in that it calmly unmasks this "philosophy" which makes the contemporary capitalist the ideal and measure of all things. And yet what effort it takes to demonstrate that if primitive man is not an entrepreneur, it is because profit does not interest him; that if he does not "optimize" his activity, as the pedants like to say, it is not because he does not know how to, but because he does not feel like it!

Sahlins does not limit himself to the case of hunters. Using something called the Domestic Mode of Production (DMP), he examines the economy of "neolithic" societies, of primitive farmers, as can be observed today in Africa or Melanesia, in Vietnam or South America. There is nothing in common, apparently, between desert or forest nomads and sedentaries who hunt, fish and collect, but are essentially dependent on what they grow. One could expect, on the contrary, as a function of the considerable change that constitutes the conversion of a hunting economy into an agrarian economy, the blossoming of absolutely new economic attitudes, not to mention, of course, transformations in the organization of society itself.

Relying on a considerable number of studies conducted in various regions of the world, Sahlins examines in detail the local configurations (Melanesian, African, South American, etc.) of the DMP whose recurrent characteristics he brings to light: the predominance of sexual division of labor; segmentary production in view of consumption; autonomous access to the means of production; a centrifugal relationship between units of production. Taking into account an economic reality (the DMP), Sahlins creates categories that are properly political in that they touch the heart of primitive social organization: segmentation, autonomy, centrifugal relations. It is essentially impossible to think of primitive economics outside of the political. What merits attention for now is that the pertinent traits we use to describe the mode of production of slash-and-burn agriculturists also allow us to define the social organization of hunting peoples. From this point of view, a band of nomads, just like a sedentary tribe, is composed of units of production and of consumption — the "homes" or the "households" — in which the sexual division of labor, indeed, prevails. Each unit functions as a segment autonomous from the whole, and even if the rule of exchange solidly structures the nomad band, the play of centrifugal force is nevertheless present. Beyond differences in living styles, religious representations, ritual activity, the framework of society does not vary from the nomad community to the sedentary village. That machines of production so different as nomadic hunting and slash-and-burn agriculture could be compatible with identical social formations is a point whose significance it would be appropriate to measure.

All primitive communities aspire, in terms of their consumer production, to complete autonomy; they aspire to exclude all relations of dependence on neighboring tribes. It is, in short, primitive society's autarkic ideal: they produce just enough to satisfy all needs, but they manage to produce all of it themselves. If the DMP is a system fundamentally hostile to the formation of surplus, it is no less hostile to allowing production slip below the threshold that would guarantee the satisfaction of needs. The ideal of economic autarky is, in fact, an ideal of political independence, which is assured as long as one does not need others. Naturally, this ideal is not realized everywhere all the time. Ecological differences, climatic variations, contacts or loans can leave a society unable to satisfy the need for this commodity or that material or an object others know how to manufacture. This is why, as Sahlins shows, neighboring tribes, or even distant ones, find themselves engaged in rather intense trade relations. But, he points out in his tireless analysis of Melanesian "commerce", Melanesian societies do not have "markets" and "the same no doubt goes for archaic societies." The DMP thus tends, by virtue of each community's desire for independence, to reduce the risk incurred in exchange determined by need as much as possible: "reciprocity between commercial partners is not only a privilege, but a duty. Specifically, it obliges each person to receive as well as to give." Commerce between tribes is not import-export.

Now the will for independence — the autarkic ideal — inherent in the DMP since it concerns the community in its relationship to other communities, is also at work within the community, where centrifugal tendencies push each unit of production, each "household" to proclaim: every man for himself! Naturally, such a principle, ferocious in its egoism, is exercised only rarely: there have to be exceptional circumstances, like the famine whose effects Firth observed on the Tikopia society, victim in 1953-54 to devastating hurricanes. This crisis, writes Sahlins, revealed the fragility of the famous we — We, the Tikopia — while at the same time clearly demonstrating the strength of the domestic group. The household seemed to be the fortress of private interest, that of the domestic group, a fortress which, in times of crisis, isolated itself from the outside world and raised its social drawbridges — when not pillaging its relatives' gardens. As long as nothing serious alters the normal course of daily life, the community does not allow centrifugal forces to threaten the unity of its Self, the obligations of kinship continue to be respected. This is why, at the end of an extremely technical analysis of the case of Mazulu, a village of Tonga Valley, Sahlins thinks it possible to explain the underproduction of certain households by their certainty that their solidarity with those best stocked will play in their favor: "for if some of them fail, is it not precisely because they know at the outset that they can count on the others?" But should an unforeseeable event occur (a natural disaster or external aggression, for example) to upset the order of things, then the centrifugal tendency of each unit of production asserts itself, the household tends to withdraw into itself, the community "atomizes," while waiting for the bad moment to pass.

This does not mean, however, that under normal conditions, kinship obligations are always willingly respected. In Maori society, the household is "constantly confronted with a dilemma, constantly forced to maneuver and compromise between the satisfaction of its own needs and its more general obligations toward distant relatives which it must satisfy without compromising its own well-being." And Sahlins also quotes several savory Maori proverbs which clearly show the irritation felt toward overly demanding relatives (when these recipients have only a weak degree of kinship), and generous acts are then grudgingly accomplished.

The DMP thus assures primitive society of abundance measured by the ratio of production to need; it functions in view of the total satisfaction of need, refusing to go beyond it. The Savages produce to live, they do not live to produce: "The DMP is a consumer production which tends to slow down output and to maintain it at a relatively low level." Such a "strategy" obviously implies a sort of wager on the future: namely, that it will be made of repetition and not of difference, that the earth, the sky and the gods will oversee and maintain the eternal return of the same. And this, in general, is indeed what happens: changes that distort the lines of strength in society, such as the natural catastrophe of which the Tikopia were victims, are exceptional. But it is also the rarity of these circumstances that strips naked a society's weakness: "The obligation of generosity inscribed in the structure does not withstand the test of bad luck." Is this the Savages' incurable shortsightedness, as the travelers' chronicles say? Rather, in this insouciance one can read the greater concern for their freedom.

Through analysis of the DMP, Sahlins offers us a general theory of primitive economy. From production adapted exactly to the immediate needs of the family, he extracts, with great clarity, the law that underlies the system: "...the DMP conceals an anti-surplus principle: adapted to the production of subsistence goods, it tends to immobilize when it reaches this point." The ethnographically founded claim that, on the one hand, primitive economies are underproductive (only a segment of society works for short periods of time at low intensity), that on the other, they always satisfy the needs of society (needs defined by the society itself and not by an exterior example), such a claim then imposes, in its paradoxical truth, the idea that primitive society is, indeed, a society of abundance (certainly the first, perhaps also the last), since all needs are satisfied. But it also summons the logic at the heart of this social system: *structurally*, writes Sahlins, *"economy" does not exist.* That is to say that the economic, as a sector unfolding autonomously manner in the social arena, is absent from the DMP; the latter functions as consumer production (to assure the satisfaction of needs) and not as production of exchange (to acquire profit by commercializing surplus goods). What is clear, finally (what Sahlins' great work asserts), is the discovery that primitive societies are societies that refuse economy.[4]

The formalist economists are surprised that the primitive man is not, like the capitalist, motivated by profit: this is indeed the issue. Primitive society strictly limits its production lest the economic escape the social and turn against society by opening a gap between rich and poor, alienating some. A society without economy, certainly, but, better yet, a society against economy: this is the brilliant truth toward which Sahlins' reflections on primitive

---

[4] We cannot overlook the equally exemplary research that Jaques Lizot has been doing for several years among the last great Amazonian ethnic group, the Yanomami Indians. Measuring the time slash-and-burn farmers spend working, Lizot has come to the same conclusions as Sahlins in his analysis of the DMP. Cf. in particular Jacques Lizot, "Économie ou société? Quelques thèmes à propos de l'étude d'une communauté d'Amérindiens," *Journal de la Société des Américanistes*, IX, 1973, pp. 137–175.

society lead us. Reflections that are rigorous and tell us more about the Savages than any other work of the same genre. But it is also an enterprise of true thought, for, free of all dogmatism, it poses the most essential questions: under what conditions is a society primitive? Under what conditions can primitive society persevere in its undivided being?

Society without a State, classless society: this is how anthropology speaks of the factors that allow a society to be called primitive. A society, then, without a separate organ of political power, a society that deliberately prevents the division of the social body into unequal and opposing groups: "Primitive society allows poverty for everyone, but not accumulation by some." This is the crux of the problem that the institution of the chieftainship poses in an undivided society: what happens to the egalitarian will inscribed at the heart of the DMP in the face of the establishment of hierarchical relations? Would the refusal of division that regulates the economic order cease to operate in the political arena? How is the chief's supposedly superior status articulated to society's undivided being? How are power relations woven between the tribe and its leader? This theme runs throughout Sahlins' work, which approaches the question most directly in its detailed analysis of Melanesian big-man systems in which the political and the economic are joined together in the person of the chief.

In most primitive societies, two essential qualities are demanded of the chief: oratorical talent and generosity. A man unskilled at speaking or avaricious would never be recognized as leader. This is not a matter, of course, of personal psychological traits but of formal characteristics of the institution: a leader must not retain goods. Sahlins thoroughly examines the origin and effects of this veritable obligation of generosity. At the start of a big-man career we find unbridled ambition: a strategic taste for prestige, a tactical sense for the means to acquire it. It is quite clear that, to lavish goods, the chief must first possess them. How does he procure them? If we eliminate the case, not pertinent here, of manufactured objects which the leader receives from missionaries or ethnologists to later redistribute to members of the community, if we consider that the freedom to earn at the expense of others is not inscribed in the relations and modalities of exchange in these societies, it remains that, to fulfill his obligation of generosity, the big-man must produce the goods he needs by himself: he cannot rely on others. The only ones to aid and assist him are those who for various reasons consider it useful to work for him: people of his kinship who from then on maintain a client relationship with him. The contradiction between the chief's solitude and the necessity to be generous is also resolved through the bias of polygyny: if, in the great number of primitive societies, the rule of monogamy largely prevails, the plurality of wives, on the other hand, is almost always a privilege of important men, that is, the leaders. But, much more than a privilege, the chief's polygyny is a necessity in that it provides the principle means of acting like a leader: the work force of supplementary wives is used by the husband to produce a surplus of consumer goods that he will distribute to the community. One point is thus solidly established for now: in the primitive society, the economy, insofar as it is no longer inscribed in the movement of the DMP, is only a political tool; production is subordinated to power relations; it is only at the institutional level of the chieftainship that both the necessity and the possibility of surplus production appears.

Sahlins rightly uncovers here the antinomy between the centrifugal force inherent to the DMP and the opposite force that animates the chieftainship; a tendency toward dispersion in terms of modes of production, a tendency toward unification in terms of the institution. The supposed place of power would thus be the center around which society, constantly wrought by the powers of dissolution, institutes itself as a unity and a community — the chieftainship's force of integration against the DMP's force of disintegration: "The big-man and his consuming ambition are means whereby a segmentary society, 'acephalous' and fragmented into small autonomous communities overcomes these cleavages... to fashion larger fields of relation and higher levels of cooperation." The big-man thus offers, according to Sahlins, the illustration of a sort of minimum degree in the continuous curve of political power which would gradually lead to Polynesian royalty, for example: "In pyramid societies, the integration of small communities is perfected, while in Melanesian big-man systems, it has hardly begun, and is virtually unimaginable in the context of hunting peoples." The big-man would thus be a minimal figure of the Polynesian king, while the king would be the maximal extension of the big-man's power. A genealogy of power, from its most diffuse forms to its most concentrated realizations: could this be the foundation of the social division between masters and subjects and the most distant origin of the state machine?

Let us consider this more closely. As Sahlins says, the big-man accedes to power by the sweat of his brow. Unable to exploit the others in order to produce surplus, he exploits himself, his wives, and his clients-relatives: self-exploitation of the big-man and non-exploitation of society by the big-man who obviously does not have at his disposal the power to force the others to work for him, since it is precisely this power he is trying to conquer. It could not be a question, then, in such societies, of the social body's division along the vertical axis of political power: there is no division between a dominant minority (the chief and his clients) which would command and a dominated majority (the rest of the community) which would obey. It is rather the opposite spectacle that Melanesian societies offer us. As far as division, we see that if there is, in fact, division, it is only that which separates a minority of rich workers from a majority of the lazy poor: but, and it is here that we touch upon the very foundation of primitive society, the rich are only rich because of their own work, the fruits of which are appropriated and consumed by the idle masses of the poor. In other words, society as a whole exploits the work of the minority that surrounds the big-man. How then can we speak of power in relation to the chief, if he is exploited by society? A paradoxical disjunction of forces that all divided societies maintain: could the chief, on the one hand, exercise power over society, and society on the other, subject this same chief to intensive exploitation? But what, then, is the nature of this strange power whose potency we seek in vain? What is it about this power, finally, what cause primitive society to shun it? Can one, quite simply, still speak of power? This is indeed the whole problem: why does Sahlins call power that which obviously is not?

We detect here the rather widespread confusion in ethnological literature between prestige and power. What makes the big-man run? What is he sweating for? Not, of course, for a power to which the people of the tribe would refuse to submit were he even to dream of exercising it, but for prestige, for the positive image that the mirror of society would reflect back onto him celebrating a prodigious and hard-working chief. It is this inability to think of prestige without power that burdens so many analyses of political anthropology and that is particularly misleading in the case of primitive societies. By confusing prestige and power, we first underestimate the political essence of power and the social relations it institutes; we then introduce into primitive society a contradiction which cannot appear there. How can society's will for equality adapt to the desire for power which would precisely found inequality between those who command and those who obey? To raise the question of political power in primitive societies forces one to think of chieftainship outside of power, to ponder this immediate given of primitive sociology: the leader is powerless. In exchange for his generosity, what does the big-man get? Not the fulfillment of his desire for power, but the fragile satisfaction of his honor, not the ability to command, but the innocent enjoyment of a glory he exhausts himself to maintain. He works, literally, for glory: society gives it to him willingly, busy as it is savoring the fruits of its chief's labor. Flatterers live at the expense of those who listen to them.

Since the big-man's prestige does not win him any authority, it follows that he is not the first rung of the ladder of political power and that we were quite mistaken to see him as a real locus of power. How, then, do we place the big-man and other figures of chieftainship on a continuum? Here, a necessary consequence of the initial confusion between prestige and power appears. Powerful Polynesian royalty does not result from a progressive development of Melanesian big-man systems, because there is nothing in these systems to develop: society does not allow the chief to transform his prestige into power. We must, therefore, utterly renounce this continuist conception of social formations, and accept and recognize that primitive societies where the chiefs are powerless are radical departures from societies where power relations unfold: the essential discontinuity in societies without a State and societies with a State.

Now, there is a conceptual instrument generally unknown to ethnologists that allows us to resolve many difficulties: it is the category of debt. Let us return for a moment to the primitive chief's obligation of generosity. Why does the institution of the chieftainship involve this obligation? It certainly expresses a sort of contract between the chief and his tribe, the terms of which offer him the gratification of his narcissism in exchange for a flood of goods he will pour over society. The obligation of generosity clearly contains an egalitarian principle that places trade partners in a position of equality: society offers prestige which the chief acquires in exchange for goods. Prestige is not recognized unless goods are provided. But this would be to misinterpret the true nature of the obligation of generosity, to see in it only a contract guaranteeing the equality of the parties concerned. Hiding beneath this appearance is the profound inequality of society and the chief in that his obligation of generosity is, in fact, a duty, that is to say, a debt. The leader is in debt to society precisely because he is the leader. And he can never get rid of this debt, at least not as long as he wants to continue being the leader: once he stops being the leader, the debt is abolished, for it exclusively marks the relationship that unites the chieftainship and society. At the heart of power relations is indebtness.

We discover, then, this essential fact: if primitive societies are societies without a separate organ of power, this does not necessarily mean that they are powerless societies, societies where political questions are not raised. It is, on the contrary, to refuse the separation of power from society that the tribe maintains its chief's indebtedness; it is society that remains the holder of power and that exercises it over the chief. Power relations certainly exist: they take the form of a debt that the leader must forever pay. The chief's eternal indebtedness guarantees society that he will remain exterior to power, that he will not become a separate organ. Prisoner of his desire for prestige, the Savage chief agrees to submit to society's power by settling the debt that every exercise of power institutes. In trapping the chief in his desire, the tribe insures itself against the mortal risk of seeing political power become separate from it and turn against it: primitive society is a society against the State.

Since debt relations belong to the exercise of power, one must be prepared to find it everywhere that power is exercised. This is indeed what royalty teaches us, Polynesian or otherwise. Who pays the debt here? Who are the indebted? They are, as we well know, those whom kings, high priests or despots name the common people, whose debt takes on the name of tribute that they owe to the rulers. Hence it follows that, in effect, power does not come without debt and that inversely, the presence of debt signifies that of power. Those who hold power in any society prove it by forcing their subjects to pay tribute. To hold power, to impose tribute, is one and the same, and the despot's first act is to proclaim the obligation of payment. The sign and truth of power, debt traverses the political arena through and through; it is inherent in the social as such.

This is to say that, as a political category, debt offers the surest criterion on which to evaluate the being of societies. The nature of society changes with the direction of the debt. If debt goes from the chieftainship toward society, society remains undivided, power remains located in the homogeneous social body. If, on the contrary, debt goes from society toward the chieftainship, power has been separated from society and is concentrated in the hands of the chief, the resulting heterogeneous society is divided into the dominating and the dominated. What does the rupture between undivided societies and divided societies consist of? It is produced when the direction of the debt is reversed, when the institution turns power relations to its profit against society, thus creating a base and a summit toward which the eternal recognition of debt climbs ceaselessly in the name of tribute. The rupture in the direction of debt's movement separates societies in such a way that continuity is unthinkable: no progressive development, no intermediary social figure between the undivided society and the divided society. The conception of History as a continuum of social formations engendering themselves mechanically one after the other fails here, in its blindness to the glaring fact of rupture and discontinuity, to articulate the true problems: why does primitive society cease at a certain moment to code the flow of power? Why does it allow inequality and division to anchor death in the social body which it had, until then, warded off? Why do the Savages implement the chief's desire for power? Where is the acceptance of servitude born?

A close reading of Sahlins' book constantly raises similar questions. It does not explicitly formulate them itself, for the continuist prejudice acts as a veritable epistemological obstacle to the logic of this analysis. But we do see that its rigor brings it infinitely closer to such a conceptual elaboration. It makes no mistake about the opposition between society's desire for equality and the chief's desire for power, an opposition which can go as far as the murder of the leader. This was the case among the people of the

Paniai who, before killing their big-man, explained to him: "...You should not be the only rich one among us, we should all be the same, so you have to be equal to us." A discourse of society against power which is echoed by the reverse discourse of power against society, clearly stated by another chief: "I am a chief not because the people love me, but because they owe me money and they are scared." The first and only among the experts in economic anthropology, Sahlins paves the way for a new theory of primitive society by allowing us to measure the immense heuristic value of the economical-political category of debt.

We must finally point out that Sahlins' work furnishes an essential piece in the dossier of a debate that, until quite recently, was not inscribed in the order of the day: what of Marxism in ethnology, and of ethnology in Marxism? The stakes in such an interrogation are vast, extending far beyond university walls. Let us simply call to mind here the terms of a problem which will be brought up sooner or later. Marxism is not only the description of a particular social system (industrial capitalism), it is also a general theory of history and of social change. This theory presents itself as the science of society and of history, it unfolds in the materialist conception of societal movement and discovers the law of this movement. There is thus a rationality of history, the being and the becoming of the sociohistorical real brings up, one last time, the economic determinations of society: ultimately, these are the play and the development of productive forces which determine the being of society, and it is the contradiction between the development of productive forces and the rapports of production which, interlocking social change and innovation, constitute the very substance and law of history. Marxist theory of society and history is an economic determinism which affirms the prevalence of the material infrastructure. History is thinkable because it is rational, it is rational because it is, so to speak, natural, as Marx says in *Das Kapital*: "The development of society's economic formation is assimilable to the progress of nature and its history...." It follows that Marxism, as a science of human society in general, can be used to consider all social formations history offers us. It can be used, certainly, but even more, it is obliged to consider all societies to be a valid theory. Marxists, thus, cannot ignore primitive society; the historical continuism affirmed by the theory they claim as their own does not allow them to.

When ethnologists are Marxists, they obviously subject primitive society to the analysis that calls for and allows the instrument that they possess: Marxist theory and its economic determinism. They must, consequently, affirm that even in societies anterior to capitalism, economics occupied a central, decisive place. There is, in effect, no reason for primitive societies, for example, to be an exception to the general law that encompasses all societies: productive forces tend to develop. We find ourselves asking two very simple questions as a result: Are economics central in primitive societies? Do productive forces develop? It is precisely the answers to these questions that Sahlins' book formulates. It informs us or reminds us that in primitive societies, the economy is not a machine that functions autonomously: it is impossible to separate it from social life, religious life, ritual life, etc. Not only does the economic field not determine the being of primitive society, but it is rather society that determines the place and limits of the economic field. Not only do the productive forces not tend toward development, but the will for underproduction is inherent in the DMP. Primitive society is not the passive toy in the blind game of productive forces; it is, on the contrary, society that ceaselessly exercises rigorous and deliberate control over production. It is the social that orders the economic game; it is, ultimately, the political that determines the economic. Primitive societies are machines of anti-production. What, then, is the motor of history? How does one deduce the social classes of a classless society, the division of an undivided society, the alienated work of a society that only alienates the work of the chief, the State of a society without a State? Mysteries. It follows that Marxism cannot be used to consider primitive society, because primitive society is not thinkable in this theoretical framework. Marxist analysis is valuable, perhaps, for divided societies or for systems where, apparently, the sphere of economy is central (capitalism). Such an analysis, when applied to undivided societies, to societies that posit themselves in the refusal of economy, is more than absurd, it is obscurantist. We do not know whether or not it is possible to be Marxist in philosophy; we see clearly, however, that it is impossible in ethnology.

Iconoclastic and salutary, we were saying of the great work of Marshall Sahlins, who exposes the mystifications and deceptions with which the so-called human sciences too often content themselves. More concerned with establishing theory starting from facts than fitting facts to theory, Sahlins shows us that research must be alive and free, for great thought can perish if reduced to theology. Formalist economists and Marxist anthropologists have this in common — they are incapable of reflecting on man in primitive societies without including him in the ethical and conceptual frameworks issued from capitalism or from the critique of capitalism. Their pathetic undertakings are born in the same place and produce the same results: an ethnology of poverty. Sahlins has helped demonstrate the poverty of their ethnology.

9

THE RETURN TO ENLIGHTENMENT

> I will explain myself: but this will be to take the most use-
> less, most superfluous precaution: for everything that I will
> tell you could only be understood by those who do not
> need to be told.
>
> Jean-Jacques Rousseau

Pierre Birnbaum does me an honor indeed, and I shall be the last to complain about the company in which he places me. But this is not the principal merit of his essay. This document seems worthy of interest in that it is, in a sense, anonymous (like an ethnographic document): I mean that a work such as this absolutely illustrates the very widespread way of approaching (or not approaching) the question of politics, that is, the question of society, in what we call the social sciences. Rather than extract the comic aspects and without spending too much time on the apparently, for some, inevitable conjunction between confident tone and blurred ideas, I

First published in *Revue française de science politique*, no. 1, Paris, Presses de la Fondation nationale des sciences politiques, February, 1977.

will attempt to zero in on little by little the "theoretical" locus from which Birnbaum has produced his text.

But first, let's correct certain errors and fill in some gaps. It seems, according to the author, that I invite my contemporaries "to envy the fate of Savages." Naïve or cunning? No more than the astronomer who invites others to envy the fate of stars do I militate in favor of the Savage world. Birnbaum confuses me with promoters of an enterprise in which I do not hold stock (R. Jaulin and his acolytes). Is Birnbaum unable, then, to locate the differences? As analyst of a certain type of society, I attempt to unveil the modes of functioning and not to construct programs: I content myself with describing the Savages, but perhaps it is he who finds them noble? So let's skip over this futile and hardly innocent chatter on the return of the Noble Savage. Besides, Birnbaum's constant references to my book on the Guayaki leave me a bit perplexed: does he imagine by chance that this tribe constitutes my only ethnological basis of support? If this is the case, he shows an unsettling gap in his information. My presentation of ethnographic facts concerning the Indian chieftainship is not at all new: it has been around, to the point of monotony, in the written documents of all the travelers, missionaries, chroniclers, ethnographers who since the beginning of the 16th century have succeeded each other in the New World. It is not I who, from this point of view, discovered America. I will add that my work is much more ambitious than Birnbaum would believe: it is not only American primitive societies on which I attempt to reflect, but on primitive society in general, which encompasses all particular primitive societies. Having brought these various clarifications to the fore, let us turn now to serious matters.

With rare clairvoyance, Birnbaum inaugurates his text with an error that augurs badly for the rest: "We have always," he writes, "questioned the origins of political domination..." It is exactly the opposite: we have never interrogated the question of origin, for, beginning with Greek antiquity, western thought has always assumed the social division of the dominating and dominated as inherent to society as such. Understood as an ontological structure of society, as the natural state of the social being, the division into Masters and Subjects has constantly been thought of as the essence of all real or possible societies. There could not be, then, in this social vision, any origin of political domination since it is inseparable from human society, since it is an immediate given of society. Hence the great stupefaction of the first observers of primitive societies: societies without division, chiefs without power, people without faith, without law, without king. What discourse could the Europeans use to describe the Savages? Either question their own conviction that society could not be thought of without division and admit that primitive peoples constituted societies in the full sense of the term; or else decide that a non-divided grouping, where chiefs do not command and where no one obeys, could not be a society: the Savages are really savages, and one must civilize them, "police" them, a theoretical and practical path which the Westerners of the 16th century unanimously took. With the exception, however, of Montaigne and of La Boétie, the former perhaps under the influence of the latter. They, and they alone, thought against the current, which, of course, has escaped Birnbaum. He is certainly neither the first nor the last to pedal in the wrong direction; but since La Boétie does not need me to defend him, I would like to return to Birnbaum's proposals.

What is he getting at? His goal (if not his approach) is perfectly clear. To him, it is a matter of establishing that "the society against the State presents itself [...] as a society of total constraint." In other words, if primitive society is unaware of social division, it is at the price of a much more frightful alienation, that which subjects the community to an oppressive system of norms that no one can change. "Social control" is absolute: it is no longer society against the State, it is the society against the individual. Ingenuously, Birnbaum explains to us why he knows so much about primitive society: he has read Durkheim. He is a trusting reader; not a doubt enters his mind: Durkheim's opinion of primitive society is really the truth about primitive society. Let us move on. It follows, thus, that the Savage society distinguishes itself not by the individual freedom of men, but by "the preeminence of mystical and religious thought which symbolizes the adoration of everything." Birnbaum has missed the chance here at a catchy phrase: I will supply it for him. He thinks, but without managing to express it, that myth is the opiate of the Savages. Humanist and progressive, Birnbaum naturally wishes the liberation of the Savages: we must detoxify them (we must civilize them). All this is rather silly. Birnbaum, in fact, is totally unaware that his suburban atheism, solidly rooted in a scientism already outmoded at the end of the 19th century, meets head on, justifies, the missionary enterprise's densest discourse and colonialism's most brutal practice. There is nothing to be proud of here.

Contemplating the relationship between society and chieftainship, Birnbaum calls to the rescue another eminent specialist of primitive societies, J.W. Lapierre, whose opinion he makes his own: "... the chief [...] has the monopoly on usage of legitimate speech and [...] no one can take speech in order to oppose it to the chief's without committing a sacrilege condemned by unanimous public opinion." This at least is clear. But Professor Lapierre is certainly peremptory. And how is he so learned? What book did he read that in? Does he consider the sociological concept of legitimacy? Thus, the chiefs of which he speaks possess the monopoly on legitimate speech? And what does this legitimate speech say? We would be very curious to know. Thus, no one can oppose this speech without committing a sacrilege? But then these are absolute monarchs, Attilas or Pharaohs! We are wasting our time then reflecting on the legitimacy of their speech: for they are the only ones to speak, it is they who command; if they command, it is they who possess political power; if they possess political power, it is because society is divided into Masters and Subjects. Off the subject: I am interested in primitive societies and not in archaic despotism. Lapierre/Birnbaum, in order to avoid a slight contradiction, should choose: either primitive society is subjected to the "total constraint" of its norms, or else it is dominated by the legitimate speech of the chief. Let us allow the professor to talk about this and go back to the pupil who needs some additional explanation, as brief as this might be.

What is a primitive society? It is a non-divided, homogeneous society, such that, if it is unaware of the difference between the rich and the poor, *a fortiori*, it is because the opposition between the exploiters and the exploited is absent. But this is not the essential matter. What is notably absent is the political division into the dominating and the dominated: the chiefs are not there to command, no one is destined to obey, power is not separate from society which, as a single totality, is the exclusive holder of power. I have written countless times before (and it seems this is still not enough[1]) that power only exists when exercised: a power that is not exercised is, in effect, nothing. What, then, does primitive society do with the power that it possesses? It exercises it, of course, and first of all, on the chief, precisely to prevent him from fulfilling an eventual desire for power, to prevent him from acting the chief. More generally, society exercises its power in order to conserve it, in order to prevent the separation of this power, in order to ward off the irruption of division into the social body, the division into Masters and Subjects. In other words, society's use of power to assure the conservation of its undivided being creates a relationship between the social being and itself. What third term establishes this relationship? It is precisely that which causes so much worry for Birnbaum/Durkheim, it is the world of myth and rites, it is the religious dimension. The primitive social being meditated by religion. Is Birnbaum unaware that there is no society except under the sign of the Law? This is probable. Religion thus assures society's relationship to it

---

[1] Cf., for example, "La question du pouvoir dans les sociétés primitives," *Interrogations*, International Journal of Anarchist Research, 7, 1976 [Chapter Six in this present book]. Cf. also my preface to M. Sahlins' book, Gallimard, 1976 [Chapter Five in this present book).

Law, that is, to the ensemble of norms that organize social relations. Where does Law come from? Where is Law as legitimate foundation of society born? In a time prior to society, mythic time; its birthplace is at once immediate and infinitely faraway, the space of the Ancestors, of cultural heroes, of gods. It is there that society institutes itself as an undivided body; it is they who decree the Law as a system of norms, this Law that religion has a mission to transmit and to make sure is eternally respected. What does this mean? It means that society's foundation is exterior to itself, society is not the founder of itself: the foundation of primitive society does not stem from human decision, but from divine action. At this, an idea developed in an absolutely original way by Marcel Gauchet, Birnbaum declares himself surprised: how surprising, indeed, that religion is not the an opiate, but that the religious component, far from acting as a superstructure over society, should be, on the contrary, inherent in the primitive social being; how surprising that this society should be read as a total social fact!

Does Birnbaum/Lapierre, a late apostle of the Age of Enlightenment, now see more clearly what is legitimate in the Savage chief's speech? This is doubtful so I will clarify it for him. The chief's discourse is one of tradition (and, in this capacity, he does not, of course, have the monopoly) – let us respect the norms taught by the Ancestors! Let us not change anything in the Law! It is a discourse of the Law that forever establishes society as an undivided body, the Law that exorcises the specter of division, the Law guarantees the freedom of men against domination. As the spokesperson of ancestral Law, the chief cannot say more; he cannot, without running serious risks, position himself as legislator of his own society, substitute the Law of the community with the law of his desire. In an undivided society, what could change and innovation lead to? To nothing else but social division, to the domination of a few over the rest of society. Birnbaum can certainly, after this, hold forth on the oppressive nature of primitive society; or even on my organicist conception of society. Could it be that he does not understand what he reads? The metaphor of the beehive (metaphor, and not model) is not mine, but the Guayaki Indians': these irrationalists, when they celebrate the festival of honey, compare themselves, indeed, against all logic, to a beehive! This would not happen to Birnbaum; he is not a poet, but a scholar of cool Reason. May he keep it.[2]

On page ten of his essay, Birnbaum declares me incapable of giving a sociological explanation of the birth of the State. But on page 19, it seems

[2] If Birnbaum is interested in organicist conceptions of society, he should read Leroi-Gourhan (*Le Geste et la Parole*); he will be gratified. Now for a riddle: In South America, the Whites call themselves *racionales*: in relation to whom?

that this birth "may now be explained by rigorous demographic determinism...." It is, in short, the reader's choice. A few clarifications may guide this choice. Actually, up until now, I have never said anything regarding the origin of the State, that is, regarding the origin of social division, the origin of domination. Why? Because this is a matter of a (fundamental) question of sociology, and not of theology or philosophy of history. In other words, to pose the question of origin depends on an analysis of the social: under what conditions can social division surge forth from the undivided society? What is the nature of the social forces that would lead Savages to accept the division into Masters and Subjects? Under what conditions does primitive society as undivided society die? A geneology of misfortune, a search for the social *clinamen* that can only be developed, of course, by questioning the primitive social being: the problem of origin is strictly sociological, and neither Condorcet nor Hegel, neither Comte nor Engels, neither Durkheim nor Birnbaum are of any help in this. In order to understand social division, we must begin with the society that existed to prevent it. As for knowing whether I can or cannot articulate an answer to the question of the origin of the State, I still do not know, and Birnbaum knows even less. Let us wait, let us work, there is no hurry.

Two words now regarding my theory on the origin of the State: "rigorous demographic determinism explains its appearance," Birnbaum has me say, with a consummate sense of the comic. It would be a great relief if we could go from demographic growth to the institution of the State in a single bound; we would have time to occupy ourselves with other matters. Unfortunately, things are not so simple. To substitute a demographic materialism for an economic materialism? The pyramid would still be poised on its tip. What is certain, on the other hand, is that ethnologists, historians and demographers have shared a false certainty for a very long time: namely, that the population of primitive societies was necessarily weak, stable, inert. Recent research shows the opposite: the primitive demography evolves, and most often, in the direction of growth. I have, for my part, attempted to show that in certain conditions, the demographic eventually has an effect on the sociological, that this parameter must be taken into account as much as others (not more, but not less) if one wants to determine the possibility of change in primitive society. From this to a deduction of the State...

Like everyone, Birnbaum passively welcomed what ethnology taught: primitive societies are societies without a State — without a separate organ of power. Very good. Taking primitive societies seriously, on the one hand, and ethnological discourse on these societies, on the other, I wonder why they are without a State, why power is not separated from the social body. And it appears to me little by little that this non-separation of power, this non-division of the social being is due not to primitive societies' fetal or embryonic state, not to an incompleteness or a noncompletion, but is related to a sociological act, to an institution of sociality as refusal of division, as refusal of domination: if primitive societies are Stateless, it is because they are against the State. Birnbaum, all of a sudden, and many others along with him, no longer hear out of this ear. This disturbs them. They don't mind the Stateless, but against the State, hold it! This is an outrage. What about Marx then? And Durkheim? And us? Can we no longer tell our little stories? No! This cannot happen! We have here an interesting case of what psychoanalysis calls resistence; we see what all these doctors are resisting, and therapy will be a deep breath.

Birnbaum's readers may tire of having to choose constantly. Indeed, the author speaks on page nine of my "voluntarism that casts aside all structural explanation of the State" only to state on page 20 that I abandon "the voluntarist dimension which animates La Boétie's *Discours*...." Apparently unaccustomed to logic, Birnbaum confuses two distinct outlines of reflection: a theoretical outline and a practical outline. The first is articulated around a historical and sociological question: what is the origin of domination? The second refers to a political question: what should we do to abolish domination? This is not the place to address the latter point. Let us return, then, to the former. It seems to me that Birnbaum quite simply has not read my brief essay on La Boétie: nothing, of course, obliges him to, but why the devil pick up his pen to write on things he knows nothing about? I will thus quote myself as to the voluntary character of servitude and to the properly anthropological stakes of La Boétie's *Discours*: "And though unintentional, this will suddenly reveals its true identity: it is desire." (See Chapter 7 of this book). A high school student already knows all this: that desire refers to the unconscious, that social desire refers to the social unconscious, and that sociopolitical life does not unfold only in the accountability of consciously expressed wills. For Birnbaum, psychological conceptions must date from the middle of the 19th century, the category of desire is no doubt pornography, while will is Reason. As for me, I attempt to zero in on the arena of desire as a political space, to establish that the desire for power cannot be realized itself without the inverse and symmetrical desire for submission, to show that primitive society is the locus of repression of this two-fold evil desire, and to ask: Under what conditions is this desire more powerful than its repression? Why does the community of Equals divide itself into Masters and Subjects? How can respect for the Law yield to the love of One?

Are we not approaching the truth? It seems so. Would not the ultimate analyzer of all this be what we call Marxism? It is true that, to describe the anthropology that claims filiation with Marxism, I used the expression (which seems to trouble Birnbaum) "Marxist swamp." This was in a moment of excessive benevolence. The study and analysis of Karl Marx's thought is one thing, the examination of all that calls itself "Marxist" is another. As for anthropological "Marxism" — Marxist anthropology — an obviousness begins (slowly) to emerge: this "anthropology" is made up of a two-fold deception. On the one hand, it deceptively and shamelessly affirms its relationship with the letter and spirit of Marxian thought; on the other hand, it deceptively, and fanatically, attempts to express the social being of primitive society scientifically. Marxist anthropologists could care less about primitive societies! They don't even exist for these obscurantist theologians who can only speak of pre-capitalist societies. Nothing but the holy Dogma! Doctrine above everything! Especially above the reality of the social being.

The social sciences (and notably, ethnology) are currently, as we know, the theater of a powerful attempt at ideological investment. Marxification! yelps the right, which has long since lost the capacity for comprehension. But Marx, it seems to me, does not have a lot to do with this cuisine. As for him, he saw a little further than Engles' nose; he saw them coming, the Marxists in reinforced concrete, ahead of time. Their somber, elementary, dominatrix ideology of combat (doesn't domination say anything to Birnbaum?) can be recognized beneath the interchangeable masks called Leninism, Stalinism, Maoism (its partisans have gotten subtle lately): it is this ideology of conquest of total power (doesn't power say anything to Birnbaum?), it is this ideology of granite, hard to destroy, which Claude Lefort has begun to chisel.[3] Wouldn't this, finally, be the place from which Birnbaum attempts to speak (the swamp where he seems to want to wallow)? Would this not be the undertaking to which he wants to bring his modest contribution? And he does not fear, after this, to speak to me of freedom, of thought, of thought of freedom. He has no shame.

As for his pranks regarding my pessimism, texts such as his are surely not the kind to make me optimistic. But I can assure Birnbaum of one thing: I am not a defeatist.

---

[3] Cf. *Un homme en trop. Réflexions sur l'Archipel du Goulag.* Éditions du Seuil, 1976.

10

MARXISTS AND
THEIR ANTHROPOLOGY

Though it is not very entertaining, we must reflect a bit on Marxist anthropology, on its causes and effects, its advantages and inconveniences. For if, ethnomarxism, on the one hand, is still a powerful current in the human sciences, the ethnology of Marxists is, on the other hand, of an absolute, or rather, radical nullity: it is null at its root. And this is why it is not necessary to enter into the works in detail: one can quite easily consider ethnomarxists' abundant production as a whole, as a homogeneous whole equal to zero. Let us ruminate then, on this nothingness, on this conjunction between Marxist discourse and primitive society.

A few historical points, first. French anthropology has developed for the past twenty years, thanks to the institutional promotion of the social sciences (the creation of numerous courses in ethnology in the Universities and

First published in *Libre,* no. 3, Paris, Payot, pp. 135–149, with the following note: "These pages were written by Pierre Clastres a few days before his death. He was not able to oversee the transcription and revision. Hence, there were some problems in deciphering the manuscript. Questionable words were placed in brackets. Illegible words or expressions were left blank."

at the Centre National de la Recherche Scientifique), but also in the wake of Lévi-Strauss' considerably original undertaking. And so, until recently, ethnology unfolded principally under the sign of structuralism. But, around ten years ago, the tendency was reversed: Marxism (what is called Marxism) has gradually emerged as an important line of anthropological research, recognized by numerous non-Marxist researchers as a legitimate and respectable discourse on the societies that ethnologists study. Structuralist discourse has thus yielded to Marxist discourse as the dominant discourse of anthropology.

For what reasons? To invoke a talent superior to that of Lévi-Strauss in this or that Marxist, for example, is laughable. If the Marxists shine, it is not due to their talent, for they sorely lack talent, by definition, one could say: the Marxist machine would not function if its mechanics had the least talent, as we shall see. On the other hand, to attribute, as is often done, the regression of structuralism to the fickleness of fashion seems absolutely superficial. Insofar as structuralist discourse conveys a strong thought (a thought), it is transconjunctural and indifferent to fashion: an empty and quickly forgotten discourse. We shall soon see what is left of it. Of course, we cannot attach the progression of Marxism in ethnology to fashion either. The latter was ready, ahead of time, to fill an enormous gap in the structuralist discourse (in reality, Marxism does not fill anything at all, as I will attempt to show). What is this gap where the failure of structuralism takes root? It is that this major discourse of social anthropology does not speak of society. What is missing, erased from the structuralist discourse (essentially, that of Lévi-Strauss: for, outside of a few rather clever disciples, capable at best of doing sub-Lévi-Strauss, who are the structuralists?), what this discourse cannot speak of, because it is not designed for it, is concrete primitive society, its mode of functioning, its internal dynamic, its economy and its politics.

But all the same, it will be said, the kinship, the myths, don't these count? Certainly. With the exception of certain Marxists, everyone agrees to recognize the decisive importance of Lévi-Strauss' work *Elementary Structures of Kinship*. This book, moreover, has inspired among ethnologists a formidable outpouring of studies of kinship: there are countless studies on the mother's brother or the sister's daughter. Are they able to speak of anything else? But let us pose the real question once and for all: is the discourse on kinship a discourse on society? Does the knowledge of the kinship system of such and such tribe inform us about its social life? Not at all: when one has skinned a kinship system, one scarcely knows any more about the society, one is still at the threshold. The primitive social body cannot be reduced to its blood ties and alliances; it is not only a machine for fabricating kinship relations. Kinship is not society: is this to say that kinship relations are secondary in the primitive social fabric? Much to the contrary: they are fundamental. In other words, primitive society, less than any other, cannot be thought of without kinship relations, and yet the study of kinship (such as it has been conducted up until now, in any case) does not teach us anything about the primitive social being. What use are kinship relations in primitive societies? Structuralism can only furnish a single answer, a massive one: to codify the prohibition of incest. This function of kinship explains that men are not animals, and nothing more: it does not explain how primitive man is a particular man, different from others. And yet kinship ties fulfill a determined function, inherent in primitive society as such, that is, an undivided society made up of equals: kinship, society, equality, even combat. But this is another story, of which we shall speak another time.

Lévi-Strauss' other great success is situated in the field of mythology. The analysis of myths has provoked fewer vocations than that of kinship: among other things, because it is more difficult and because no one, no doubt, could ever manage to do it as well as the master. On what condition can his analysis be deployed? On the condition that myths constitute a homogeneous system, on the condition that "myths reflect upon each other," as Lévi-Strauss says himself. The myths thus have a rapport with each other, they can be reflected upon. Very good. But does the myth (a particular myth) limit itself to reflecting upon its neighbors so that the mythologist might reflect upon them together? Surely not. Here again, structuralist thought abolishes, in a particularly clear manner, the rapport with the social: it is the relation of the myths among themselves that is privileged at the outset, by elision of the place of the production and invention of the myth, the society. That the myths think themselves among each other, that their structure can be analyed, is certain: Lévi-Strauss brilliantly provides the proof; but it is in a secondary sense: for they first consider the society which considers itself in them, and therein lies their function. Myths make up primitive society's discourse on itself; they have a sociopolitical dimension that structural analysis naturally avoids taking into consideration lest it break down. Structuralism is only operative on the condition of cutting the myths from society, of seizing them, ethereal, floating a good distance from the space of origin. And this is indeed why it is almost never a question of primitive social life: namely, the rite. What is there that is more collective, indeed, more social, than a ritual? The rite is the religious mediation between myth and society: but, for structuralist analysis, the difficulty stems from the fact that rites do not reflect upon each other. It is impossible to reflect upon them. Thus, exit the rite, and with it, society.

Whether one approaches structuralism from its summit (the work of Lévi-Strauss), whether one considers this summit according to its two major components (analysis of kinship, analysis of myths), an observation emerges, the observation of an absence: this elegant discourse, often very rich, does not speak about the society. It is a structuralism like a godless theology: it is a sociology without society.

Combined with the increase in strength of the human sciences, a strong — and legitimate — demand has thus emerged among researchers and students: we want to talk about the society, tell us about the society! This is when the scene changes. The graceful minuet of the structuralists, politely dismissed, is replaced by a new ballet, that of the Marxists (as they call themselves): they do a robust folk dance in their big, studded clogs, stomping clumsily on the ground of research. For various reasons (political and not scientific), the public applauds. It is, in effect, because Marxism, as a social and historical theory, is entitled by nature to extend its discourse to the field of primitive society. Better: the logic of Marxist doctrine forces i not to neglect any type of society, it is in its nature to speak the truth regarding all social formations that mark history. And this is why there is inherent in the global Marxist discourse, a discourse prepared in advance on primitive society.

Marxist ethnologists make up an obscure but numerous phalanx. We search in vain for a marked individuality, an original mind in this disciplined body: all devout followers of the same doctrine, they profess the same belief, intone the same credo, each surveying the other to make sure the letter of the canticles sung by this scarcely angelic choir are respected in orthodoxy. Tendencies, however, are confronted aggressively, one might argue. Indeed: each of them spends his time calling the other a pseudo-Marxist impostor, each claims the correct interpretation of the Dogma as his own. It is not up to me, naturally, to hand out diplomas for Marxist authenticity to whoever deserves them (let them deal with that themselves). But I can, however, (it is not a pleasure, it is a duty) attempt to show that their sectarian quarrels stir the same parish, and that the Marxism of one is not worth more than that of another.

Take for example Meillassoux. He would be, they say, one of the thinking (thinking!) heads of Marxist anthropology. In this particular case, painstaking efforts have been spared me, thanks to the detailed analysis that A. Adler has devoted to this author's recent work.[1] Let the reader refer, then, to this work and to its criticism: Adler's work is serious, rigorous, more than attentive (Adler, like Meillassoux — or rather, unlike him — is, in fact, a specialist on Africa). The Marxist thinker should be proud to have as conscientious

---

[1] C. Meillassoux, *Femmes, Greniers et Capitaux*, Paris, Maspero, 1976; A. Adler, "L'ethnologie marxiste: vers un nouvel obscurantisme?" *l'Homme*, XVI (4) pp. 118-128.

reader and show appreciation: and yet, this is not at all the case. To Adler's very reasonable objections (who destroys, as we might expect, the author's undertaking), Meillassoux responds[2] in a way that can be summed up easily: those who do not agree with Marxist anthropology are partisans of Pinochet. Cekomça. This is short but to the point. Why bother with nuances when one is the supercilious protector of the doctrine? He is a sort of *integriste*, there is something of a Monseigneur Lefebvre in this man: the same stubborn fanaticism, the same incurable allergy to doubt. From this wood, harmless puppets are made. But when the puppet is in power, he becomes unsettling and is named, for example, Vichinsky: To the gulag, nonbelievers! We'll teach you to doubt the dominant relations of production in primitive social life.

Meillassoux, however, is not alone, and it would be unjust to the others to give the impression that he has the monopoly on anthropological Marxism. We must, for equity's sake, make room for his deserving colleagues.

Take, for example, Godelier. He has acquired quite a reputation (at the bottom of rue de Tournon) as a Marxist thinker. His Marxism attracts attention, for it seems less rugged, more ecumenical than Meillassoux's. There is something of a radical-socialist in this man (red on the outside, white on the inside). Could this be an opportunist? Come now. This is an athlete of thought: he has undertaken to establish the synthesis between structuralism and Marxism. We see him hop from Marx to Lévi-Strauss. (Hop! As though it were a question of a little bird! These are the lurches of an elephant.)

Let us flip through his last work,[3] notably the preface of the second edition: a task, which, let it be said in passing, offers little pleasure. Style, indeed, makes the man, and this one is not exactly Proustian (this boy does not have his eye on the French Academy). In short the conclusion to this preface is a bit tangled. Godelier explains that Lefort and I pose the question of the State's origin (in our work on La Boétie) (this is not what it is about at all), that Deleuze and Guattari have already addressed this in *Anti-Oedipus*, but that their remarks were probably inspired by Clastres (p. 25, n. 3). Go figure. Godelier is, in any case, honest: he admits that he does not understand anything he reads (he quotes things and then peppers them with exclamation points and question marks). Godelier does not like the category of desire, which suits him well, by the way. It would be a waste of time to try to explain, because he wouldn't understand, that what Lefort and I identify under this term has very little to do with how Deleuze and Guattari use it.

---

2 C. Meillassoux, "Sur deux critiques de *Femmes, Greniers et Capitaux* ou Fahrenheit 450,5," *l'Homme*, XVII (1), pp. 123-128.

3 M. Godelier, *Horizon, trajets marxistes en anthropologie*, 2nd edition, Paris, Maspero, 1977.

Let us move on. In any case, these ideas are suspect to him, for the bourgeoisie applauds them, and he is doing everything necessary to insure that the bourgeoisie remain the only ones to applaud.

Godelier, on the other hand, is applauded by the proletariat. To his proud remarks, what ovations in Billancourt! There is, let us admit, something moving (and unexpected) in this ascetic rupture: he renounces the University of the bourgeoisie, its pomp and careers, its work and promotions. This is the Saint Paul of the human sciences. Amen. But all the same, the reader loses patience; can this oaf utter anything but silliness? He must have an idea from time to time! Godelier's ideas are very difficult to find in this overwhelming Marxist rhetoric. If we put aside the quotations of Marx, and the banalities of which everyone is guilty in moments of laziness, there isn't much left. Let us admit, however, that in the foreword of the first edition, and the preface of the second, our pachyderm has made a considerable effort (good intentions are not lacking). Embarking on a veritable journey, as he says himself, this hardy navigator has crossed oceans of concepts. What has he discovered? That the representations, for example, of primitive societies (religions, myths, etc.) belong to the field of ideology. Now, it is appropriate here to be Marxist (unlike Godelier), that is, faithful to the text of Marx: what, in effect, is ideology to Marx? It is the discourse that a divided society holds on itself, structured around a social conflict. This discourse has the mission to mask the division and the conflict, to give the appearance of social homogeneity. In a word, ideology is the lie. For the ideological to exist, there at least has to be social division. Godelier is unaware of this; how, then, could he know that ideology, in the sense in which Marx speaks of it, is a modern phenomenon, appearing in the 16th century, contemporaneous, as it happens, to the birth of the modern, democratic State? It is not historical knowledge that weighs upon Godelier's head: and so, religion, myth are ideology for him. He no doubt thinks that ideas are ideology. He believes that everyone is like him. It is not in primitive society that religion is ideology, but in Godelier's head: to him, his religion is certainly his Marxist ideology. What does it mean to speak of ideology in regard to primitive societies, that is, undivided societies, classless societies, since by nature they exclude the possibility of such a discourse? It means, first of all, that Godelier does what he wants with Marx, secondly, that he does not know anything about what a primitive society is. Neither Marxist, nor ethnologist! A master stroke!

Quite logically, his "ideological" conception of primitive religion would lead him to determine myth as the opiate of the Savages. Let us not prod him along, he is doing what he can, he will say it another time. But, if his logic is null, his vocabulary is poor. This vigorous mountaineer in effect goes trudging through the Andes (pp. 21–22). And what does he discover there? That the relation between the dominant caste of the Incas and the dominated peasantry constituted an *unequal* exchange (his emphasis, on top of it). Where did he go to fish this up? So, between the Master and the Subject, there is an unequal exchange? And no doubt also between the capitalist and the worker? Doesn't that spell corporatism? Godelier/Salazar, same fight? Who would have thought! Let us thus enrich Godelier's vocabulary: unequal exchange is simply called theft, or in Marxist terms, exploitation. This is the price for wanting to be both a structuralist (exchange and reciprocity) and a Marxist (inequality); one is left with nothing. Godelier attempts here to plaster the category of exchange (which is only valuable for primitive societies, that is, for societies of equals) onto societies divided into classes, that is, structured on inequality: (he mixes everything and writes — reactionary, of course — nonsense), sometimes cramming religion into ideology, sometimes exchange into inequality.

Everything is the same to him. Is he interested, for example, in Australian societies? He notices, with his usual finesse, that there *"the relations of kinship were also relations of production,* and constituted the economic structure"(p. 9, this is still his emphasis). Halt! Production is present! This proposition severely lacks content. Or else, it signifies that the said relations of production are established between kin: whom else would they be established with? With the enemies perhaps? Outside of war, all social relations are established between relatives, of course. Any beginning ethnologist knows this; this is banality without interest as a result. But this is not what Godelier the Marxist wants to tell us. He wants to introduce, to drop-kick, Marxist categories into primitive society (where they have no business) — relations of production, productive forces, development of productive forces — this hard, wooden language that they constantly have in their mouths — all while clinging to structuralism: primitive society=kinship relations=relations of production. Cekomça.

A few brief remarks on this. First, on the category of production. More competent and attentive to the facts than Godelier (this is not hard), specialists in primitive economy such as Marshall Sahlins in the United States or Jacques Lizot here, who are concerned with ethnology and not with catechism, have established that primitive society functions precisely like a machine of anti-production; that the domestic mode of production still operates below its possibilities; that there are no production relations because there is no production, for this is the last concern of primitive society (cf. my preface to Marshall Sahlins' *Stone Age Economics* [Trans.: Chapter Eight of this book]). Naturally, Godelier (whose Marxism, as we see here, is exactly the same brand as that of his rival Meillassoux: they are the Marx Brothers) cannot renounce Holy Production: otherwise, he would go bankrupt, he would be unemployed. That said, Godelier is not crazy: here is a good-natured fellow who, with the good-naturedness of a bulldozer, crushes ethnographic facts under the doctrine by which he makes his living, and who has the nerve to reproach others for total disdain for all the facts that contradict them (p. 24). He knows what he is talking about.

On kinship, finally. Though a structuralist, a Marxist cannot understand kinship relations. What use is a kinship system? This, pupil Godelier, is used to fabricate relatives. But what use is a relative? Surely not to produce anything. It is used precisely to bear the name of the relative until the new order. This is the principal sociological function of kinship in primitive society (and not to institute the prohibition of incest). I could no doubt be more clear. I will limit myself for now (for a little suspense always produces the best effects) to saying that the function of nomination, inscribed in kinship, determines the entire sociopolitical being of primitive society. It is there that the tie between kinship and society is located. We shall untie this knot another time. If Godelier manages to say a little more about this, we'll offer him a free subscription to *Libre*.

Godelier's preface is a bouquet: the most exquisite flowers compose it. A work of art. Let us pick one last quote: "For — and many are not aware of this — there have existed and still exist numerous societies divided into orders or castes or classes, into exploiters and exploited, and who, nevertheless, do not know the State." Why doesn't he tell us first, for precision is important, to what societies he is alluding? Coy of him. As for the rest, he clearly wants to say that one cannot think of social division without the State, that the division into the dominating and the dominated does not necessarily implicate the State. What exactly is the State for Godelier? Surely, the ministers, the Élysée, the White House, the Kremlin. This innocence of the bumpkin in the capital is charming. Godelier forgets one thing, the principle (which the Marxists manage to remember when they control the State apparatus): namely, that the State is the exercise of political power. We cannot think power without the State and the State without power. In other words: there where one locates an effective exercise of power by a part of society over the rest, we find ourselves confronted with a divided society, that is, a society with a State. Social division into the dominating and dominated is, through and through, political; it divides men into Masters of power and Subjects of power. That the economy, the tribute, the debt, the alienated work appear as signs and effects of political division along the axis of power, I have demonstrated sufficiently elsewhere (and Godelier is not the last to have profited from it, p. 22, for example, but without quoting me, the scoundrel... As Kant said, there are those who do not like paying their debts).

Primitive society is not divided because it does not comprise a separate organ of political power. Social division first involves the separation between society and the organ of power. Thus, all non-primitive (that is, divided) societies comprise a more or less developed figure of the State. Where there are masters, where there are subjects who pay their tribute, where there is a debt, there is power, there is the State. Of course, between the minimal figure of the State as certain Polynesian, African, and other royalties embody it, and the more State-like forms of the State (linked, pell-mell, to demography, to the urban phenomenon, to division of labor, to writing, etc.), there exist considerable degrees in the intensity of the power exercised, in the intensity of the oppression undergone, the final degree being reached by the type of power that fascists and communists put into place: there the power of the State is total, the oppression, absolute. But it remains irreducible, the central point: just as we cannot think of undivided society without the absence of the State, we cannot think of divided society without the presence of the State. And to reflect on the origin of inequality, social division, classes, domination is to reflect on the political, on power, on the State, and not on the economy, production, etc. The economy arises from the political, the relations of production come from power relations, the State engenders classes.

And now having savored the spectacle of this tomfoolery, let us approach the important question: what of the Marxist discourse in anthropology? I was speaking, in the beginning of this text, of the radical nullity of Marxist ethnology (read, readers, the works of Meillassoux, Godelier and company: it is edifying). Radical, that is, at first. Why? Because such a discourse is not a scientific discourse (that is, concerned with truth), but a purely ideological discourse (that is, concerned with political efficacy). In order to see this clearly, we must distinguish first between the thought of Marx and Marxism. Marx was, along with Bakunin, the first critic of Marxism. Marx's thought is a grandiose attempt (sometimes successful, sometimes failed) to reflect on the society of his time (western capitalism) and the history which brought it into being. Contemporary Marxism is an ideology in the service of politics. The result is that Marxists have nothing to do with Marx. And they are the first to admit it. Do not Godelier and Meillassoux call themselves pseudo-Marxist impostors? It is absolutely true, I agree with them, they are both right. Shamelessly, they take refuge in Marx's beard in order to palm off their merchandise more efficiently. A beautiful case of false advertising. But it would take more than one to dishonor Marx.

Postmarxian Marxism, besides becoming the dominant ideology of the workers' movement, has become the principal enemy of the workers' movement, has constituted itself as the most arrogant form of the stupidest thing the 19th century has produced: scientism. In other words, contemporary Marxism institutes itself as *the* scientific discourse on the history of society, as the discourse that enunciates the laws of historical movement, the laws of societal transformations that are each engendered by the other. Thus, Marxism can speak of all types of societies, since it understands the principle of their workings in advance. But there is more: Marxism must speak of all types of societies, whether possible or real, for the universality of the laws that it discovers cannot suffer a single exception. Otherwise, the doctrine as a whole crumbles. As a result, in order to maintain not only coherence, but the very existence of this discourse, it is imperative for the Marxists to formulate the Marxist conception of primitive society, to constitute a Marxist anthropology. In default of which there would be no Marxist theory of history, but only the analysis of a particular society (the capitalism of the 19th century) elaborated by someone named Marx.

But here the Marxists get trapped in their Marxism. Indeed they do not have a choice: they must subject primitive social facts to the same rules of function and of transformation that order other social formations. It could not be a question here of two weights and two measures: if there are laws of history, they must be as legitimate at the start of history (primitive society) as in the continuation of its course. Thus a single weight, a single measure. What is the Marxist measure of social facts? It is the *economy*.[4] Marxism is an economism, it reduces the social body to economic infrastructure, the social is the economical. And this is why the Marxist anthropologists, perforce, slap onto the primitive social body that which they think functions elsewhere: the categories of production, relations of production, development of the productive forces, exploitation, etc. To the foreceps, as Adler says. And it is thus that the elders exploit the young (Meillassoux), that kinship relations are relations of production (Godelier).

Let us not go back to this collection of nonsense. Let us shed light, rather, on the militant obscurantism of Marxist anthropologists. Brazenly, they traffic facts, trample and crush them to the point of letting nothing remain. For the reality of social facts they substitute the ideology of their discourse. Who are Meillassoux, Godelier and their consorts? They are the Lyssenkos of the human sciences. Just how far does their ideological frenzy, their will to pillage ethnology, go? All the way, that is, as far as the elimination, pure and simple, of primitive society as a specific society, as an inde-

---

4 And on this point, there certainly is a root of Marxism, in Marx; it would be derisive to take this away from the Marxists. Did he not, in effect, allow himself to write, in *Das Kapital* that: [quotation missing in Clastres' original manuscript].

pendent social being. In the logic of Marxist discourse, primitive society quite simply cannot exist, it does not have the right to autonomous existence, its being is only determined according to that which will come much later, its necessary future. For the Marxists, primitive societies are only, they proclaim eruditely, pre-capitalist societies. Here, then, is a society's mode of organization which was that of all humanity for millennia, but for the Marxists. For them, primitive society only exists insofar as it can be reduced to the figure of society that appeared at the end of the 18th century, capitalism. Before that, nothing counts: everything is precapitalist. They do not complicate their lives, these guys. It must be relaxing to be a Marxist. All of this can be explained starting with capitalism, for they possess the good doctrine, the key that opens capitalist society and thus, all historical social formations. The result: what [measures] society for Marxism in general is the economy, and for the ethnomarxists who go even further, what measures primitive society is capitalist society. Cekomça. But those who do not recoil before a bit of fatigue pose the question in the manner of Montaigne or La Boétie or Rousseau and judge what has come after in relation to what has come before: what of post-primitive societies? Why have inequality, social division, separate power, the State appeared?

But, one will wonder, how can something so suspicious work? For, though in recession for some time, it still attracts customers. It is quite obvious that these customers (the listeners and readers of these Marxisms) are not demanding about the quality of the products they consume, to say the least. Too bad for them! If they like that soup, they can swallow it. But to limit ourselves to this would be at once very cruel and too simple: first, by denouncing the enterprise of ethnomarxists, we can prevent a certain number of the intoxicated from dying idiots (this Marxism is the opiate of the dim-witted). But it would be very frivolous, practically irresponsible, to limit oneself to emphasizing (if I may say so) the nullity of a Meillassoux or of a Godelier. Their work is not worth a nail, this is understood, but it would be a great mistake to underestimate it: the nothingness of the discourse masks in effect the being on which it feeds, namely, its capacity to diffuse an ideology of the conquest of power. In contemporary French society, the University occupies a considerable place. And in the University, notably in the field of the human sciences (for it seems more difficult to be Marxist in mathematics or in biology), this political ideology that is the Marxism of today attempts to gain a foothold as dominant ideology.

In this global apparatus, our ethnomarxists occupy a place that is certainly modest but not negligible. There is a political division of labor and they accomplish their part of the general effort: to assure the triumph of their common ideology. Sapristi! Would these not quite simply be Stalinists, good aspiring bureaucrats? One wonders... This would explain, in any case, why they mock primitive societies, as we have seen: primitive societies are only a pretext for them to spread their ideology of granite and their wooden language. This is why it is less a matter of mocking their stupidity than of flushing them out of the real place where they situate themselves: the political confrontation in its ideological dimension. The Stalinists are not, in effect, just any conquerors of power: what they want is total power, the State of their dreams is the totalitarian State: enemies of intelligence and freedom, like fascists, they claim to hold total knowledge to legitimate the exercise of total power. There is every reason to be suspicious of people who applaud the massacres in Cambodia or Ethiopia because the massacrers are Marxists. Should Amin Dada one day proclaim himself Marxist, we will hear them yell: bravo Dada.

And now let us wait and keep our ears to the ground: perhaps the brontosauruses will bray.

11

ARCHEOLOGY OF VIOLENCE: WAR IN PRIMITIVE SOCIETIES

For the past few decades an abundance of ethnographic literature has been devoted to describing primitive societies, to understanding their mode of operation: if violence is dealt with (rarely), it is primarily to show how these societies work toward controlling it, codifying it, ritualizing it, in short, tend to reduce, if not abolish it. We evoke the violence, but mostly to demonstrate the horror that it inspires in primitive societies, to establish that they are, finally, societies against violence. It would not be too surprising, then, to observe in the field of research in contemporary ethnology the quasi-absence of a general reflection on violence in at once its most brutal and most collective, most pure and most social form: war. Consequently to limit oneself to ethnological discourse, or more specifically, to the nonexistence of such a discourse on primitive war, the curious reader or researcher in social sciences will justifiably deduce that (with the exception of secondary anecdotes) violence does not at all loom over the horizon of the Savages' social life, that the primitive social being unfolds outside of armed

First published in *Libre*, no. 1, Paris, Payot, 1977, pp. 137–173.

conflict, that war does not belong to the normal, habitual functioning of primitive societies. War is thus excluded from ethnological discourse; one can think of primitive society without at the same time thinking of war. The question, clearly, is to determine whether this scientific discourse is speaking the truth on the type of society it targets: let us stop listening to it for a moment and turn toward the reality of which it speaks.

The discovery of America, as we know, provided the West with its first encounter with those we would from then on call Savages. For the first time, Europeans found themselves confronted with a type of society radically different from all they had known up until then; they had to think of a social reality that could not exist in their traditional representation of the social being: in other words, the world of the Savages was literally unthinkable for European thought. This is not the place to analyze in detail the reasons for this veritable epistemological impossibility: they have to do with the certainty, coextensive to all history of western civilization, of what human society is and should be, a certainty expressed starting with the Greek dawn of European political thought, of the *polis*, in the fragmented work of Heraclitus. Namely that the representation of society as such must be embodied in the figure of the One exterior to the society, in the hierarchical configuration of political space, in the function of the command of the chief, king, or despot: there is no society without the characteristic division into Masters and Subjects. A human grouping without the characteristic division could not be considered a society. Now, whom did the discoverers see arise from the Atlantic shores? "People without faith, without law, without king," according to the chroniclers of the 16th century. The cause was clear: these men in a state of nature had not yet acceded to a state of society. There was quasi-unanimity in this judgment on the Indians of Brazil, upset only by the discordant voices of Montaigne and La Boétie.

But, on the other hand, there was not unrestricted unanimity when it came to describing the Savages' customs. Explorers or missionaries, merchants or learned travelers, from the 16th century until the (recent) end of world conquest, all agreed on one point: whether Americans (from Alaska to Tierra del Fuego) or Africans, Siberians from the steppes or Melanesians from the isles, nomads from the Australian deserts or sedentary farmers from the jungles of New Guinea, primitive peoples were always presented as passionately devoted to war; it was their particularly bellicose character that struck European observers without exception. From the enormous documentary accumulation gathered in chronicles, travel literature, reports from priests and pastors, soldiers or peddlers, one image continuously emerged from the infinite diversity of the cultures described: that of the warrior. An image dominant enough to induce a sociological observation: primitive societies are violent societies; their social being is a being-for-war.

This is the impression, in any case, of direct witnesses in many climates and throughout several centuries, many of whom participated in the life of the indigenous tribes for years. It would be both easy and useless to make up an anthology of these judgments concerning the populations of very different regions and periods. The aggressive dispositions of the Savages are almost always severely judged: how, indeed, could one Christianize, civilize or convince people of the virtues of work and commerce, when they were primarily concerned with warring against their neighbors, avenging defeats or celebrating victories? In fact, the French or Portuguese missionaries' opinion of the Tupi Indians of the Brazilian coast in the mid-16th century anticipates and condenses all the discourses to come: were it not, they said, for the incessant war these tribes wage against each other, the country would be overpopulated. It is the apparent prevalence of war in primitive life that retains the attention of social theoreticians in the first place. To the state of Society, which, for him, is the society of the State, Thomas Hobbes contrasts not the real but the logical figure of man in his *natural condition,* the state of men before living in society, that is, under "a common Power to keep them all in awe." Now, by what means is the natural condition of men distinguished? Through war of every man against every man. But, one will say, this war which opposes abstract men against each other, invented for the needs of the cause that the thinker of the civil State is defending, this imaginary war does not in any way concern the empirical, ethnographical reality of war in primitive society. Nevertheless, Hobbes himself thinks it possible to illustrate the cogency of his deduction from an explicit reference to a concrete reality: the natural condition of man is not only the abstract construction of a philosopher, but, in effect, the actual, observable fate of a newly discovered humanity. "It may peradventure be thought, there was never such a time, nor condition of warre as this; and I believe it was never generally so, over all the world: but there are many places, where they live so now. For the savage people in many places of America, except the government of small families, the concord where of dependeth on naturall lust, have no government at all; and live at this day in that brutish manner, as I said before."[1] One will not be overly surprised by Hobbes' quietly disdainful point of view concerning the Savages; these are the received ideas of his time (but ideas rejected, let us repeat, by Montaigne and La Boétie): a society without government, without State, is not a society; thus, the Savages remain exteri-

---

[1] Hobbes, *Leviathan,* edited by Richard Tuck, Cambridge, New York, Cambridge University Press, p. 88.

or to the social, they live in the natural condition of men where the war of each against each reigns. Hobbes was not unaware of the American Indians' intense bellicosity; this is why he saw in their real wars the striking confirmation of his certainty: the absence of the State permits the generalization of war and makes the institution of society impossible.

The equation: world of Savages=world of war, finding itself constantly verified in the field, traverses all popular or scholarly representation of primitive society. It is thus that another English philosopher, Spencer, writes in his *Principles of Sociology*: "In the life of the savages and barbarians, the dominant events are wars," as an echo to that which three centuries before him the Jesuit Soarez de Souza said of the Tupinamba of Brazil: "Since the Tupinamba are very bellicose, they are preoccupied with how they will make war on their contraries." But did the inhabitants of the New World hold the monopoly on the passion for war? Hardly. In an already ancient work,[2] Maurice R. Davie, reflecting on the causes and functions of war in primitive societies, undertook a systematic sampling of what the ethnography of the time taught on this subject. Now, it follows from his meticulous prospecting that with extremely rare exceptions (the Central and Eastern Eskimos) no primitive society escapes violence; none among them, whatever their mode of production, their techno-economic system or their ecological environment, is unaware of or refuses the warlike deployment of violence which engages the very being of each community implicated in armed conflict. It thus seems well established that one cannot think of primitive society without also thinking of war which, as an immediate given of primitive sociology, takes on a dimension of *universality*.

This massive presence of the fact of war is answered, so to speak, by the silence of the most recent ethnology, according to which it would seem violence and war exist only insofar as they are warded off. Where does this silence come from? First, certainly, from the conditions under which the societies ethnologists are interested in are currently living. We know well that throughout the world there scarcely exist primitive societies that are absolutely free, autonomous, without contact with the white socioeconomic environment. In other words, ethnologists no longer have the opportunity to observe societies isolated enough so that the play of traditional force which define and support them can be given free course: primitive war is invisible because there are no more warriors to wage it. In this regard, the situation of the Amazonian Yanomami is unique: their secular isolation has permitted these Indians, no doubt the last great primitive society in the world, to live up to the present as though America had not been discov

---

[2] M.R. Davie, *La Guerre dans les sociétés primitives*, Payot, 1931

ered. And so one can observe there the omnipresence of war. Still, this is not a reason to draw up, as others have done, a caricatured portrait, where the taste for the sensational far eclipses the capacity to understand a powerful sociological mechanism.[3] In short, if ethnology does not speak of war, it is because there is no reason to speak of it; it is because primitive societies, when they become the object of study, have already started down the road of dislocation, destruction and death: how could they display the spectacle of their free warlike vitality?

But perhaps this is not the only reason. One can indeed suppose that ethnologists, when starting their work, bring to the chosen society not only their notebook and tape recorder, but also the conception, previously acquired, of the social being of primitive societies and, consequently, of the status of violence there, the causes that unleash it and the effects that it has. No general theory of primitive society can economize a consideration of war. Not only does the discourse on war belong to the discourse on society but it assigns it its meaning: the idea of war measures the idea of society. This is why the absence of reflections on violence in current ethnology could be explained first by the actual disappearance of war following the loss of freedom that installs the Savages in a forced pacifism, but also by the adhesion to a type of sociological discourse which tends to exclude war from the field of social relations in primitive society. The obvious question is whether such a discourse is adequate to the primitive social reality. And so, before examining this reality, we should briefly outline the received discourse on primitive society and war. Heterogeneous, the discourse on war develops in three major directions: a naturalist discourse, an economist discourse, and an exchangist discourse.

The *naturalist discourse* is articulated with particular stringency by A. Leroi-Gourhan in his work *Le Geste et la Parole* and notably in the next-to-last chapter of volume II, where the author develops, in a view of unquestionable (yet very questionable) vastness, his historical-ethnological conception of primitive society and the transformations that modify it. In conformance with the indissoluble conjunction between archaic society and the phenomenon of war, Leroi-Gourhan's general undertaking logically includes a vision of primitive war, a vision whose meaning is sufficiently indicated by the spirit that runs throughout the work and by the title of the chapter in which it appears: the social organism. Clearly asserted, the organicist point of view on society appeals to and encompasses, in an absolutely coherent

---

[3] Cf. N.A. Chagnon, *Yanomamö. The Fierce People*, Holt, Rinehart & Winston, 1968.

manner, a certain idea of war. What about violence, then, according to Leroi-Gourhan? His answer is clear: "Aggressive behavior has been part of human reality at least since the Australanthropes, and the accelerated evolution of the social apparatus has not changed anything in the slow development of phyletic maturation," (p. 237). Aggression as behavior, that is, the use of violence, is thus related to humanity as a species; it is coextensive with it. In sum, as a zoological property of the human species, violence is identified here as an irreducible fact, a sort of *natural* given rooted in the biological being of man. This specific violence, realized in aggressive behavior, is not without cause or end; it is always oriented and directed toward a goal: "Throughout the course of time, aggression appears as a fundamental technique linked to acquisition, and in the primitive, its initial role is hunting where aggression and alimentary acquisition are merged" (p. 236). Inherent in man as a natural being, violence is defined thus as a means of subsistence, as a means of assuring subsistence, as a means to a natural end inscribed at the heart of the living organism: to survive. Hence, the identification of primitive economy as predatory economy. The primitive man, as man, is devoted to aggressive behavior; as primitive, he is both apt and determined to synthesize his naturalness and his humanity in the technical coding of an aggressivity henceforth useful and profitable: he is a hunter.

Let us admit this link between violence, which is harnessed in the technique of acquiring food, and man's biological being, whose integrity violence must maintain. But where is this very particular aggression, manifested in the violence of war, situated? Leroi-Gourhan explains to us: "Between hunting and its double, war, a subtle assimilation is progressively established, as one and the other are concentrated in a class that is born of the new economy, that of men with weapons," (p. 237). Here then, in a sentence, the mystery of the origin of social division is solved: through "subtle assimilation," hunters gradually become warriors who, as holders of armed force, possess the means to exercise political power over the rest of the community to their profit. One may be surprised by the frivolity of such a remark from the pen of a scholar whose work is exemplary in his field, prehistory. All this would require further exposition, but the lesson to draw is clear: in the analysis of human facts, one cannot reduce the social to the natural, the institutional to the biological. Human society stems not from zoology but from sociology.

Let us return then to the problem of war. War would thus inherit its charge of aggression from hunting — a technique of alimentary acquisition; war would only be a repetition, a double, a redeployment of the hunt: more prosaically, war, for Leroi-Gourhan, is *the hunting of men*. Is this true or false? It is not difficult to find out, since it suffices to consult those of whom

Leroi-Gourhan believes he speaks, the contemporary primitives. What does ethnographic experience teach us? It is quite obvious that if the goal of the hunt is to acquire food, the means of attaining it is aggression: the animal must be killed in order to be eaten. But then one must include in the area of the hunt as a technique of acquisition all behaviors that destroy another form of life so that it can be eaten: not only animals, fish and carnivorous birds, but also insectivores (the aggression of the fledgling against the fly it swallows, etc.). In fact, all violent techniques of alimentary acquisition would logically have to be analyzed in terms of aggressive behavior. There is no reason to privilege the human hunter over the animal hunter. In reality, what principally motivates the primitive hunter is appetite, to the exclusion of all other sentiments (the case of non-alimentary, that is, ritual, hunt pertains to another domain). What radically distinguishes war from the hunt is that the former relies entirely on a dimension absent from the latter: aggressiveness. And that the same arrow can kill a man or a monkey is not enough to make war and hunting identical.

This is indeed why we can compare one to the other: war is pure aggressive behavior and aggressiveness. If war is hunting and war is the hunting of man, then hunting would have to be war on the buffalo, for example. Outside of supposing that the goal of war is always alimentary, and that the object of this type of aggression is man as game destined to being eaten, Leroi-Gourhan's reduction of war to hunting has no foundation. For if war is indeed the "double" of the hunt, then generalized anthropology is its horizon. We know that this is not the case: even among the cannibal tribes, the goal of war is never to kill the enemies in order to eat them. Rather, this "biologization" of an activity such as war inevitably takes away its properly social dimension. Leroi-Gourhan's problematic conception leads to a dissolution of the sociological in the biological; society becomes a social organism, and all attempts to articulate a non-zoological discourse on society reveals itself as vain. The question on the contrary will be to establish that primitive war owes nothing to the hunt, that it is rooted not in the reality of man as a species but in the social being of the primitive society, that through its universality it points not toward nature but toward culture.

The *economist discourse* is somewhat anonymous in that it is not the particular work of a specific theoretician, but rather the expression of a general conviction, a vague certainty of common sense. This discourse was formed in the 19th century, when in Europe the idea of savagery and the idea of happiness were beginning to be thought of separately, when, rightly or wrongly, the belief that primitive life was a happy life fell apart. There was then a reversal of the old discourse into its opposite: the world of the Savages from then on became, rightly or wrongly, the world of poverty and misery. Much more recently, this popular knowledge has received scientific status from the so-called human sciences; it has become a scholarly discourse, a discourse of scholars: the founders of economic anthropology, welcoming the certainty of primitive poverty as truth, have devoted themselves to extracting the reasons for this poverty and unveiling its consequences. Thus, from this convergence between common sense and scientific discourse results a proclamation constantly reiterated by ethnologists: primitive economy is a subsistence economy which only allows the Savages to subsist, that is, to survive. If the economy of these societies cannot go past the pitiful threshold of survival — of non-death — it is because of its technological underdevelopment and its powerlessness before the natural environment which it has not managed to dominate. Primitive economy is thus an economy of poverty, and it is against this background that the phenomenon of war takes place. The economist discourse accounts for primitive war by the weakness of productive forces; the scarcity of available material goods leads to competition between groups, pushed into appropriating these goods by need, and this struggle for life ends in armed conflict: there is not enough for everyone.

One should note that this explanation of primitive war based on the poverty of the Savages is accepted as an obviousness which cannot be questioned. In his essay cited earlier, Davie perfectly illustrates this point of view: "But each tribe, outside of its struggle against nature for its existence, must maintain a competition against all other tribes with which it comes into contact; rivalries and clashes of interest are produced, and when these degenerate into disputes by force, we call that war" (p. 28). And again: "War has been defined: a dispute by force born between political groupings, under the action of vital competition... Thus, the importance of war in a given tribe varies depending on the intensity of its vital competition" (p. 78). This author, as we have seen, proclaims the universality of war in primitive society based on ethnographic information: only the Eskimos of Greenland escape this condition, an exception, explains Davie, due to the extreme hostility of the natural environment which prevents them from devoting energy to anything but looking for food: "Cooperation in the struggle for existence is absolutely imperative in their case" (p. 79). But, one might observe, the Australians seem no better off in their hot deserts than the Eskimos in their snow, and yet they are no less warlike than other peoples. We should note, too, that this scholarly discourse, the simple, "scientific" utterance of the popular postulate on primitive poverty, is adjusted exactly, *volens nolens*, to the most recent avatar of the Marxist conception of society, namely, Marxist anthropology. As far as the question of primitive war is concernced, it is to North American anthropologists that we owe (so to speak) the Marxist interpretation. More quickly than their French coreligionists, who are nevertheless ready to speak the Marxist truth on African age groups or American potlatch, or the rapports between men and women anywhere, researchers such as Harris or Gross explain the reason for war among the Amazonian Indians, notably the Yanomami.[4] Whoever expects sudden illumination from this Marxism will be quite disappointed: its supporters say nothing more of it (and no doubt think even less of it) than all their non-Marxist predecessors. If war is particularly intense among the South American Indians, it is due, according to Gross and Harris, to a lack of protein in their food, to the resulting need for conquering new hunting territories, and to the inevitable armed conflict with the occupants of these territories. In short, the very old thesis formulated by Davie, among others, of the inability of primitive economy to provide society with adequate nourishment.[5] Let us simply make a point that cannot be developed here further. If the Marxist discourse (an economist discourse if there ever was one) so easily assimilates the most summary representations of common sense, it is either that this common sense is spontaneously Marxist (o, spirits of Mao!) or else that this Marxism only distinguishes itself from common sense by the comic pretension of posing as scientific discourse. But there is something more. Marxism, as a general theory of society and also of history, is obliged to postulate the poverty of the primitive economy, that is, the very low yield of productive activity. Why? Because the Marxist theory of history (and this is a matter of the very theory of Karl Marx) uncovers the law of historical motion and of social change in the irrepressible tendency of productive forces to develop themselves. But, so that history can get underway, so that the productive forces can take wing, these same productive forces must first exist at the start of this process in the most extreme weakness, in the most total underdevelopment: lacking this, there would not be the least reason for them to tend to develop themselves and one would not be able to articulate social change and the development of productive forces. This is why Marxism, as a theory of history founded on the tendency of the development of productive forces, must give itself, as a starting point, a sort of degree zero of productive forces: this is exactly the primitive economy, henceforth thought of as an economy of poverty, as an economy

---

[4] D.R. Gross, "Protein Capture and Cultural Development in the Amazon Basin," *American Anthropologist,* 77, 1975, pp. 526-549; M. Harris, "The Yanomamö and the Causes of War in Band and Village Societies."

[5] J. Lizot, an expert on the Yanomami, shows how flawed the work of Gross and Harris is. Cf. "Population, Ressources et Guerre chez les Yanomami," in *Libre,* 2, 1977.

which, wanting to wrest itself from poverty, will tend to develop its productive forces. It would be a great satisfaction for many to know the Marxist anthropologists' viewpoint on this: though they go on at length about forms of exploitation in primitive societies (elder/youth, man/woman, etc.), they are less eloquent as to the foundation of the doctrine they claim to support. For primitive society poses a crucial question to Marxist theory: if the economical does not constitute the infrastructure through which the social being becomes transparent, if the productive forces, not tending to develop themselves, do not function as a determinant of social change, what, then, is the motor that starts the movement of History?

That said, let us return to the problem of the primitive economy. Is it or is it not an economy of poverty? Do its productive forces represent the most minimal development or not? The most recent, and most scrupulous, research in economic anthropology shows that the economy of the Savages, or the Domestic Mode of Production, in fact allows for the total satisfaction of society's material needs, at the price of a limited period of productive activity at a low intensity. In other words, far from constantly exhausting themselves in the attempt to survive, primitive society, selective in the determination of its needs, possesses a machine of production capable of satisfying them, and functions in fact according to the principle: to each according to his needs. This is why Sahlins was able to speak of the primitive society as the first affluent society. Sahlins' and Lizot's analyses on the quantity of food necessary to a community and on the time devoted to procuring it indicate that primitive societies, whether it be a question of nomad hunters or sedentary farmers, are, in reality, in light of the small amount of time devoted to production, veritable *leisure societies*. The work of Sahlins and that of Lizot thus mesh with and confirm the ethnographic material furnished by the ancient travelers and chroniclers.[6]

The economist discourse, in its popular, scholarly or Marxist variations, explains war as tribes competing to obtain scarce goods. It would already be difficult to understand where the Savages, engaged full time in the exhausting quest for food, would find the extra time and energy to wage war against their neighbors. But current research shows that the primitive economy is, on the contrary, an economy of abundance and not of scarcity: violence, then, is not linked to poverty, and the economist explanation of primitive war sees its supporting argument sink. The universality of primitive abundance precisely prohibits linking it to the universality of war. Why are the tribes at war? At least we already know what the materialist answer is

---

6 Cf. M. Sahlins, *Age de pierre, Age d'abondance. L'économie des sociétés primitives*, Paris, Gallimard, 1976.

worth. And since economics has nothing to do with war, then perhaps it is necessary to turn our gaze toward the political.[7]

The *exchangist discourse* on primitive war supports the sociological undertaking of Claude Lévi-Strauss. Such an assertion would appear, first of all, paradoxical: in this author's considerable work, war occupies only a thin volume. But beyond the fact that the importance of an issue is not necessarily measured by the space allotted to it, it so happens, under the circumstances, that the general theory of society elaborated by Lévi-Strauss narrowly depends on his conception of violence: structuralist discourse itself is at stake. Let us, then, examine it.

Lévi-Strauss considers the question of war in only one text, analyzing the relationship between war and commerce among the South American Indians.[8] War, here, is clearly situated in the field of social relations: "Among the Nambikwara, as no doubt among the numerous populations of pre-Columbian America, war and commerce are activities that are impossible to study in isolation" (p. 136). And again: "... martial conflicts and economic exchanges do not merely constitute two types of coexistent relations in South America, but rather two aspects, opposed and indissoluble, of a single and identical social process" (p. 138). We cannot, then, according to Lévi-Strauss, think of war in and of itself; it does not possess its own specificity, and this type of activity, far from requiring a particular examination, can, in fact, only be understood in "the context of other elements making up the social whole." (p. 138). In other words, violence, in primitive society, is not an autonomous sphere: it only takes on meaning in relation to the general network of tribal relations; violence is only a particular case of this global system. If Lévi-Strauss wants to indicate by this that primitive war is an activity of a strictly sociological order, no one, of course, would contest it, with the exception, however, of Leroi-Gourhan, who merges warlike activity into the biological order. Certainly, Lévi-Strauss does not limit himself to these vague generalities: he furnishes, on the contrary, a precise idea on the mode of operation of primitive society, Amerindian, in any case. The

---

7 Natural catastrophes (droughts, floods, earthquakes, the disappearance of an animal species, etc.) can provoke a local scarcity of resources. Still, this would have to last a rather long time to lead to conflict. Another type of situation could, it seems, confront a society with rarity, without nature being responsible: does the conjunction of an absolutely closed space and an absolutely open (that is, growing) demography conceal the risk of a social pathology bordering on war? This is not obvious, but it is up to the specialists of Polynesia or Melanesia (islands, that is, closed spaces) to answer.

8 Cf. Lévi-Strauss, "Guerre et commerce chez les Indiens de l'Amérique du Sud," *Renaissance*, vol. I, New York, 1943.

identification of this mode of operation assumes the highest importance, since it determines the nature and significance of violence and of war. What does Lévi-Strauss find in the relationship between war and society? The answer is clear: "Commercial exchanges represent potential wars peacefully resolved, and wars are the outcome of unfortunate transactions" (p. 136). Thus, not only does war inscribe itself in the field of the sociological, but it receives its ultimate meaning from the particular functioning of primitive society: the relations between communities (whether tribes, bands or local groups) are first commercial, and depending on the success or failure of these commercial enterprises, there will be peace or war between the tribes. Not only are war and commerce to be thought of in continuity, but it is commerce that holds sociological priority over war, a somewhat ontological priority in that it takes place at the very heart of the social being. Let us add, finally, that far from being new, the idea of a conjunction between war and commerce is in fact an ethnological banality, on the same level as the idea of scarcity in the primitive economy. Thus the intrinsic relationship between war and commerce is asserted, in exactly the same terms as Lévi-Strauss, by Davie, for example: "In primitive cases, commerce is often an alternative to war, and the manner in which it is conducted shows that it is a modification of war" (op. cit., p. 302).

But, one might object, the text in question is minor and does not in any way compromise the general theory of the social being such as Lévi-Strauss has developed it in more comprehensive works. Such is not the case. In fact, the theoretical conclusions of this supposedly minor text are integrally repeated in Lévi-Strauss's great sociological work, *Elementary Structures of Kinship*, at the end of one of the most important chapters, "The Principle of Reciprocity": "There is a link, a continuity, between hostile relations and the provision of reciprocal prestations: exchanges are peacefully resolved wars, and wars are the result of unsuccessful transactions."[9] However, on the same page, the idea of commerce is explicitly (and without explanation) eliminated. Describing the exchange of gifts between foreign Indian groups, Lévi-Strauss takes care to indicate his abandonment of the reference to commerce: "It is a matter, thus, of reciprocal goods, and not of commercial operations." Let us examine this more closely.

Lévi-Strauss' firm distinction between the reciprocal gift and the commercial operation is absolutely legitimate. Still, it would not be superfluous

---

[9] *Structures Élmentaires de la parenté*, p. 86 of the first edition (PUF, 1949) or p. 78 of the second edition (Mouton, 1967). [*The Elementary Structures of Kinship*, Boston, Beacon Press, 1969. Edited by Rodney Needham, trans. by James Harle Bell, John Richard von Sturmer, and Rodney Needham.]

to explain why, in a quick detour through economic anthropology. If the material life of primitive societies develops against a backdrop of abundance, the Domestic Mode of Production is also characterized by *an ideal of autarky:* each community aspires to produce all that is necessary for its members' subsistence. In other words, the primitive economy tends toward the community's withdrawal into itself, and the ideal of economic autarky conceals another: the ideal of political independence. In deciding to depend only on itself for its consumer production, the primitive community (village, band, etc.) has no need for economic relations with neighboring groups. It is not need that gives rise to international relations in the primitive society, which is perfectly capable of satisfying all its needs without having to solicit the assistance of others: we produce all that we need (food and tools), we are therefore in a position to do without others. In other words, the autarkic ideal is an anti-commercial ideal. Like all ideals, it is not always accomplished everywhere: but should circumstances demand it, the Savages can boast of doing without others.

This is why the Domestic Mode of Production excludes commercial relations: the primitive society, in its being, refuses the risk, inherent in commerce, of sacrificing its autonomy, of losing its freedom. And so, it is appropriate that the Lévi-Strauss of *Elementary Structures* guarded himself from repeating what he wrote in "War and Commerce." To understand anything about primitive war, one must avoid articulating a commerce that does not exist.

Thus, it is no longer commerce that gives meaning to war, it is exchange; the interpretation of war stems from *the exchangist conception of society;* there is a continuity between war ("the result of unsuccessful transactions") and exchange ("peacefully resolved wars"). But, just as war in the first version of the Lévi-Straussian theory of violence was targeted as the potential non-success of commerce, in the exchangist theory we see an equivalent priority attributed to exchange of which war is but the failure. In other words, war does not possess any positivity by itself; it expresses not the social being of primitive society, but the non-realization of this being which is a being-for-exchange: war is the negative and the negation of primitive society in so far as primitive society is primarily a place of exchange, in so far as exchange is the very essence of primitive society. According to this conception, war, as a skidding, a rupture of the movement toward exchange, could only represent the non-essence, the non-being of the society. It is the accessory in relation to the principal, the accident in relation to the substance. What the primitive society wants is exchange: such is its sociological desire, which tends constantly toward realizing itself, and in fact, almost always realizes itself, except in the case of an accident. Then violence and war arise.

The logic of the exchangist conception leads thus to a quasi-dissolution of the phenomenon of war. By giving priority to exchange and viewing war as devoid of positivity, war loses all institutional dimension: it does not belong to the being of primitive society, it is only an accidental, uncertain, unessential characteristic of it; primitive society is thinkable without war. This exchangist discourse on primitive war, a discourse inherent in the general theory that Lévi-Strauss develops on primitive society, does not take into account the ethnographic given: the quasi-universality of the phenomenon of war, whatever the societies under consideration, their natural environment or their socioeconomic mode of organization; the intensity, naturally variable, of warlike activity. Thus, in a way, the exchangist conception and its object fall outside of one another; primitive reality extends beyond Lévi-Strauss' discourse. Not because of the author's negligence or ignorance, but because taking war into account is incompatible with his analysis of society, an analysis that can only support itself by excluding the sociological function of war in primitive society.

Is this to say that one must, in order to respect primitive reality in all its dimensions, abandon the idea of society as a place of exchange? Not at all. It is not, in effect, an alternative: either exchange or violence. It is not exchange in and of itself that is contradictory to war, but the discourse that reduces the social being of primitive society exclusively to exchange. Primitive society is a space of exchange, and it is also a place of violence: war, on the same level as exchange, belongs to the primitive social being. One cannot, and this is what must be established, think of primitive society without thinking, at the same time, of war. For Hobbes, primitive society was war of each against each. Lévi-Strauss' point of view is symmetrical and inverse to that of Hobbes: primitive society is the exchange of each with each. Hobbes left out exchange, Lévi-Strauss leaves out war.

But, on the other hand, is it simply a matter of juxtaposing the discourse on exchange and the discourse on war? Does reestablishing war as an essential dimension of primitive society leave intact the idea of exchange as the essence of the social? It is obviously impossible: to be mistaken on war is to be mistaken on society. To what is Lévi-Strauss' error due? To a confusion of the sociological levels on which warlike activity and exchange function respectively. By wishing to situate them on the same level, one is fatally led to eliminate one or the other, to deform primitive social reality by mutilating it. Exchange and war are obviously to be thought of, not in terms of a continuity that would allow gradually passing from one to the other, but in terms of a radical discontinuity that alone manifests the truth of primitive society.

The extreme segmentation that characterizes primitive society everywhere would be the cause, it has often been written, of the frequency of war in this type of society. Scarcity of resources would lead to vital competition, which would lead to isolation of groups, which would produce war. Now, if there is indeed a profound relationship between the multiplicity of sociopolitical entities and violence, one can only understand this link by reversing the habitual order of their presentation: it is not war that is the effect of segmentation, it is segmentation that is the effect of war. It is not only the effect, but the goal: war is at once the cause of and the means to a sought-after effect and end, the segmentation of primitive society. In its being, primitive society wants dispersion; this wish for fragmentation belongs to the primitive social being which institutes itself as such in and by the realization of this sociological will. In other words, primitive war is the means to a political end. To ask oneself, consequently, why the Savages wage war is to probe the very being of their society.

Each particular primitive society equally and wholly expresses the essential properties of this type of social formation, which finds its concrete reality in the primitive community. The latter is made up of an ensemble of individuals, each of whom recognizes and claims his appurtenance to this ensemble. Together the community gathers and goes beyond the diverse units that constitute it, most often inscribed along the axis of kinship, by integrating them into a whole: elementary and extended families, lineages, clans, moieties, etc., but also, for example, military societies, ceremonial brotherhoods, age groups, etc. The community is thus more than the sum of its groups, and this establishes it as a political unity. The political unity of the community is incribed in the spatial unity of the habitat: the people who belong to the same community live together in the same place. According to the rules of postmarital residence, an individual can naturally be brought to leave his community of origin in order to join that of his spouse: but the new residence does not abolish the old appurtenance, and primitive societies, moreover, invent numerous ways to overturn the rules of residence if they are thought to be too painful.

The primitive community is thus a local group. This determination transcends the economic variety of modes of production, since it is indifferent to the fixed or mobile character of the habitat. A local group may be made up of nomadic hunters as well as sedentary farmers; a wandering band of hunters and collectors, as much as a stable village of gardeners, possess the sociological properties of the primitive community. The latter, as political unity, not only inscribes itself in the homogeneous space of its habitat, but extends its control, it coding, its territorial right. It is obvious in the case of hunters; it is also true of farmers who still maintain, beyond their plantations, a wild space where they can hunt and pick useful plants: simply, the territory of a band of hunters is likely to be more vast than that of a village of farmers. The locality of the local group is thus its territory, as a natural reserve of material resources, certainly, but especially as an exclusive space for the exercise of community rights. The exclusivity in the use of the territory implies a movement of exclusion, and here the properly political dimension of primitive society as a community including its essential relationship to the territory clearly appears: the existence of the Other is immediately posited in the act that excludes him; it is against the other communities that each society asserts its exclusive right to a determined territory; the political relationship with neighboring groups is immediately established. A relationship that institutes itself in the political order and not in the economical order, let us recall: the domestic mode of production being what it is, no local group has any need, in principle, to encroach upon neighbors' territory for provisions.

Control of the territory allows the community to realize its autarkic ideal by guaranteeing it self-sufficiency in resources: thus, it does not depend on anyone; it is independent. One would assume, all things being equal for all local groups, a general absence of violence: it could only arise in rare cases of territorial violation; it would only be defensive, and thus never produce itself, each group relying on its own territory which it has no reason to leave. Now, as we know, war is widespread and very often offensive. Territorial defense, thus, is not the cause of war; the relationship between war and society has yet to be illuminated.

What of the being of primitive society, insofar as it is realized, identical, in the infinite series of communities, bands, villages, or local groups? The answer is present in all ethnographic literature since the West has taken interest in the Savage world. Primitive society has always been considered a place of absolute difference in relation to western society, a strange and unthinkable space of absence — absence of all that constitutes the observers' sociocultural universe: a world without hierarchy, people who obey no one, a society indifferent to the possession of wealth, chiefs who do not command, cultures without morals for they are unaware of sin, classless societies, societies without a State, etc. In short, what the writings of ancient travelers or modern scholars constantly cry out and yet never manage to say is that primitive society is, in its being, undivided.

Primitive society is unaware of — because it prevents the appearance of — the difference between rich and poor, the opposition between exploiters and the exploited, the domination of the chief over society. The Domestic Mode of Production, which assures the economic autarky of the community as such, also allows for the autonomy of kinship groups which compose the social ensemble, and even the independence of individuals. Outside of gender-related division, there is, in effect, no division of labor in primitive society: each individual is polyvalent in a way; men know how to do everything men should know how to do, women know how to do everything women should know how to do. No individual is less knowledgable or less capable; no individual can fall victim to the enterprises of another more talented or better-off: the relatives of the victim would soon discourage the vocation of the apprentice-exploiter. Vying with each other, ethnologists have noted the Savages' indifference before their goods and possessions which are easily refabricated once worn or broken, have noted the absence among them of all desire for accumulation. Why, indeed, would such a desire appear? Productive activity is exactly measured by the satisfaction of needs and does not go beyond that: surplus production is perfectly possible in the primitive economy, but it is also totally useless: what would be done with it? Moreover, the activity of accumulation (producing a useless surplus) could only be, in this type of society, a strictly individual enterprise: the entrepreneur could only count on his own strengths, the exploitation of others being sociologically impossible. Let us imagine, nevertheless, that despite the solitude of his effort, the savage entrepreneur manages to constitute, by the sweat of his brow, a stock of resources which, let us recall, he would not know what to do with since it is already a matter of a surplus, that is, goods that are unnecessary in that they no longer have anything to do with the satisfaction of needs. What will happen? Simply, the community will help him consume these free resources: the man who has become rich by the strength of his own hand will see his wealth disappear in the blink of an eye into his neighbors' hands or stomachs. The realization of the desire of accumulation would reduce itself thus at once to a pure phenomenon of self-exploitation of the individual by himself, and the exploitation of the rich man by the community. The Savages are wise enough not to abandon themselves to this folly; primitive society functions in such a way that inequality, exploitation, division are impossible there.

At its actual level of existence — the local group — primitive society presents two essential sociological properties that touch upon its very being, the social being that determines the reason for being and the principle of the intelligibility of war. The primitive community is at once a totality and a unity. A totality in that it is a complete, autonomous, whole ensemble, ceaselessly attentive to preserving its autonomy, a society in the full sense of the word. A unity in that its homogeneous being continues to refuse social division, to exclude inequality, to forbid alienation. Primitive society is a single totality in that the principle of its unity is not exterior to it: it does not allow any configuration of One to detach itself from the social body in order to represent it, in order to embody it as unity. This is why the criterion of non-division is fundamentally political: if the savage chief is powerless, it is because society does not accept power separated from its being, division established between those who command and those who obey. And this is also why, in primitive society, it is the chief who is commissioned to speak in the name of society: in his discourse, the chief never expresses the flights of his individual desire or the statement of his private law, but only the sociological desire that society remain undivided, and the text of Law that no one has established, for it has nothing to do with human decision. The legislators are also the founders of society — the mythical ancestors, the cultural heroes, the gods. It is of this Law that the chief is spokesperson: the substance of his discourse always refers to the ancestral Law that no one can transgress, for it is the very being of society: to violate the Law would be to alter the social body, to introduce into it the innovation and change that it absolutely rejects.

Primitive society is a community that assures control of its territory in the name of the Law guaranteeing its non-division. The territorial dimension already includes the political in that it excludes the Other. It is precisely the Other as mirror — the neighboring groups — who reflect back onto the community the image of its unity and totality. Faced with neighboring communities or bands, a particular community or band posits itself and thinks of itself as absolute difference, as irreducible freedom, as a body possessing the will to maintain its being as a single totality. Here then is how primitive society concretely appears: a multiplicity of separate communities, each watching over the integrity of its territory, a series of neo-monads each of which, in the face of others, asserts its difference. Each community, in that it is undivided, can think of itself as a We. This We in turn thinks of itself as a totality in the equal relationship that it maintains with the equivalent We's that constitute other villages, tribes, bands, etc. The primitive community can posit itself as a totality because it institutes itself as a unity: it is a whole, because it is an undivided We.

At this level of analysis, the general structure of primitive organization can be thought of as purely static, as totally inert, as void of movement. The global system seems to be able to function only in view of its own repetition, by making all emergence of opposition or conflict impossible. Now, ethnographic reality shows the opposite: far from being inert, the system is in perpetual movement; it is not static but dynamic, and the primitive monad, far from remaining closed upon itself, actually opens itself to others in the extreme intensity of the violence of war. How then do we think of both the system and war? Is war a simple diversion that would translate the occasional failure of the system, or would the system be unable to function without war? Wouldn't war simply be a prerequisite for the primitive social being? Wouldn't war be, not the threat of death, but the condition of primitive society's life?

One point is clear: the possibility of war is inscribed in the being of primitive society. Indeed, the will of each community to assert its difference is strong enough so that the least incident quickly transforms the sought-after difference into a real dispute. The violation of territory, the assumed aggression of the neighbors' shaman: this is all that is required for war to break out. A fragile equilibrium, as a result: the possibility of violence and armed conflict is an immediate given. But could one imagine this possibility never being realized and instead of war of each against each, as Hobbes thought, having, on the contrary, exchange of each with each, as Lévi-Strauss' viewpoint implies?

Take for instance the hypothesis of generalized friendship. We quickly discover that this is impossible for several reasons. First of all, because of spatial dispersion. Primitive communities maintain a certain distance between each other, both literally and figuratively: between each band or village there are their respective territories, allowing each group to keep its distance. Friendship does not adapt well to distance. It is maintained easily with nearby neighbors who can be invited to parties, from whom one can accept invitations, whom one can visit. With distant groups, these types of relations cannot be established. A primitive community is loathe to travel very far or stay away for long from its own, familiar territory: as soon as they are no longer "at home," the Savages experience, rightly or wrongly but most often rightly, a strong feeling of distrust and fear. Amiable relations of exchange only develop between groups close to one another; distant groups are excluded: they are, at best, Foreigners.

But the hypothesis of friendship of all with all contradicts each community's profound, essential desire to maintain and deploy its being as single totality, that is, its irreducible difference in relation to all other groups, including neighbors, friends and allies. The logic of primitive society, which is a logic of difference, would contradict the logic of generalized exchange, which is a logic of identity, because it is a logic of identification. Now, it is this, above all, that primitive society refuses: identifying with others, losing that which constitutes it as such, losing its very being and its difference, losing the ability to think of itself as an autonomous We. In the identification of all with all, which generalized exchange and friendship of all with all would entail, each community would lose its individuality. The exchange of all with all would be the destruction of primitive society: identification is a movement toward death, the primitive social being is an affirmation of life. The logic of identicalness would give way to a sort of equalizing discourse, the motto of friendship of all with all being: We are all the same! The unification of the multiplicity of partial We's into a meta-We, the elimination of the difference unique to each autonomous community would abolish the distinction between the We and the Other, and primitive society itself would disappear. This is not a matter of primitive psychology but of sociological logic: there is, inherent in primitive society, a centrifugal logic of crumbling, of dispersion, of schism such that each community, to consider itself as such (as a single totality), needs the opposite figure of the foreigner or enemy, such that the possibility of violence is inscribed ahead of time in the primitive social being; war is a structure of primitive society and not the accidental failure of an unsuccessful exchange. This structural status of violence is illustrated by the universality of war in the Savage world.

Structurally, generalized friendship and exchange of all with all are impossible. Consequently, should we say that Hobbes was right, and from the impossibility of friendship of all with all conclude the reality of war of each against each? Take for example, now, the hypothesis of generalized hostility. Each community is in a confrontational situation with all the others, the war machine is functioning at full speed, global society is composed only of enemies aspiring to reciprocal destruction. Now all wars, as we know, leave a victor and a vanquished. What, in this case, would be the principal result of war of all against all? It would institute precisely the political relationship that primitive society works constantly to prevent; the war of all against all would lead to the establishment of domination and power that the victor could forcibly exercise over the vanquished. A new social configuration would then appear, introducing a relationship of command obedience and the political division of society into Masters and Subjects. In other words, it would be the death of primitive society insofar as it is and considers itself an undivided body. As a result, generalized war would produce exactly the same effect as generalized friendship: the negation of the primitive social being. In the case of friendship of all with all, the community would lose its autonomous totality through the dissolution of its difference. In the case of war of all against all, it would lose its homogeneous unity through the irruption of social division: primitive society is a single totality. It cannot consent to universal peace which alienates its freedom; it cannot abandon itself to general war which abolishes its equality. It is not possible, among the Savages, to be either friend of all or enemy of all.

And yet, war is part of the essence of primitive society; like exchange, it is a structure of it. Is this to say that the primitive social being would be a sort of compound of two heterogeneous elements — a little exchange, a little war — and that the primitive ideal consists of maintaining the equilibrium between these two components in the quest for a sort of happy medium between contrary, if not contradictory, elements? This would be to persist in the Lévi-Straussian idea that war and exchange are developed on the same level and that one is always the limit and the failure of the other. From this perspective, generalized exchange eliminates war, but at the same time eliminates primitive society. General war eliminates exchange, with the same result. The primitive social being, thus, simultaneously needs exchange and war, in order to be able to combine at once the autonomist point of honor and the refusal of division. It is to this twofold demand that the status and function of exchange and war are related, unfolding on different levels.

The impossibility of war of all against all for a given community immediately classifies the people surrounding it: Others are immediately classified into friends and enemies. With the former, one will attempt to form alliances, with the others, one accepts — or one seeks — the risk of war. We would be mistaken to gather from this description only the banality of an absolutely general situation in primitive society. For it is necessary now to pose the question of alliance: why does a primitive society need allies? The answer is obvious: because it has enemies. It has to be assured of its strength, certain of repeated victory over its adversaries, in order to do without the military support, indeed, even the neutrality, of the allies. This is never the case in practice: a community never launches into a war adventure without first protecting itself by means of diplomatic acts — parties, invitations — after which supposedly lasting alliances are formed, but which must constantly be renewed, for betrayal is always possible, and often real. Here a trait appears, described by travelers or ethnographers as the Savages' inconstancy and taste for betrayal. But, once again, it is not a matter of primitive psychology: the inconstancy here signifies simply that the alliance is not a contract, that its rupture is never perceived by the Savages as a scandal, and that finally, a given community does not always have the same allies or the same enemies. The terms of alliance and war can change, and, following fortuitous events, group B, allied with group A against group C, would be perfectly capable of turning against A to side with C. Experience in the field constantly offers the spectacle of such turnabouts, for which the people responsible always have reasons. What one should keep in mind is the permanence of the apparatus as a whole — the division of Others into allies and enemies — and not the conjunctural and variable place occupied in this apparatus by the communities implicated.

But this mutual, and justified, distrust that allied groups feel indicates clearly that alliances are often consented to unwillingly, that alliance is not a desired goal but only a means: the means to attain at the lowest risk and at the least cost a goal that is the war enterprise. Which amounts to saying that one is resigned to alliance because it would be too dangerous to engage in military operations alone, and that, if one could, one would gladly do without allies who are never absolutely reliable. There is, as a result, an essential property of international life in primitive society: war relates first to alliance;

war as an institution determines alliance as a tactic. The strategy is the same for all communities: to persevere in their autonomous being, to conserve themselves as what they are, undivided We's.

We have already observed that through the will for political independence and exclusive control of its territory manifested by each community, the possibility of war is immediately inscribed in the functioning of these societies: primitive society is a locus of a permanent state of war. We see now that seeking an alliance depends on actual war: there is a sociological priority of war over alliance. Here, the true relationship between exchange and war emerges. Indeed, where are relations of exchange established, which sociopolitical units assume a principle of reciprocity? These are precisely the groups implicated in the networks of alliance; exchange partners are allies, the sphere of exchange is that of alliance. This does not mean, of course, that were it not for alliance, there would no longer be exchange: exchange would simply find itself circumscribed within the space of the autonomous community at the heart of which it never ceases to operate; it would be strictly intra-communal.

Thus, one exchanges with allies; there is exchange, because there is alliance. It is not only a question of the exchange of good behavior — a cycle of parties to which people take turns inviting each other — but the exchange of gifts (without veritable economic significance, let us repeat), and especially the exchange of women. As Lévi-Strauss writes, "... the exchange of brides is merely the conclusion of an uninterrupted process of reciprocal gifts..." (p. 79). In short, the reality of alliance establishes the possibility for complete exchange, which affects not only goods and services but matrimonial relations. What is the exchange of women? At the level of human society as such, it assures this society's humanity, that is, its non-animality; it signifies that human society does not belong to the order of nature but to that of culture: human society unfolds in the universe of the rule and not in that of need, in the world of the institution and not in that of instinct. The exogamic exchange of women founds society as such in the prohibition of incest. But it is precisely a matter of exchange insofar as it institutes human society as non-animal society, and not exchange as instituted in the framework of a network of alliances between different communities, which unfolds on another level. In the framework of alliance, the exchange of women assumes a clear political significance; the establishment of matrimonial relations between different groups is a way of concluding and reinforcing political alliance in order to confront inevitable enemies under the best conditions. From allies who are also relatives, one may hope for more constancy in warlike solidarity, though the links of kinship are in no way a definitive guarantee of fidelity to the alliance. According to Lévi-Strauss, the exchange of women is the conclusion of an "uninterrupted process of reciprocal gifts." In reality, when two groups enter into relations, they do not at all seek to exchange women: what they want is a politico-military alliance, and the best means of reaching this is to exchange women. This is why if the field of matrimonial exchange is indeed more restricted than the field of political alliance, it cannot in any case surpass it: alliance at once permits exchange and interrupts it, it is its limit, exchange never goes beyond alliance.

Lévi-Strauss confuses the end with the means. A confusion caused by his very conception of exchange, which situates on the same level exchange as a founding act of human society (prohibition of incest, exogamy) and exchange as a consequence and means of political alliance (the best allies, or the least bad, are relatives). In the end, the point of view that supports the Lévi-Straussian theory of exchange is that primitive society wants exchange, that it is a society-for-exchange, that the more exchange there is, the better it works. Now, we have seen as much on an economical level (the autarkic ideal) as on a political level (will for independence), that primitive society constantly develops a strategy destined to reduce the need for exchange as much as possible: this is not at all a society for exchange, but rather a society against exchange. And this appears with the greatest clarity precisely at the juncture between the exchange of women and violence. We know that one of the goals of war asserted most insistently by all primitive societies is the capture of women: one attacks enemies in order to seize their women. It matters little whether the reason invoked is a real cause or a simple pretext for hostility. Here, war clearly manifests primitive society's profound repugnance toward reentering the exchangist game: in the exchange of women, a group gains women but loses just as many, while in the war for women, the victorious group wins women without losing any. The risk is considerable (injury, death), but so are the benefits: they are total, the women are free. Interest would thus always command the preference of war to exchange: but this would be a situation of war of all against all, the impossibility of which we have seen. War, thus, involves alliance; alliance founds exchange. There is exchange of women because one cannot do otherwise: since one has enemies, one must procure allies and attempt to transform them into brothers-in-law. Inversely, when for one reason or another (imbalance of the sex ratio in favor of men, extension of polygyny, etc.) the group desires to procure supplementary wives, it will attempt to obtain them through violence, through war and not through exchange in which they would win nothing.

Let us sum up. The exchangist discourse on primitive society, in reducing this society wholly to exchange, is mistaken on two distinct but logically connected points. It is first of all unaware — or refuses to acknowledge — that primitive societies, far from always seeking to extend their field of exchange, tend on the contrary to reduce its significance constantly. This discourse consequently underestimates the real importance of violence, for the priority and exclusivity accorded to exchange leads in fact to abolishing war. To be mistaken about war, as we were saying, is to be mistaken about society. Believing that the primitive social being is a being-for-exchange, Lévi-Strauss is led to say that primitive society is society-against-war: war is failed exchange. Though his discourse is very coherent, it is false. The contradiction is not internal to this discourse, it is the discourse that is contrary to the ethnographically readable sociological reality of primitive society. War implies alliance, alliance entails exchange (understood not as the difference between man and animal, as the passage from nature to culture, but, of course, as the unfolding of the sociality of primitive society, as the free play of its political being). It is through war that one can understand exchange, and not the reverse. War is not the accidental failure of exchange, exchange is a tactical effect of war. It is not, as Lévi-Strauss believes, the fact of exchange that determines the non-existence of war, it is the fact of war that determines the existence of exchange. The constant problem of the primitive community is not: whom will we trade with? but: how can we maintain our independence? The Savages point of view on exchange is simple: it is a necessary evil; since we need allies, they might as well be brothers-in-law.

Hobbes believed, wrongly, that the primitive world is not a social world, because war there prevents exchange, understood not only as exchange of goods and services, but especially as exchange of women, in accordance with the exogamic rule in the prohibition of incest. Doesn't he say that the American Savages live in "that brutish manner" and that the absence of social organization is revealed in their submission to "natural lust" (there is no universe of the rule among them)? But Hobbes' error does not make Lévi-Strauss' truth. For the latter, primitive society is a world of exchange: but at the price of a confusion between the founding exchange of human society in general and exchange as a mode of relation between different groups. And so he is forced to eliminate war, in that it is the negation of exchange: if there is war, there is no exchange, and if there is no more exchange, there is no more society. Certainly, exchange is inherent in the human social: human society exists because the exchange of women exists, because incest is prohibited. But this exchange has nothing to do with the properly sociopolitical activity that is war, and this in no way puts into question exchange as respect for the prohibition of incest. War puts into question exchange as an ensemble of sociopolitical relations between different communities, but it puts it into question precisely in order to found and establish it through the mediation of alliance. Confusing these two levels of exchange, Lévi-Strauss inscribes war on this same level, where it doesn't belong, and from which it must thus disappear. For this author, the implementation of the principle of reciprocity is translated in the search for alliance; the latter permits the exchange of women, and the exchange ends in the negation of war. This description of the primitive social fact would be absolutely satisfying, providing war did not exist: we know of its existence but also of its universality. The ethnographic reality thus holds the opposite discourse: the state of war between groups makes the search for alliance necessary, which provokes the exchange of women. The successful analysis of kinship systems or of mythological systems thus coexists with a failed discourse on society.

An examination of ethnographic facts reveals the properly political dimension of warlike activity. It is related neither to a zoological specificity of humanity, nor to the vital competition of communities, nor, finally, to a constant movement of exchange toward the suppression of violence. War is linked to primitive society as such (and so it is universal there); it is its mode of operation. It is the very nature of this society that determines the existence and meaning of war, which, as we have seen, because of the extreme specificity displayed by each group, is present ahead of time as a possibility in the primitive social being. For all local groups, all Others are Foreigners: the figure of the Foreigner confirms, for every given group, the conviction of its identity as an autonomous We. That is, the state of war is permanent, since with foreigners there can only be hostile relations, whether actually implemented in a real war or not. It is not the limited reality of armed conflict or combat that is essential, but the permanence of its possibility, the permanent state of war that maintains all communities in their respective difference. What is permanent, structural, is the state of war with Foreigners which sometimes culminates, in rather regular intervals, rather frequently depending on the society, in actual battle, in direct confrontation: the Foreigner is thus the Enemy, which engenders in turn the figure of the Ally. The state of war is permanent, but the Savages do not necessarily spend their time waging war.

War, as external policy of primitive society, relates to its internal policy, to what one might call the intransigent conservatism of this society, expressed in the incessant reference to the traditional system of norms, to the ancestral Law which must always be respected, which cannot be altered. What is primitive society seeking to conserve with its conservatism? It is seeking to conserve its very being; it wants to persevere in its being. But what is this being? It is an undivided being; the social body is homogeneous; the community is a We. Primitive conservatism thus seeks to prevent innovation in society; it wants the respect of the Law to assure the maintenance of non-division; it seeks to prevent the appearance of division in society. This is primitive society's internal policy, as much on the economic level (the impossibility of accumulating wealth) as on the level of power relations (the chief is there not to command): to conserve itself as an undivided We, as a single totality.

But we see clearly that the will to persevere in its undivided being equally animates all We's, all communities: each position of the Self implies opposition and hostility to others; the state of war will last as long as each primitive community can assert its autonomy in relation to the others. If one proves itself incapable of this, it will be destroyed by the others. The capacity to implement structural relations of hostility (dissuasion) and the capacity to resist effectively the enterprises of others (to fend off an attack), in short, the warlike capacity of each community, is the condition of its autonomy. In other words: the permanent state of war and actual war periodically appear as the principal means used by primitive society to prevent social change. The permanence of primitive society has to do with the permanence of the state of war; the application of internal policy (to maintain the undivided and autonomous We intact) has to do with the implementation of external policy (to form alliances in order to wage war): war is at the very heart of the primitive social being, war constitutes the very motor of social life. In order to think of themselves as a We, the community must be both undivided (one) and independent (totality): internal non-division and external opposition are combined; each is a condition for the other. Should war cease, the heart of primitive society will cease to beat. War is its foundation, the very life of its being, it is its goal: primitive society is *society for war*, it is, by definition, warlike...[10]

The dispersion of local groups, which is primitive society's most immediately perceptible trait, is thus not the cause of war, but its effect, its specific goal. What is the function of primitive war? To assure the permanence of the dispersion, the parceling, the atomization of the groups. Primitive war is the work of a *centrifugal logic*, a logic of separation, which is expressed from time to time in armed conflict.[11] War serves to maintain each community's political independence. As long as there is war, there is autonomy: this is

---

[10] Here let us recall not the discourse of Westeners on primitive man as warrior, but that, perhaps less expected but which stems from the same logic, of the Incas. The Incas said of the tribes that stirred at the steps of the Empire that these were savages *in a constant state of war*: which legitimated all attempts to integrate them by means of conquest into the *pax incaïca*.

[11] This logic concerns not only intercommunal relations, but also the operation of the community itself. In South America, when the demographic size of a group goes beyond the threshold considered optimum by its society, some of the people will establish another village further away.

why war cannot cease, why it must not cease, why it is permanent. War is the privileged mode of existence of primitive society, made up of equal, free and independent sociopolitical units: if enemies did not exist, they would have to be invented.

Thus, the logic of primitive society is a centrifugal logic, a logic of the multiple. The Savages want the multiplication of the multiple. Now what is the major effect of the development of centrifugal force? It faces an insurmountable barrier, the most powerful sociological obstacle to the opposite force, centripetal force, the logic of unification, the logic of One: the more dispersion there is, the less unification there is. We see henceforth that the same rigorous logic determines both the internal policy and external policy of primitive society. On the one hand, the community wants to persevere in its undivided being and prevent a unifying authority — the figure of the commanding chief — from separating itself from the social body and introducing social division between Master and Subjects. The community, on the other hand, wants to persevere in its autonomous being, that is, remain under the sign of its own Law: it thus refuses all logic that would lead it to submit to an exterior law; it is opposed to the exteriority of the unifying Law. Now, what is the legal power that embraces all differences in order to suppress them, that exists precisely to abolish the logic of the multiple and to substitute it with the opposite logic of unification? What is the other name of this One that primitive society by definition refuses? It is the State.

Let us go back. What is the State? It is the total sign of division in society, in that it is a separate organ of political power: society is henceforth divided into those who exercise power and those who submit to it. Society is no longer an undivided We, a single totality, but a fragmented body, a heterogeneous social being. Social division and the emergence of the State are the death of primitive society. So that the community might assert its difference, it has to be undivided; its will to be a totality exclusive of others rests on the refusal of social division: in order to think of themselves as We exclusive of Others, the We must be a homogeneous social body. External segmentation, internal non-division are two faces of a single reality, two aspects of the same sociological functioning and of the same social logic. So that the community might be able to confront the enemy world, it must be united, homogeneous, division-less. Reciprocally, in order to exist in non-division, it needs the figure of the Enemy in which it can read the unified image of its social being. Sociopolitical autonomy and sociological non-division are conditions for each other, and the centrifugal logic of the crumbling is a refusal of the unifying logic of the One. This concretely signifies that primitive communities can never attain great sociodemographic dimensions, for the fundamental tendency of primitive society is toward dispersion and not toward concentration, toward atomization and not toward assembly. If, in a primitive society, one observes the action of centripetal force, the tendency toward reorganization visible in the constitution of social macro-units, it is because this society is losing the primitive logic of the centrifuge, it is because this society is losing its properties of totality and unity, it is because this society is in the midst of no longer being primitive.[12]

Refusal of unification, refusal of the separate One, society against the State. Each primitive community wants to remain under the sign of its own Law (auto-nomy, political independence) which excludes social change (society will remain what it is: an undivided being). The refusal of the State is the refusal of exo-nomy, of exterior Law, it is quite simply the refusal of submission, inscribed as such in the very structure of primitive society. Only fools can believe that in order to refuse alienation, one must have first experienced it: the refusal of alienation (economical or political) belongs to the very being of this society, it expresses its conservatism, its deliberate will to remain an undivided We. Deliberate, indeed, and not only the effect of the functioning of a social machine: the Savages know well that any alteration of their social life (any social innovation) could only translate into the loss of freedom.

What is primitive society? It is a multiplicity of undivided communities which all obey the same centrifugal logic. What institution at once expresses and guarantees the permanence of this logic? It is war, as the truth of relations between communities, as the principal sociological means of promoting the centrifugal force of dispersion against the centripetal force of unification. The war machine is the motor of the social machine; the primitive social being relies entirely on war, primitive society cannot survive without war. The more war there is, the less unification there is, and the best enemy of the State is war. Primitive society is society against the State in that it is society-for-war.

Here we are once again brought back to the thought of Hobbes. With a lucidity that has since disappeared, the English thinker was able to detect the profound link, the close relationship between war and the State. He was able to see that war and the State are contradictory terms, that they cannot exist together, that each implies the negation of the other: war prevents the State, the State prevents war. The enormous error, almost fatal amongst a man of this time, is to have believed that the society which persists in war of each against each is not truly a society; that the Savage world is not a social

---

12 Such is the absolutely exemplary case of the Tupi-Guarani of South America, whose society, from the moment of the discovery of the New World, was wrought by centripetal forces, by a logic of unification.

world; that, as a result, the institution of society involves the end of war, the appearance of the State, an anti-war machine par excellence. Incapable of thinking of the primitive world as a non-natural world, Hobbes nevertheless was the first to see that one cannot think of war without the State, that one must think of them in a relation of exclusion. For him, the social link institutes itself between men due to "a common Power to keep them all in awe:" the State is against war. What does primitive society as a sociological space of permanent war tell us in counterpoint? It repeats Hobbes' discourse by reversing it; it proclaims that the machine of dispersion functions against the machine of unification; it tells us that war is against the State.[13]

---

[13] At the end of this attempt at an archeology of violence, various ethnological problems arise, this one in particular: What will be the destiny of primitive societies that let the war machine run rampant? By permitting the autonomy of the group of warriors in relation to the community, would not the dynamic of war carry within it the risk of social division? How do primitive societies react when this occurs? Essential questions, for behind them lurks the transcendental question: under what conditions can social division appear in an undivided society? We shall attempt to answer these questions and others in a series of studies which the present text inaugurates.

12

SORROWS OF THE SAVAGE WARRIOR

One cannot think of primitive society, I recently wrote,[1] without at the same time thinking of war. Inherent in the primitive social being, an immediate and universal given of its mode of operation, warlike violence appears in the Savages' universe as the principal means of maintaining this society's non-division, of maintaining each community's autonomy as *single totality*, free and independent of others: war, a major obstacle erected by Stateless societies against the machine of unification that is the State, is part of the essence of primitive society. One might as well say, consequently, that all primitive society is warlike: hence, the ethnographically established universality of war in the infinite variety of known primitive societies. If war is a societal attribute, then warlike activity functions as a determining factor of the male being-in-the-world: in primitive society, man is, by definition, a warrior. An equation that, as we shall see, when brought to light, illuminates the frequently and often foolishly debated question of social relations between men and women in primitive society.

---

[1] Cf. "Archéologie de la violence," *Libre,* 77-1 [Chapter Eleven of this book].

Primitive man, as such, is a warrior; each male adult is equal to the warlike function, which, though it allows — even calls for — acknowledged differences in individual talents, particular qualities, personal bravery and know-how (in short, a hierarchy of prestige), it excludes, on the other hand, any unegalitarian disposition of the warriors on the axis of political power. Warlike activity does not tolerate, any more than economic activity or social life in times of peace, the division of the warrior community — as in all military organizations — into soldiers-performers and chiefs-commanders: discipline is not the principal force of primitive armies; obedience is not the first duty of the basic combatant; the chief does not exercise any commanding power. For, contrary to an opinion that is as false as it is widespread (that the chief has no power, *except in times of war*), the warrior leader is at no moment of the expedition (preparation, battle, retreat) in a position — should such be his intention — to impose his will, to give an order which he knows ahead of time will not be obeyed. In other words, war does not, any more than peace, allow the chief to act the chief. To describe the true figure of the savage chief in his warrior dimension (what use is a war chief?) requires special treatment. Let us note for now that war does not open a new field in the political relations between men: the war chief and the warriors remain Equals; war never creates, even temporarily, division in primitive society between those who command and those who obey; the will for freedom is not canceled by the will for victory, even at the price of operational efficiency. The war machine, by itself, is incapable of engendering inequality in primitive society. Travelers' and missionaries' ancient chronicles and ethnologists' recent work concur on this observation: when a chief seeks to impose his own desire for war on the community, the latter abandons him, for it wants to exercise its free collective will and not submit to the law of a desire for power. At best, a chief who wants to act the chief is shunned; at worst, he is killed.

Such, then, is the structural relationship primitive society generally maintains with war. Now, a certain type of primitive society exists (existed) in the world in which the relationship to war went far beyond what was said above. These were societies in which warlike activity was somehow subdivided or overdetermined: on the one hand, it assumed, as in all primitive societies, the properly sociopolitical function of maintaining communities by ceaselessly digging and redigging the gap between them; on the other hand, it unfolded on a completely different level, no longer as a political means of a sociological strategy — letting centrifugal forces play themselves out in order to ward off all forces of unification — but indeed as a private goal, as *the warrior's personal end*. War at this level is no longer a structural effect of a primitive society's mode of operation; it is an absolutely free and individual enterprise in that it proceeds only from the warrior's decision: the warrior obeys only the law of his desire or will.

Would war, then, be the sole affair of the warrior in this case? Despite the extremely personalized aspect of warlike activity in this type of society, it is rather clear that it does have an effect on the sociological level. What new figure does the twofold dimension that war assumes here assign to the social body? It is upon this body that a strange space — a foreign space — is outlined; an unforeseeable organ is attached to it: *the particular social group constituted by the ensemble of warriors.*

And not by the ensemble of men. For not all men in these societies are necessarily warriors; all do not hear the call to arms with equal intensity; only some realize their warlike vocation. In other words, the warrior group is made up of a minority of men in this type of society: those who have deliberately chosen to devote themselves, full time, so to speak, to warlike activity, those for whom war is the very foundation of their being, the ultimate point of honor, the exclusive meaning of their lives. The difference between the general case of primitive societies and the particular case of these societies appears immediately. Primitive society being warlike by essence, all men there are warriors: potential warriors, because the state of war is permanent; actual warriors, when, from time to time, armed conflict erupts. And it is precisely because all men are always ready for war that a special group, more warlike than the others, cannot differentiate itself from the heart of the masculine community: the relation to war is equal for all. In the case of "warrior societies," however, war also assumes the character of a personal vocation open to all males, since each is free to do what he wants, but which only some, in fact, realize. This signifies that, in the general case, all men go to war from time to time, and that, in the particular case, *some men go to war constantly.* Or, to say it even more clearly: in "warrior" societies, all men go to war from time to time, when the community as a whole is concerned (and we are brought once again to the general case); but, in addition, a certain number among them are constantly engaged in warlike expeditions, even if the tribe for the time being finds itself in relative peace with neighboring groups: they go to war on their own and not in response to a collective imperative.

Which, of course, does not in any way signify that society remains indifferent or inert before the activism of its warriors: war, on the contrary, is exalted, the victorious warrior is celebrated, and his exploits are praised by all in great festivals. A positive relation thus exists between society and the warrior. This is indeed why these societies are distinctly warlike. Still, it will be necessary to elucidate the very real and unexpectedly profound relationship that links a community such as this to the slightly enigmatic group of its warriors. But where does one find such societies?

We should first note that the warlike societies do not represent a specific, irreducible, immutable essence of primitive society: they are only a particular case, this particularity having to do with the special place occupied by warlike activity and warriors. In other words, all primitive societies could transform themselves into warlike societies, depending on local circumstances, either external (for example, neighboring groups' increased aggressiveness, or, on the contrary, their weakening, inciting an increase of attacks on them) or internal (the exaltation of the warlike ethos in the system of norms that orders collective existence). Furthermore, the path can be traveled in the opposite direction: a warlike society could very well cease to be one, if a change in the tribal ethic or in the sociopolitical environment alters the taste for war or limits its field of application. A primitive society's becoming warlike, or its eventual return to the classic, previous situation, pertains to specific, local history and ethnography, which is sometimes possible to reconstitute. But this is another problem.

Becoming warlike is thus a possibility for all primitive societies. Assuredly, then, all over the world, throughout the course of the millennia that this primordial mode of human social organization has lasted, there have been warrior societies here and there, emerging then disappearing. But naturally it would not be enough to refer only to the sociological possibility of all primitive societies becoming warlike societies, and to the probability of such an evolution. The ethnologist, fortunately, has access to rather ancient documents in which warlike societies are described in great detail. He may even be lucky enough to conduct fieldwork among one of these societies, a rare occurrence and all the more precious. The American continent, as much in the North as in the South, offers a rather large sampling of societies which, beyond their differences, have a remarkable commonality: they have, to varying degrees, pushed their warlike vocation quite far, institutionalized brotherhoods of warriors, allowed war to occupy a central place in the political and ritual life of the social body, accorded social recognition to this original, almost asocial form of war and to the men who wage it. Explorers' reports, adventurers' chronicles, missionaries' accounts inform us that such was the case with the Huron, the Algonkin and the Iroquois; more recent narratives have been added to these old accounts, confirming them: the narratives of Indian captives, official American documents (civil and military), and the autobiographies of vanquished warriors, speak to us of the Cheyenne and the Sioux, the Blackfoot and the Apache.

Just as bellicose but less well-known, South America provides anthropological research and reflection with an incomparable field of study constituted by the Grand Chaco. Situated at the heart of the South American continent, this austere and vast tropical region covers a good part of Paraguay, Argentina and Bolivia. The climate (very contrasting seasons), the hydrography (very few rivers), the flora (abundance of thorny vegetation adapted to the scarcity of water) combine to make the Chaco very homogeneous from the point of view of nature. But it is even more so from the point of view of culture; it stands out on the South American ethnographic horizon with the sharpness of a determined cultural area. Of the numerous tribes that occupied this territory, most of them, in effect, illustrate perfectly, no doubt better than any other society, what is habitually understood by warlike culture: war is the activity most highly valorized by society, it is the quasi-exclusive occupation of a select number of men. The first Spanish Conquistadors, who, having barely reached the edge of the Chaco, had to confront the repeated assaults of the *chaquenos* Indians, quickly learned this at their own expense.

Now it so happens that, thanks to the luck of history and to the Jesuits' tenacity, we have considerable documentation on the principles of these tribes. During the 18th century, until their expulsion in 1768, the Jesuits, encouraged by their successes amongst the Guarani Indians, attempted to integrate the Chaco into their missionary enterprise. The failure, starting before the expulsion, was almost total and, as the Jesuits themselves emphasize, somewhat inevitable: against the evangelical mission rose the insurmountable obstacle of the Indians' diabolical warlike passion. Unable to assess the positive results of a successful spiritual conquest, the missionaries resigned themselves to reflecting on their failure and explaining it by the particular nature of the societies that fate had assigned to them: hence, luckily for us, the missionaries' superb descriptions, enriched by years of daily contact with the Indians, by the knowledge of their languages, by the Jesuits' genuine fondness toward these ferocious warriors. And thus, the name of Martin Dobrizhoffer is henceforth associated with the Abipone tribe, that of Florian Paucke with the Mocovi, that of José Sanchez Labrador with the famous Guaicuru-Mbaya, as well as the work of Pedro Lozano, historian of the Society of Jesus, devoted especially to the Chaco societies.[2]

These tribes have, for the most part, disappeared. The exemplary testimonies kepping alive their memory are thus doubly precious. But no matter how precise and detailed, these books cannot take the place of direct observation of a living society. This possibility was offered to me in 1966 in the Paraguayan part of the Chaco, close to the Pilcomayo river which separates Argentina from Paraguay. This river's middle current borders the territory of the Chulupi Indians to the south, better known in ethnographic literature by the (inaccurate) name of Ashluslay but whose self-designation is Nivaklé, a

2 Cf. bibliography.

term which, as one might expect, simply means "Men." Estimated at 20,000 at the beginning of the century, the Chulupi now seem to have halted the demographic decline which threatened them: today there are around 10,000. I stayed with them for six months (May-October 1966), accompanied in my travels by two Indian interpreters who, in addition to their own language, spoke Spanish and Guarani fluently.[3]

Until the early 1930s, the Paraguayan Chaco was an almost exclusively Indian territory, a terra incognita which the Paraguayans had hardly attempted to penetrate. And so the tribes there led their traditional, free, autonomous lives, where war, especially among the Chulupi-Nivaklé, occupied a preponderant place. Following attempts by the Bolivian State to annex this region, a murderous war erupted in 1932, the Chaco war, which set the Bolivians against the Paraguayans until 1935, and which saw the defeat of the Bolivian army. The Indians, extraneous to this international conflict, were nevertheless its first victims: this fierce war (50,000 deaths on each side) occurred on their territory, and notably on that of the Nivaklé, forcing the Indians to flee the combat zones and irremediably upheaving traditional social life. Wanting to consolidate their victory, the Paraguayans erected a chain of forts along the frontiers, and the garrisons also protected colonists and religious missions installed on this virgin territory, against potential Indian attacks. The tribe's age-old freedom was now over: fairly continuous contact with the whites and the usual effects (epidemics, exploitation, alcoholism, etc.) did not take long to spread destruction and death.

The most warlike communities nevertheless reacted better than the others: this is the case of the Chulupi[4] who, relying on a powerful war ethos and tribal solidarity, were able to maintain relative autonomy. That is to

---

[3] All these societies (Abipone, Mocovi, Toba, Guaicuru, Chulupi, etc.) were equestrian tribes which had acquired horses well before the North American Indians. Horses are seen among the Abipone from the beginning of the 17th century; the Chulupi became horsemen toward the beginning of the 19th century. The acquisition of the horse had, of course, profound effects on the life of these societies, but did not alter their rapport with war: war was simply intensified by the mobility that the horses assured the combatants, and their techniques were adapted to this new war machine that is a mount (one does not fight in the same way on foot and on horseback).

[4] Of the abundant ethnographic material gathered amongst the Chulupi-Nivaklé, only a very small portion of it has been published to this day. Cf. "De quoi rient les Indiens," in la Société contre l'état, Éditions de Minuit, 1974 [Society Against the State, New York, Zone Books, 1987]. This warlike tribe will be the subect of a subsequent publication.

say that at the time of my stay amongst these Indians, the war had been over for them long ago. And yet, many men, then fifty or sixty years old, were former warriors (former combatants) who, twenty or twenty-five years before (in the early '40s) still pitilessly ambushed their hereditary enemies, the Toba Indians, who occupied the opposite bank of the Pilcomayo in Argentina. I had frequent conversations with several of them. The fresh memory of rather recent combats, the warriors' desire to exalt their war exploits, the passionate attention of the young men who listened to their fathers' stories: all of this made me want to know more about the "warrior" society, about the rites and techniques of Indian warfare, about the relation between society and its warriors. As much as to the chronicles of a Sanchez Labrador or a Dobrizhoffer, I am indebted to these men — for clarifying the status of the warrior in their own community — for allowing me to glimpse the traits that make up the proud figure of the Warrior, to locate the necessary lincs of movement that describe the warlike life, to understand (for they told me: they know) the savage warrior's destiny.

Let us consider, for example, the case of three tribes of the Chaco, because they illustrate perfectly the singular world of warrior societies and because the documentation concerning them is very rich: the Abipone, the Guaicuru, and the Chulupi. Institutionally accepted and recognized by society as a determined place in the sociological field, or as a particular organ of the social body, the warrior groups are called, respectively: Höchero, Niadagaguadi, Kaanoklé. These terms denote not only these men's principal activity (war), but also their appurtenance to an order whose superiority is socially admitted (a "nobility," say the chroniclers), to a sort of chivalry whose prestige reflects on the entire society: the tribe is proud of its warriors. To earn the name of warrior is to win a title of nobility.

This superiority of the warrior group rests exclusively on the prestige that war exploits procure: society functions here as a mirror that gives the victorious warrior a rather flattering image of himself, not only so that he will deem legitimate the efforts deployed and the risks taken, but also so that he will be encouraged to pursue and carry out his bellicose vocation, to persevere, in sum, in his warrior being. Festivals, ceremonies, dances, chants and drinking parties collectively celebrate or commemorate his exploits, and the Abipone Höchero or Chulupi Kaanoklé experiences, in the secret depths of his being, the truth of this recognition, meshing the ethical world of tribal values and the private warrior's individual point of honor.

This is to say that this hierarchical arrangement — not only accepted by society but desired — which acknowledges the warrior's superior social status, does not go beyond the sphere of prestige: it is not a hierarchy of power which the warrior group possesses and exercises over society. No relation of dependence forces society to obey the warlike minority. Warlike society does not allow social division to rupture the homogeneity of the social body any more than any other primitive society; it does not let the warriors institute themselves as an organ of political power separated from society; it does not let the Warrior incarnate the new figure of Master. Still, it would be necessary to analyze in depth the procedures that society implements in order to maintain the distance between warriors and power. It is this essential disjunction that Sanchez Labrador observes, having noted the propensity of the Guaicuru noblemen-warriors to boasting and bragging:

...there is, in truth, little difference between all of them (I, p. 151).

Who are the warriors? As one might well imagine, aggressiveness and bellicosity generally diminishing with age, warriors are primarily recruited from a select age group: that of young men over 18. The Guaicuru in particular developed a complex ensemble of ceremonial activities around war, celebrating a boy's reaching the age to carry arms (after 16) with a veritable rite of passage. In the course of the ritual, the adolescents underwent painful physical trials and had to distribute all their goods (weapons, clothing, ornaments) to the people of the tribe. This is a specifically military ritual, and not an initiation rite: the latter is celebrated earlier, for boys 12 to 16 years old. But the young men who successfully underwent the warrior ritual nevertheless did not belong to the group of the Niadagaguadi, the brotherhood of warriors, to which only a particular type of exploit gave access. Beyond the ritual differences of these societies, a military career was open to all young men in all the tribes of the Chaco. As for the ennoblement resulting from entrance into the warrior group, it depended exclusively on the novice's personal valor. A totally *open* group, consequently, (which should prevent viewing this group as a closed caste in gestation), but a *minority* group at the same time, for all young men did not come to accomplish the exploit required, and among those who did succeed, *not all desired* (as we shall see) to be socially recognized and named warriors: that a Chulupi or Abipone combatant refuse the coveted title of Kaanoklé or Höchero suffices to show, through the importance of the renouncement, the greatness of what he hopes to preserve in exchange. In this one can read precisely what being a warrior signifies.

The warrior has passion for war. A singularly intense passion in the tribes of the Chaco, as their chroniclers explain. Of the Guaicuru, Sanchez Labrador writes:

They are totally indifferent to everything, but take care of
their horses, their labrets, and their weapons with great zeal.
(I, p. 288).

Dobrizhoffer confirms this disabused observation regarding the same
Guaicuru:

Their principal and unique care and knowledge are of horses
and weapons (I, p. 190).

But this also goes for the Abipone who, from this point of view, are no
better than the Guaicuru. Dobrizhoffer, horrified by the wounds inflicted on
children, notes that this is

a prelude to war for which they are trained at a very young
age (II, p. 48).

The consequence of this pedagogy of violence was a major one for a
missionary priest: hardly prepared to practice Christian virtues, the Abipone
actively avoided the ethics of *loving one another*. Christianization, writes the
Jesuit, was destined to failure:

... the young Abipone are an obstacle to the progress of religion. In their ardent desire for military glory and spoils, they
are avidly cutting the heads of the Spanish and destroying
their carts and their fields... (II, p. 148).

Young men's taste for war is no less intense in otherwise very different
societies. It is thus that at the other end of the American continent in
Canada, Champlain often fails in his efforts to maintain peace among the
tribes with whom he would like to forge an alliance: always the same insti-
gators of war, the young men. His long-term strategy, based on establishing
peaceful relations between the Algonkin and the Iroquois, would have succeeded, perhaps, were it not for

...nine or ten scatterbrained young men [who] undertook to
go to war, which they did without anyone being able to stop
them, for the little obedience they give to their chiefs... (p.
285).

The French Jesuits experienced the same disappointments in these regions as their German and Spanish counterparts in the Chaco a century later. Wanting to stop the war that their allies the Huron were waging on the Iroquois, and at the very least save the prisoners of war from the terrible tortures that the victors would inflict, they systematically attempted to buy back the Iroquois captives from the Huron. To such an offer of ransom, here is what an indignant Huron chief answered:

> I am a man of war and not a merchant, I have come to fight and not to bargain; my glory is not in bringing back presents, but in bringing back prisoners, and leaving, I can touch neither your hatchets nor your cauldrons; if you want our prisoners so much, take them, I still have enough courage to find others; if the enemy takes my life, it will be said in the country that since Ontonio[5] took our prisoners, we threw ourselves into death to get others (III, year 1644, p. 48).

As for the Chulupi Indians, their veterans told me how, between 1928 and 1935, in preparation for a particularly decisive and dangerous raid against the Bolivian and Argentinean soldiers, then determined to exterminate them, they had to turn away dozens of very young men whose impetuosity and lack of discipline threatened to compromise the success of the expedition, indeed, to turn it into a disaster. We do not need you, said the Kaanoklé, there are enough of us. There were sometimes no more than twelve.

Warriors are thus young men. But why are young men so enamored of war? Where does their passion originate? What, in a word, makes the warrior tick? It is, as we have seen, the desire for prestige, which society alone can bestow or refuse. Such is the link that unites the warrior to his society, the third term that connects the social body and the warrior group by establishing a relationship of dependence at the outset: the warrior's self-realization involves social recognition; the warrior can only think of himself as such if society recognizes him as such. Carrying out an individual exploit is but a necessary condition for acquiring the prestige that only social approval can confer. In other words, depending on the circumstances, society could very well refuse to recognize the valor of a warlike action judged inopportune, provocative or premature: a game is played between society and the warrior in which only the tribe makes the rules. The chroniclers measure the potency of the desire for prestige by the passion for war, and what Dobrizhoffer writes of the Abipone goes for all warlike societies:

---

[5] Indigenous name of the French governor.

> They consider the nobility most worthy of honor to be not
> that which is inherited through blood and which is like patri-
> mony, but rather that which one obtains through one's own
> merits [...] For them, nobility resides not in the worth and
> honor of lineage, but in valor and rectitude (II, p. 454).

The warrior acquires nothing in advance; he does not profit from the situation; glory is not transferable and is not accompanied by privilege.

Love of war is a secondary passion, derived from a primary passion: the
more fundamental desire for prestige. War here is a means to achieve an individual goal: the warrior's desire for glory, the warrior himself is his own goal.
Will not to power but to glory: for the warrior, war is by far the quickest and
most efficient means to satisfy his will. But how does the warrior make society recognize him? How does he force society to confer upon him the prestige
that he expects? What proof, in other words, does he advance to establish his
victory? There are, first of all, the spoils. Their at once real and symbolic
importance in the tribes of the Chaco is all the more remarkable since generally in primitive society, war is not waged for economic ends. Having noted
that the Guaicuru do not wage war in order to augment their territory,
Sanchez Labrador defines the main reasons for war:

> The principal reason that makes them bring war to a foreign
> territory is solely the interest for spoils and vengeance for
> what they consider offenses (I, p. 310).

To Dobrizhoffer, the Abipone explained that

> war against the Christians procured for them more benefits
> than did peace (II, p. 133).

What do the spoils of war consist of? Essentially, metallic instruments,
horses and prisoners, men, women or children. Metal's purpose is obvious: to
increase the technical efficiency of weapons (arrowheads, lance tips, knives,
etc.). Horses are much less useful. Indeed, the Abipone, Mocovi, Toba,
Guaicuru did not lack horses at all: on the contrary, they had thousands;
some Indians had up to 400 animals and only used a few (for war, travel,
cargo). Most Abipone families had at least fifty horses. They therefore had no
need for others' horses, yet at the same time felt they could never have
enough: it was a sort of sport to capture the enemies' herds (Spanish or
Indian). A risky sport, naturally, since each tribe jealously watched over its

most precious good, the immense herd of horses. It was a precious good, certainly, but one of pure prestige, spectacular in its weak use and exchange value. Possessing thousands of horses was also quite a burden for each community because of the obligations it created: constant vigilance in order to protect them from the neighbors, the constant search for pastures and abundant sources of water. Nevertheless, the Indians of the Chaco risked their lives to steal other people's horses, knowing well that increasing their livestock at the enemies' expense would cloak them in twice the glory. Dobrizhoffer indicates how massive these thefts were:

> Once, in a single assault, the young Abipone men, who are more ferocious than the adults, stole 4,000 horses (III, p. 16).

Finally, the most prestigious spoils: prisoners, as Sanchez Labrador explains:

> Their desire for prisoners and children of any other nation, even the Spanish, is inexpressible and frenzied (I, p. 310).

Less marked than among the Guaicuru, the desire to capture enemies is nevertheless strong among the Abipone or the Chulupi. When I stayed with the Chulupi, I met two old people in one of their villages, a man and a woman who had spent long years in captivity among the Toba. A few years earlier, they had been returned in exchange for some Toba prisoners held by the Chulupi. Comparing what Sanchez Labrador and Dobrizhoffer write of the status of captives among the Guaicuru and the Abipone, there is a considerable difference in the way they are treated. According to the Sanchez Labrador, the prisoners of the Guaicuru were serfs or slaves. Due to their presence, adolescents were allowed to run free:

> They do what they want, without even helping their parents. This is the servants' occupation (I, p. 315).

Dobrizhoffer, on the contrary, notes regarding the Abipone:

> They would never consider their prisoners of war, whether Spanish, Indian or Negro, as serfs or slaves (II, p. 139).

In reality, the tasks demanded of the prisoners by their Guaicuru masters were hardly more than daily chores: gathering firewood, fetching water, cooking. For the rest, the "slaves" lived like their masters, participating with them in military enterprises. Common sense explains why the victors could not transform the vanquished into slaves whose labor could be exploited: what tasks would they perform? There are no doubt worse conditions than being a slave of the Guaicuru, as Sanchez Labrador himself explains:

> While the masters sleep, they get drunk or do other things (I, p. 251).

The Guaicuru, moreover, hardly took an interest in the subtleties of social distinctions:

> Their self-glorification makes them consider the rest of the nations of which they have knowledge, including the Spanish, as slaves (II, p. 52).

Though it cannot be resolved here, we should at least raise this problem: that of the particular demography of these warlike societies. In the middle of the 18th century, the Guaicuru numbered 7,000, the Abipone, 5,000. Shortly after the arrival of the Spanish in these regions, the first war took place in 1542 between the Conquistadors led by A.N. Cabeza de Vaca and the Guaicuru, who at that time numbered around 25,000. In little more than two centuries, their population thus fell by more than two thirds. The Abipone certainly underwent the same demographic drop. What are the causes for this? We must obviously take into consideration the epidemics introduced by the Europeans. But, as the Jesuits remark, the Chaco tribes, in contrast to the others (the Guarani, for example), were hostile to contact — unless bellicose — with the Spanish, and therfore were relatively sheltered from the deadly microbial impact. If the epidemics are, at least in this case, beside the point, then to what can the depopulation of the tribes be attributed? The missionaries' observations on this point are very specific. Surprised by the small number of children among the Guaicuru, Sanchez Labrador notes that altogether he has only met four couples with two children each, the others having only one or none (II, p. 31). Dobrizhoffer makes the same observation: the Abipone have few children. Among them, moreover, the number of women far exceeds that of men. The Jesuit records the surely exaggerated proportion of 100 men to 600 women; hence, the great frequency of polygyny (II, pp.102-103).

There is no doubt that the mortality of young men was very high and that the Chaco tribes paid a heavy price for their passion for war. This is not, however, what accounts for the low demographic: the polygynous marriages would have had to compensate for the losses in men. It seems evident that the drop in population was provoked not by the excess mortality of men, but by the lack of natality: there were not enough children. To be more specific: there were few births *because the women did not want to have children.* And this is why one of the goals of war was to *capture the children of others.* An operation that was often successful, by the way: the tribes" captive children and adolescents, particularly the Spanish, generally refused to leave when they had the chance. Nevertheless, these societies (especially the Abipone, Mocovi and Guaicuru), by the very fact of the warlike dynamic, found themselves confronted with the question of their own survival. For should not these two distinct and convergent desires be linked: the desire of society to bring war and death elsewhere, the individual desire of women not to have children? The will to give death, on the one hand, the refusal to give birth, on the other. In satisfying its warlike passion, the haughty chivalry of the Chaco pointed, tragically, toward the possibility of its own death: sharing this passion, young women agreed to be the wives of warriors, but not the mothers of their children.

War's mid-term socioeconomic effects in these societies remain to be outlined. Some of these societies (Abipone, Mocovi, Guaicuru) had long since abandoned agriculture, because permanent war and pastoral needs (seeking new pastures for the horses) were not suited to sedentary life. Thus, they became nomads on their territory in groups of 100 to 400 people, living from hunting, fishing and collecting (wild plants, honey). If the repeated raids against the enemies at first aimed at conquering prestige goods (horses, prisoners), they also assumed a properly economic dimension: to procure not only equipment goods (weapons), but also consumer goods (edible cultivated plants, cotton, tobacco, beef, etc.). In other words, without exaggerating the extent of these functional tendencies of war, the raids *also* become enterprises of pillaging: the Indians found it easier to procure the goods they needed with weapons in hand. Such a practice could in the long-run create a two-fold relation of economic dependence: society's external dependence on the places producing the desired goods (essentially the Spanish colonies); the tribe's internal dependence on the group that at least partially assured its subsistence, namely the warrior group. And so, it is not too surprising to learn that the term the Guaicuru used to designate not only hunters, but warriors, was Niadagaguadi, those thanks to whom we eat.

Would not this economic "perversion" of war in societies totally devoted to it, be, rather than a local accident, the effect of a logic inherent to war itself? Does not the warrior fatally transform himself into a looter? This is what we are led to believe by primitive societies who followed an analogous path. The Apache, for example (cf. bibliography), having abandoned agriculture, gradually allowed war to assume an economic function: they systematically pillaged Mexican and American settlements, under the command of the famous Geronimo, among others, whose tribe only tolerated military action if enough spoils were produced. The logic of war, perhaps, but strongly aided by possession of the horse.

The detailed analysis of the elements that comprised the spoils of war could suggest that they alone established recognition of the warrior as such, that spoils were the essential source of the sought-after prestige. This is not the case, and the appurtenance to the Höchero or the Kaanoklé group was not in any way determined by the number of horses or prisoners captured: *it was necessary to bring back the scalp of an enemy killed in combat.* We are generally unaware that this tradition is as old in South America as it is in North America. Almost all the Chaco tribes respected it. To scalp the fallen enemy explicitly signified the young victor's desire to be admitted into the club of warriors. Impressive ceremonies celebrated the entrance of the new member, recognizing his definitive right to the title — for this was an ennoblement — of *warrior*. It is necessary, thus, to posit this double equation: the warriors occupy the summit of the social hierarchy of prestige; a warrior is a man who, not content to kill his enemies, scalps them. Immediate consequence: a man who kills the enemy without scalping him *is not a warrior*. A seemingly insignificant distinction, but one that reveals itself to be of extreme importance.

There is a hierarchy of scalps. Spanish heads of hair, though not disdained, were not, by far, as esteemed as those of Indians. Thus for the Chulupi, nothing could equal a Toba scalp, their eternal enemies. Before and during the Chaco war, the Chulupi warriors stubbornly resisted the Bolivian army which wanted to seize their territory and exterminate its occupants. Admirable experts of the terrain, the Chulupi watched for and attacked the invaders near the rare sources of water. The Indians told me of these combats. Silent arrows decimated the troops, who were panic-stricken by thirst and the terror of an invisible enemy. Hundreds of Bolivian soldiers thus perished; so many, in any case, the old warriors said, that the Indians gave up on scalping mere soldiers and brought back only officers' locks. All these scalps are still kept by their owners, carefully arranged in cases of leather or basket: when they die, their relatives will burn the scalps on the tomb so that the smoke will mark a path of easy access to Kaanoklé paradise for the soul of the deceased. There is no smoke more noble than that of a Toba warrior scalp.[6] Enemy scalps were now hung from the ceiling of huts or tied to war lances. They were surrounded by intense ritual activity (festivals of celebra-

---

[6] I have attempted several times, always in vain, to trade for or to buy a scalp: this would have been, for the Indians, like selling their soul to the devil.

tion or of commemoration): this illustrates the depth of the personal link that united the warrior to his trophy.

Here, then, essentially, is the ethnographic context in which the life of warrior societies unfolds, and the horizon upon which the most secret web of relations between warrior and tribe is spun. Let us note immediately that if these relations were static, if the relations between a particular warrior group and society as a whole were stable, inert or sterile, the present enterprise of reflection would have to end here. We would have, in such a hypothesis, a minority of young men – the warriors – waging a permanent war for their own account – the quest for prestige which society would tolerate because of the primary and secondary benefits that the warriors would procure for it: collective security assured by the constant weakening of enemies, the captures and spoils of war resulting from the pillage of enemy settlements. A similar situation could reproduce itself and repeat itself indefinitely, with no innovation altering the being of the social body and the traditional functioning of society. We would have to observe, with Marcel Duchamp, that there is no solution because there is no problem. The entire question is precisely this: is there a problem? How should it be articulated?

It is a question of knowing whether primitive society is running a risk by letting a particular social group, that of the warriors, grow in its breast. There is some basis, then, to examining them: the existence in primitive society of a group of singers or dancers, for example, does not in any way affect the established social order. But it is a question here of warriors, namely, the men who hold a quasi-monopoly on society's military capacity, a monopoly, in a sense, on organized violence. They exercise this violence on their enemies. But could they eventually exercise it as well on their own society? Not physical violence (a civil war of warriors against society), but *a taking of power* by the warrior group which would from then on exercise it on, and if necessary, against society? Could the warrior group, as a specialized organ of the social body, become *a separate organ of political power*? In other words, does war harbor within it the possibility of what all primitive societies, in essence, are devoted to warding off: namely, the division of the social body into Masters (the warlike minority) and Subjects (the rest of society)?

We have just seen, in the tribes of the Chaco and among the Apache, how the dynamic of war could transform the search for prestigious spoils into the pillage of resources. If society allows the proportion of its provisions attained from the spoils of war to grow, it would thereby establish a relation of growing dependence on its providers, that is, the warriors, who would be in a position to guide the tribe's sociopolitical life as they pleased. Though minor and temporary in the specific cases evoked, the economic effects of war nevertheless show that society is in no way sheltered from such an evolution. But rather than look at local and conjunctural situations, it is the logic inherent in the existence of a body of warriors and the ethics belonging to this body that we should interrogate. Which amounts, in fact, to posing a single question: what is a warrior?

It is a man who puts his warlike passion to the service of his desire for prestige. This desire is realized when a young combatant is authorized to claim his integration into the warrior brotherhood (in the strict sense) and his confirmation as warrior (Kaanoklé, Höchero, etc.): when he brings back an enemy scalp. One could then suppose that such a fact would guarantee the new warrior an irrevocable status and a definitive prestige which he could peacefully savor. This is not the case. Far from being finished, his career has, in effect, only just begun. The first scalp is not the crowning, but, on the contrary, the point of departure. Just as in these societies, a son does not inherit the glory acquired by his father, the young warrior is not freed by his initial prowess: he must continuously start over, for each exploit accomplished is both a source of prestige and a questioning of this prestige. The warrior is in essence *condemned to forging ahead*. The glory won is never enough in and of itself; it must be forever proven, and every feat realized immediately calls for another.

The warrior is thus a man of permanent dissatisfaction. The personality of this restless figure results from a convergence of the individual desire for prestige and the social recognition that alone confers it. For each exploit accomplished, the warrior and society utter the same judgment: the warrior says, That's good, but I can do more, I can increase my glory. Society says, That's good, but you should do more, obtain our recognition of a superior prestige. In other words, as much by his own personality (glory before everything) as by his total dependence in relation to the tribe (who else could confer glory?) the warrior finds himself, *volens nolens*, a prisoner of a logic that relentlessly makes him want to do a little more. Lacking this, society would quickly forget his past exploits and the glory they procured for him. The warrior only exists in war; he is devoted as such to action: the story of his valorous acts, declaimed at festivals, is only a call for further valorous acts. The more the warrior goes to war, the more society will confer prestige upon him.

It follows that if society alone bestows or refuses glory, the warrior is dominated, alienated by society. But couldn't this relationship of subordination be reversed to the benefit of the warrior, to the detriment of the tribe? This possibility is, in effect, inscribed in the same logic of war which alienates the warrior in the ascending spiral of the ever more glorious feat. This dynamic of war, originally the purely individual enterprise of the warrior, could gradually transform it into the collective enterprise of society: it is within the warrior's reach to alienate the tribe in war. The organ (the warrior group) can develop the function (the warlike activity). In what way? We must first consider that the warriors, though devoted by nature to the individual fulfillment of their vocation, together constitute a group determined by the identity of their interests: ceaselessly organizing new raids to increase their prestige. They wage war, moreover, not against personal enemies, but against enemies of the tribe. It is, in other words, in their interest never to leave the enemies in peace, always to harass them, never to give them any respite. As a result the existence in this or that society of an organized group of "professional" warriors tends to transform the *permanent state of war* (the general situation of the primitive society) into *actual permanent war* (the particular situation of warrior societies).

Such a transformation, pushed to its conclusion, would have considerable sociological consequences since, in affecting the very structure of society, it would alter the undivided being. The power to decide on matters of war and peace (an absolutely essential power) would in effect no longer belong to society as such, but indeed to the brotherhood of warriors, which would place its private interest before the collective interest of society and would make its particular point of view the general point of view of the tribe. The warrior would involve society in a cycle of wars it wanted nothing to do with. The tribe's foreign policy would no longer be determined by itself, but by a minority that would push it toward an impossible situation: permanent war against all neighboring nations. First a group seeking *prestige*, the warlike community would then transform itself into a *pressure* group, in order to push society into accepting the intensification of war, then finally into a *power* group, which alone would decide peace and war for all. Having traveled this trajectory, inscribed ahead of time in the logic of war, the warrior group would hold power and exercise it over society in order to force it to pursue its goal: it would thus be instituted as a separate organ of political power; the entire society would be radically changed, divided into the dominating and the dominated.

War carries within it, then, the danger of the division of primitive society's homogeneous social body. A remarkable paradox: on the one hand, war permits the primitive community to persevere in its undivided being; on the other hand, it reveals itself as the possible basis for division into Masters and Subjects. Primitive society as such obeys a logic of non-division; war tends to substitute this with a logic of division. In a primitive society that is not protected from dynamic conflict, from social innovation, or, quite simply, from internal contradiction, there is conflict between the group's social desire (to maintain the social body as a single totality) and the warrior's individual desire (to increase glory), contradiction between two opposite logics such that one must triumph through radical exclusion of the other. Either the sociological logic carries it away in order to abolish the warrior, or else the warlike logic emerges in order to destroy society as an undivided body. There is no middle road. How do we posit the relationship between society and the warriors from now on? It depends on whether society can erect defense mechanisms likely to protect it from the lethal division toward which the warrior fatally leads society. It is, for society, a problem of survival: either the tribe, or the warrior. Which of the two will be the stronger? In the concrete social reality of these societies, which solution finds the problem? To know, we must look once again to the ethnology of these tribes.

Let us first locate the limits assigned to the warrior group as an autonomous organization. In fact, this group is only instituted and socially recognized as such on the level of acquired prestige: warriors are men who have won the right to certain privileges (title, name, hairdo and special paintings, etc.) not counting the erotic repercussions of their prestige among women. The very nature of their vital goal — prestige — prevents them from forming an ensemble that could elaborate a unified policy and strategy, a part of the social body that could promote and attain its own collective objectives. It is, in fact, the obligatory individualism of each warrior that prevents the warrior group from emerging as a homogeneous collectivity. The warrior desirous of acquiring prestige is only able and only wants to rely on his own forces: he has no use for the potential solidarity of his companions in arms with whom, in this case, he would have to share the benefits of an expedition. A band of warriors does not necessarily lead to a team sport mentality: ultimately, the savage warrior's only possible motto is every man for himself. Savoring prestige is a purely personal affair: so is acquiring it.

But we also see that by virtue of the same logic, the acquired prestige (the accomplished exploit) only assures the warrior of temporary satisfaction, ephemeral enjoyment. Each exploit welcomed and celebrated by the tribe obligates him, in fact, to aim higher, to look beyond, to start again at zero, in a sense, by renewing the source of his prestige, by constantly expanding the series of his exploits. The warrior's task, in other words, is an *infinite task*, always incomplete. He never attains the goal which is always out of reach: no rest for the warrior, except at the end of his quest.

Thus, his is an individual enterprise, and one that is increasingly unprofitable: the warrior's life is perpetual combat. But that still does not say everything. In order to respond to this at once personal and social demand of reconquering prestige through an exploit, it is indeed not enough for the warrior to repeat the same exploit, to settle peacefully into repetition by bringing an enemy's scalp back to the camp: neither he nor the tribe would be satisfied by this facile (so to speak) solution. Each time, the undertaking must be more difficult, the danger confronted more terrible, the risk run more considerable. Why? Because this is the only way for the warrior to maintain his individual difference in relation to his companions, because there is competition between the warriors for prestige. Each warrior's exploit, precisely because it is recognized as such, is a challenge to the others: let them do better. The novice tries to equal the veteran, thereby forcing the latter to maintain the gap of prestige by demonstrating more bravery. The cumulative effect of the individual point of honor, the tribe's social pressure and the group's internal competition is to fling the warrior into the escalation of temerity.

How does this escalation translate concretely in the field? For the warriors it is a matter of seeking out maximal difficulty which would bestow upon their victory even greater valor. Thus, for example, they will undertake longer and longer expeditions, penetrating further and further into enemy territory, renouncing the security offered by the proximity of their own territory. Or else they will confront an enemy group known for its courage or ferocity and whose scalps are therefore more esteemed than others. They will also risk their lives by leading raids at night, which Indians never do, because of the added danger of souls, spirits and phantoms. Similarly when an attack is organized, the warriors will move ahead of the front lines to launch the first assault themselves. This is because there is more glory in beating the enemy on his turf, in his camp or in his village, dashing through arrows or *arquebusades*. Explorers' testimonies, missionaries' chronicles, soldiers' reports all contain a great number of stories that illustrate the bravery of the savage warriors, sometimes deemed admirable, more often, senseless. Their bravery is of course undeniable. But it stems less from a warrior's individual personality than from war's own logic as war for prestige. From the point of view of the Europeans (in North America as well as in South America), who were blind to this logic of glory, the Indian temerity could only seem senseless, abnormal. But from the indigenous point of view, it simply corresponded to the norm common to warriors.

War for prestige, the logic of glory: to what ultimate degree of bravery could these lead the warrior? What is the nature of the exploit that procures the most glory because it is unsurpassable? It is the individual exploit, it is the act of the warrior who *alone* attacks the adversaries' camp, who in this major challenge, where the most absolute inequality is inscribed, equals himself to all the power of his companions, who claims and asserts his superiority over the enemy group. *Alone against all*: this is the culminating point of escalation in the exploit. Here, the experienced warrior's skill is hardly worth anything, his cunning is of little help to him; henceforth he finds himself starting from scratch in this confrontation where the only thing in his favor is the overwhelming surprise of his solitary presence.

Champlain, for example, tells of trying to convince a valiant Algonkin warrior not to leave by himself to attack the Iroquois and he answered:

> ... that it would be impossible for him to live if he did not kill his enemies and did not avenge himself, and that his heart told him that he had to leave as early as possible: which he was indeed determined to do (p.165).

This is also what the Iroquois do, as the French Jesuits staying with the Huron were surprised to find:

> ... and sometimes an enemy, totally naked and with only a hatchet in hand, will even have the courage to enter the huts of a town at night, by himself, then, having murdered some of those he finds sleeping there, to take flight for all defense against a hundred and two hundred people who will follow him one and two entire days (III, year 1642, p. 55).

We know that Geronimo, failing to lead the Apache into the constant war he desired, did not hesitate to attack Mexican villages, accompanied by only two or three other warriors. In his very beautiful memoirs (cf. bibliography), the Sioux Black Elk recalls how a Crow warrior was killed when, alone during the night, he attempted to steal the Sioux's horses. Black Elk also reports that in a famous battle against the American army, a Cheyenne horseman charged alone, ahead of his brothers, into the rapid fire of the fusillade: he was killed. Among the Amazonian Yanomami, more than one warrior died in a combat that he led alone against an enemy tribe, such as the famous Fusiwe (cf. bibliography). The Chulupi still celebrate the end of one of their people, a Kaanoklé of great renown. Having reached the peak of glory, he thus had no choice: mounting his best war horse, he penetrated the territory of the Toba, alone, for several days, attacked one of their camps and died in combat. In the memory of the Chulupi remains the vivacious figure of Kalai'in, the famous Toba war chief. They told me how, at the beginning of the century, he would come into the sleepy Chulupi camps at night, alone, slitting the throats and scalping one or two men each visit, always escaping. Several Chulupi warriors resolved to capture him and managed this by trapping him. Kalali'in's exploits are evoked with hatred, his death, with admiration: for he perished under torture without uttering a sound.

What good is multiplying the examples? It is enough to read the texts: swarms of anecdotes all converge to show that among the warrior, the disdain for danger always accompanies the desire for glory. This conjunction explains moreover the behavior of the warriors which confused the Europeans: namely, that a combatant captured by his enemies *never tried to escape*. Now, in numerous cases, the future of the prisoner of war was all laid out: at best he survived the terrible tortures that his masters inflicted on him, at worst (and this was the more frequent destiny) he was killed. But let us listen to Champlain narrate the consequences of a battle which he won over the Iroquois in 1609, allied with the Algonkins, capturing a dozen of them:

> Yet ours lit a fire, and as it was well aglow, each took an ember and burnt the miserable wretch little by little to make him suffer more torment. They left him for some time, throwing water on his back: then they tore out his nails, and put fire on the tips of his fingers and his member. After scorching the top of his testicles, they made him eat a certain very hot gum: then they pierced his arms close to the fists, and with sticks pulled the nerves and tore them with force: and as they saw that they could not have them, they cut them (p. 145).

More than thirty years later, nothing has changed, as the Jesuits contest in 1642:

> one of the prisoners not showing any sign of pain at the height of his torments and agonies, the Iroquois, infuriated to see his constancy, which they took as a bad omen, for they believe that the souls of warriors who disdain their rage will make them pay for the death of their bodies, seeing, as I say, this constancy, they asked why he was not screaming: he responded, I am doing what you would not do, if you were treated with the same fury with which you treat me: the iron and the fire that you apply to my body would make you scream out loud and cry like children, and I do not flinch. To these words the tigers throw themselves on the half-burned victim; they skin his testicles, and throw sand that is all red and burning with fire onto his bloody skull; they rush him to the bottom of the scaffold, and drag him around the huts (III, year 1642, p. 42).

We know that among the Tupi-Guarani a prisoner of war could be safe and sound, even free, in the village of the victors: but sooner or later he was inevitably executed and eaten. He knew this and yet did not attempt to flee. Where would he find refuge, anyway? Certainly not among his own people: indeed, for them, the captured warrior no longer belongs to the tribe, he is definitively excluded from the community which only waits to learn of his death in order to avenge it immediately. Should he attempt to escape, the people of his village would refuse to welcome him: he is a prisoner, his destiny must thus be fulfilled. In fact, the flight of a prisoner of war, as the Jesuits write in regard to Canadian Indians, is "an unpardonable crime" (III, year, p. 42).

Here, then, on all sides, this irreducible affinity, this tragic proximity between the warrior and death becomes clear. Victorious, he must immediately leave again for war in order to assure his glory with an even greater feat. But in ceaselessly testing the limits of the risk confronted and forging ahead for prestige he invariably meets this end: solitary death in the face of enemies. Vanquished, that is, captured, he ceases through this itself to exist socially in the eyes of his own people: an ambiguous nomad, he will henceforth wander between life and death, even if the latter is not granted him (this is the case of the tribes of the Chaco where prisoners were rarely executed). There is no alternative for the warrior: a single outcome for him, death. His is an infinite task, as I was saying: what is proven here, in short, is that *the warrior is never a warrior* except at the end of his task, when, accomplishing his supreme exploit, he wins death along with absolute glory. The warrior is, in his being, a being-for-death.

This is why, on this point at least, Dobrizhoffer is half-mistaken when he writes:

The Abipone seek glory, but never death (II, p. 360).

Warriors, Abipone or others, do not seek death in and of itself perhaps, but it inevitably comes at the end of the path they have decided to travel: seeking glory, they meet death. One cannot be surprised then by the very high rate of mortality among the warriors. The ancient chronicles have retained the names and figures of the best among the warriors, namely the war chiefs: almost all died sooner or later in combat. We must also remember that these losses decimated a specific age group: men between the ages of twenty and forty-five, that is, in a sense, the prime of this savage chivalry. So much perseverance in this being-for-death suggests that perhaps the passion for glory acted in the service of a more profound passion, that which we call the *death instinct,* an instinct which not only traversed the warrior group, but more seriously contaminated society as a whole: did not the women, in effect, refuse to have children, thereby condemning the tribes to rapid disappearance? A collective death wish of a society no longer aspiring to reproduce itself...

One last point is illuminated here. I indicated above that only a segment of the men in the Chaco tribes aspired to be warriors, that is, to be called such after having brought back an enemy scalp. In other words, the rest of the men went to war, but killed the enemies without scalping them, that is, did not aspire to the title of warrior. They renounced glory deliberately. All that precedes would henceforth allow one to anticipate the reason for this somewhat unexpected choice. Nevertheless, let us allow the Indians to explain it themselves: one will thereby be able to observe in their discourse the absolute freedom of their thought and of their action, as well as the cool lucidity of their political analysis. The men of these societies each do what they want and know why.

During my stay in the Chaco, I had the opportunity time and again to converse with old Chulupi combatants. A few among them were institutional warriors, the Kaanoklé: they possessed the heads of hair of enemies they had killed. As for the others, they were not veritable warriors, for they had never scalped the enemies. In the group of old combatants, the Kaanoklé were rare: most of their companions had long since perished in battle, which is expected in the warrior world. Yet it was the non-warriors who explained to me the truth of the warrior. For if they were not Kaanoklé, it was because they did not want to be. Why would valorous combatants not desire to be Kaanoklé? This was the case of Aklamatsé, a shaman of high repute, and of Tanu'uh, immensely knowledgeable about mythology, among others. Both around sixty-five years old, they had led countless battles against the Bolivians, the Argentineans, and the Toba, especially Tanu'uh; but neither of them were Kaanoklé. Tanu'uh's body, studded with scars (from steel blades, arrows and bullets) indicated sufficiently that he had narrowly escaped death more than once. Tanu'uh had no doubt killed one or two dozen men. Why aren't you a Kaanoklé? Why haven't you ever scalped your enemies? In his ambiguity, the answer was almost comic: Because it was too dangerous. I didn't want to die. In short, this man who had almost perished ten times had not wanted to become a warrior because he was afraid of death.

It was thus obvious for him: the Kaanoklé, as such, is condemned to being killed. To insist on the glory attached to the title of warrior amounts to accepting the more or less long-term price: death. Tanu'uh and his friends described the movement that propels the warrior. To be a Kaanoklé, they said, you must bring back a scalp. But once he has taken this first step, the man must leave again for war, bring back other scalps: if not, he is no longer taken seriously, he is forgotten. This is why the Kaanoklé die quickly.

We could not have a clearer analysis of the relations that link society to its warriors. The tribe accepts an autonomous group of men of war forming in its breast, encouraging their vocation by a generous recognition of prestige. But doesn't this prestige group have a good chance of becoming a pressure group, then a power group? Now it is too late for the warrior: either he renounces his status and shamefully loses face, or he finds himself irremediably trapped in his own vocation, a prisoner of his desire for glory which leads him straight to death. There is an exchange between society and the warrior: prestige for exploit. But in this confrontation, it is society, mistress of the rules of the game, that has the last word: for the ultimate exchange is that of eternal glory for the eternity of death. Ahead of time, the warrior is condemned to death by society: no joy for the savage warrior, only the certainty of sorrow. But why? Because the warrior could cause the sorrow of the society by introducing the germ of division, by becoming a separate organ of power. Such is the defense mechanism that primitive society erects to ward off the risk that the warrior, as such, bears: the undivided social body's life for the warrior's death. The text of tribal law becomes clear here: primitive society is, in its being, a *society-for-war*; it is at the same time, and for the same reasons, a *society against the warrior*.[7]

In conclusion let us leave the specific case of warrior societies to come back to the general situation of primitive societies. The preceding reflections provide some of the elements of a response to the problem of relations between men and women in this type of society: or rather they allow us to establish how this is a false problem. The promoters of Marxist anthropology — manufacturers of this indigent catechism which has to do neither with the thought of Marx nor with the primitive social reality — for lack of being able to find class struggle in primitive society, discover in the end that the social conflict is the battle of the sexes, a battle where the losers are women: in this society, the woman is alienated, exploited, oppressed by man. This pious credo is curiously echoed by a certain feminist discourse: supporters of this discourse tenaciously want primitive society to be sexist, want the woman to be the victim of masculine domination. Thus, it would not at all be a matter of a society of equality.

---

[7] There existed among certain North American tribes (Crow, Hidatsa, Mandan, Pawnee, Cheyenne, Sioux, etc.) a special club of warriors: the Crazy Dog society, a brotherhood of suicide-warriors who never retreated in combat (cf. bibliography).

The real and symbolic, conscious and unconscious relations between men and women in primitive society constitute an absolutely fascinating field of reflection for the ethnologist. Why? Because the internal social life of the community essentially rests not so much on relations between men and women — a truism of no interest — as on the very particular mode according to which these cultures understand and think of differences between the sexes in their myths, and better yet, in their rites. To state it more clearly: in primitive societies, often marked by masculinity in certain aspects, indeed by a cult of virility, men are nevertheless *in a defensive position in regards to women,* because they recognize the superiority of women — myths, rites and daily life attest to this sufficiently. To determine the nature of this superiority, to measure its significance, to locate the means used by men to protect themselves from women, to examine the efficiency of these means, all of this would require long and serious study.

I will limit myself for now to pointing out how the structural relationship that unites war and primitive society at least partially determines relations between the sexes. This society, in its being, is warlike. That is to say all men, in their beings, are warriors, the sexual division of tasks making warlike activity a masculine function. Man must thus be constantly available for war; from time to time, he actually goes. We know well that primitive war in general is hardly deadly, except, of course, in the very special case of the warrior societies. Nevertheless, since the possibility of war is constantly present, the possibility of risk, injury or death is inscribed in advance in the masculine destiny. Man in primitive society thus finds himself, by definition, marked by his condition: with more or less intensity, he is a being-for-death. Death only comes to a few individuals during combat, but before battle, it is equally threatening for all. Through the mediation of war, there is an intimate relationship, an essential proximity between *masculinity and death.*

What, in counterpoint, of women? Let us evoke, just to refresh our memory, the idea, as summary as it is accepted, of woman as a very precious "good" that men would spend their time exchanging and circulating; let us also evoke the simplistic idea of woman as the warrior's recreation, which would correspond moreover with the preceding conception: woman as a good of exchange and as a good of consumption. At this point we must discuss the defects and effects of the structuralist discourse on women. The essential property of women, which integrally defines their being, is to assure the biological, and beyond that, social reproduction of the community: women bring children into the world. Far from existing as consumed object, or as exploited subject, they are as producers of those whom society cannot do without: namely, children, as the tribe's immediate and distant future. Obvious, no doubt, but necessary to remember. The warrior's wives know a little bit more about it, who, as we saw in the case of the Chaco, *decided* the death of the tribes by *refusing* to have children. Femininity is maternity, first as a biological function, but especially as sociological command exercised over the production of children: whether there are children or not depends exclusively on women. And this is what assures women's command over society.

In other words, an immediate proximity is revealed here between *life and femininity*, such that the woman, in her being, is a being-for-life. Henceforth, the difference between man and woman in primitive society is made abundantly clear: as warrior, man is a being-for-death; as mother, woman is a being-for-life. It is their respective relations to social and biological life and death that determine the relations between men and women. In the collective unconscious of the tribe (culture), the masculine unconscious understands and recognizes the difference between the sexes as the irreversible superiority of women over men. Slaves of death, men envy and fear women, mistresses of life. Such is the primitive and primordial truth that a serious analysis of certain myths and rites would reveal. The myths, by reversing the real order, attempt to think of society's destiny as masculine destiny; the rituals, a theatrical setting in which men play out their victory, are used to ward off, to compensate for the too obvious truth that this destiny is feminine. Weakness, dereliction, inferiority of men in the face of women? This is indeed what myths almost everywhere in the world that imagine the lost golden age or paradise to conquer as an asexual world, as *a world without women*, recognize.

MYTHOLOGICAL REPRESENTATIONS OF THE WARRIOR

I have, in the preceding text, envisioned war and the warrior as reality and as politics, and not as representation. Which does not in any way signify that there is not, among the Savages, representation of war and the warrior. It is expressed, essentially, in myths. Here are two of them, extracts from a Chulupi mythological corpus which I gathered in 1966. The first concerns the origin of war, the second develops a certain representation of the warrior.

The Origin of War
Before, the Chulupi and the Toba made up a single tribe. But young people never want to be equal to each other, one always wants to be stronger than the other. Everything began when the hostility between two young people was born. They lived together, ate their fish together, went to harvest

together. Once, they went to bathe in the Pilcomayo and were wrestling.[8] One hit the other a bit hard; the one that received the blow avenged himself: he hit his adversary on the head with a piece of wood, wounding his forehead. The other did the same. This was the time when the Chulupi and the Toba were a single tribe: they spoke the same language; there were only small differences between them.

The brothers and the companions of each of the two young men gathered around them, and each went to find his father. The Toba declared that the other had started it first: and yet it was he who had started it! Before, there had never been the least discord between the Indians. In this time, the Mataco were the only enemies of the Chulupi. As for the Toba, their only enemies were the Parrot People, the Choroti.[9]

Following these events, a party was being prepared, a great drinking party of fermented honey. During the party, the Toba father got up and declared: Now, I think again of my son who was wounded![10] And he had hardly said this before he started piercing the relatives and friends of his son's adversary. A Chulupi warrior got up as well and riddled with arrows several Toba, who had been standing and singing accompanying themselves with their hatchets. Then combat began between all men who were drunk. And the cause of all of this was the two young men. The fight spread to the women, who began to fight at their husbands' sides. The combatants had a hard time separating themselves, for the fight was fierce on both sides. They stopped, parleyed, and decided to meet again the next day to begin the fight again.

The next day at dawn everything was ready. The horsemen provoked each other. Dressed only in small loincloths of caraguata fiber, they were armed with their bows and war arrows with smooth tips. The two groups were very large. The Chulupi began to dominate. There were a lot of deaths, but less on the Chulupi side, who were more agile and could dodge the arrows. The Toba ran away and abandoned a lot of their people, children, newborns. The Chulupi women nursed them, for the mothers of many of these infants had been killed during the fight. Among the prisoners, there were also women. The men devoted the entire day to scalping the dead Toba warriors. These

---

[8] Wrestling is one of the Chulupis' preferred sports. It is more a game of agility than of strength, consisting of throwing the adversary to the ground.

[9] The Mataco occupy the right bank of the upper current of the Pilcomayo; the Choroti occupied its left bank. They constituted, with the Chulupi, a single linguistic group.

[10] Drinking parties are often opportunities for brawls. Drunk, the men let resentments, sometimes ruminated over for months, explode. This is why during a party the women keep all weapons out of the mens reach.

events happened just after the appearance of night. At the time of the per-
manent day, Chulupi and Toba lived together.[11]

This myth calls for a few brief remarks. It considers at once the origin of
war and the birth of society. Before war the order of things, cosmic and
human, is not yet established: it is the prehuman time of the eternal day, not
punctuated by the succession of day and night. Social order, as multiplicity
of differences, as plurality of tribes, has yet to be born: Chulupi and Toba do
not differentiate themselves from each other. In other words, savage thought,
in its mythological expression, thinks of society's appearance and war's
appearance in conjunction; it thinks of war as consubstantial to society; war
belongs to the primitive social order. The indigenous discourse here validates
anthropological reflection.

We observe, moreover, that at the outset, the myth attributes responsibil-
ity for the launching of the war to the young men. Young men do not like
equality, they want a hierarchy between them, they want glory, and that is
why they are violent, they use force, they abandon themselves to their passion for prestige. The myth clearly says that young men are made to be warriors, that war is made for young men. The affinity between warlike activity
and age group could not be more clearly marked.

The Blind Warriors
Once, many Kaanoklé went on an expedition. At the end of several days
of walking, they stopped to sleep. The chief said: Tonight, my sons, we shall
sleep here and tomorrow we shall take up our path.

During the night, the Vuot-vuot[12] bird began to sing. And all the war-
riors burst out laughing, because it sang very badly. The bird got angry to see
that he was being made fun of in this way. He began singing again, and the
men began laughing again: How badly it sings! One man among them
laughed less than the others. The next day, when they got up, they noticed
that they had all gone blind: it was the vengeance of the bird. I am blind! So
am I! And so am I! they cried. As for the one who laughed less than the oth-
ers, he could see a little and proclaimed: I am not completely blind! I am the
only one who can see something. Then you must be our guide! And he
became the leader.

---

11 The war between the Toba and Chulupi ended sometime between 1945 and
1950.8 Wrestling is one of the Chulupis' preferred sports. It is more a game of agility
than of strength, consisting of throwing the adversary to the ground.

12 *Vuot-vuot*: unidentified bird. *Foh-foh* (in Guarani, *cavure'i*): glaucidium,
brasilianum. *Iunutah* (in Spanish, chuña): cariama cristata.

They all held each other's hands and formed a long line. They came to the woods; the one who could see a little called a swarm of bees: Where are you, bees? A nearby bee answered him:

Here I am! But I have very little honey! Just enough for my children!

Then that is not enough for us! We will go further.

Yes! Yes! Let's go further! Let's go further! cried the others in chorus.

They continued to walk and came to another place. There, the guide called once again:

Bee, where are you?

Here! And I have a lot of honey!

Well! It's yours that we will eat!

Yes! Yes! That's it! We will eat it! We will eat it! cried the chorus of blind men.

The man who could see a little began to enlarge the opening of the bee-hive in the tree and to extract the honey; and everyone began to eat. But there was still an enormous amount of honey. So they rubbed it all over their bodies, and started bumping and hitting each other:

Why have you covered me with honey?

What about you?

And they continued to fight. The one who could see a little advised them not to fight, to eat well. There was still a lot of honey, but the men were very thirsty: and so they began to look for water.

Their guide then called a lagoon:

Lagoon, where are you?

Here I am! But I have very little water! And very few eels as well!

In that case, we will go further.

Yes! Yes! We will go further! repeated the blind men together. They began to walk again, and after a while, the leader called out once again.

Lagoon, where are you?

Here I am! answered a very large lagoon. I have a lot of water and a lot of eels!

Then it's your water that we will drink!

Yes! Yes! That's it! That's it! We will drink! cried the others. They plunged into the water and quenched their thirst.

Then they began to fish for eels with their hands. They had left their sacks at the edge of the lagoon. And when a man had caught an eel, he ordered his sack to open: the sack opened itself and he threw an eel into it. When the sack was full, its owner ordered it to empty itself: the sack emptied itself, and the man filled it up all over again. When they had emptied the sacks twice, they got out of the water and the one who could see a little lit a great fire. They began to grill the eels. Meanwhile, the Foh-foh bird arrived.

It amused him very much to see all these blind men eating eels. He flew down and seized an eel and shook it above the men's heads, sprinkling them with droplets of burning hot grease. They got angry:

Why did you burn me?

Why did you?

They began bumping each other and fighting again. Foh-foh flew back to the top of his tree. He almost burst out laughing but held it in, so that they wouldn't know it was he.

He flew away and met the Iunutah bird, to whom he told the whole story:

There are men down there! I burnt them, and they started to fight each other! It's hilarious! I wanted to laugh so badly, but I held it in.

I want to see, too!

No! No! Don't go! We mustn't laugh, and the littlest thing makes you laugh.

But Iunutah insisted:

No! No! I want to go! If I start laughing uncontrollably, I will leave right away and only laugh from far away.

Foh-foh agreed finally, and led him to the place where the warriors were. There, he began his little game once again, burnt the men once again who started fighting again. Iunutah could not resist and fled far enough away so that he could laugh in peace. But the blind men soon realized that someone was laughing: Where is that laughter coming from? they asked. One of them grabbed his itoicha[13] and flung it in the direction of the laughter. The prarie grass where Iunutah was hiding caught on fire. He had hidden himself in a hole, with his legs outside: and so, they were burnt.

And that's why the feet of the Iunutah bird are red.

A classical analysis of this myth would no doubt conclude that this is a myth about the origins of a bird's physical characteristic. It seems to me, however, that this is not the essential thing, and that this myth is mostly about humor and derision. Whom does the myth ridicule? It is the warriors, grotesque cripples, more vulnerable and stripped than an infant. It is precisely the opposite of the portrait of the real warrior, a man who is confident, reckless, powerful and respected by the tribe. That is to say that the myth inverts reality, that indigenous thought mythologically does what no one would dream of actually doing: making fun of warriors, ridiculing them. This myth's mocking humor thereby expresses the gap that a warrior society maintains in relation to its warriors. And what fills the gap is precisely laughter, this same laughter that brings the warriors their sorrow in the

---

[13] *Itoicha*: tool for starting a fire.

myth. But society is not really laughing at the warrior (in reality, it makes him die), it only laughs at him in myth: who knows whether real laughter would not be turned against it?

Another aspect of the myth: it constitutes a sort of discreet guard against inequality. Does it not say, in effect, that in a kingdom of blind men, the one-eyed are king? So that its moral could be: there is no good society except under the sign of equality and non-division. It is a matter of opening one's eyes! It is a political morality tale. The classic or structuralist analysis of myths obscures the political dimension of Savage thought. Myths no doubt reflect upon each other, as Lévi-Strauss writes, but they reflect upon society first: they are primitive society's discourse on itself.*

BIBLIOGRAPHY

I. NORTH AMERICA.

Champlain, S., *Les Voyages de Samuel Champlain...*, Paris, PUF, 1951.
Élan Noir, *Mémoires d'un Sioux*, Paris, Stock, 1977.
Géronimo, *Mémoires de Géronimo*, Paris, Maspero, 1972.
Grinnell, G.B., *The Cheyenne Indians*, University of Nebraska Press, 1972.
Lowie, R.H., *The Crow Indians*, New York, Holt, Rinehart & Winston,1966.
Relations des jésuites, Montréal, Éditions du Jour, 1972 (vol. III,1642-1646; vol. IV, 1647-1655).

II. SOUTH AMERICA.

Biocca, E., *Yanoama*, Paris, Plon, 1968 (French translation).
Dobrizhoffer, M., *Historia de los Abipone*, Facultad de Humanidades, Universidad Nacional del Nordeste (Argentina), 1967-1970. Vol. 3 (Spanish translation of the Latin original).
Lozano, P., *Descripcion corografica del Gran Chaco Gualamba*. Tucumán (Argentina), 1941.
Paucke, F., *Hacia allá y para acá (una estada entre los Indios Mocobies)*, 1749-1767, Tucumán-Buenos Aires, 1942-1944, Vol. 4 (Spanish translation).
Sanchez Labrador, J., *El Paraguay Catolico*, Buenos Aires, 1910, Vol. 2.

---

* This text and the preceding one (*Libre*, 77-1) were to inaugurate a larger work, which will remain incomplete. Pierre Clastres left a few brief indications in his notes on the field he intended to explore. Here are what seemed to be the other principal articulations of his book: the nature of the war chief's power; the war of conquest in primitive societies as the possible beginning of a change in the political structure (the case of the Tupi); the role of women in relation to war; the war of the State (the Incas). [*Libre's* note.]

HANNIBAL LECTER, MY FATHER
Kathy Acker

SICK BURN CUT
Deran Ludd

THE MADAME REALISM COMPLEX
Lynne Tillman

HOW I BECAME ONE OF THE INVISIBLE
David Rattray

THE ORIGIN OF *THE* SPECIES
Barbara Barg

AUTONOMEDIA NEW AUTONOMY SERIES
Jim Fleming & Peter Lamborn Wilson, Editors

TAZ
The Temporary Autonomous Zone, Ontological Anarchy, Poetic Terrorism
Hakim Bey

THIS IS YOUR FINAL WARNING!
Thom Metzger

FRIENDLY FIRE
Bob Black

CALIBAN AND THE WITCHES
Silvia Federici

FIRST AND LAST EMPERORS: THE ABSOLUTE STATE & THE BODY OF THE DESPOT
Kenneth Dean & Brian Massumi

WARCRAFT
Jonathan Leake

THIS WORLD WE MUST LEAVE AND OTHER ESSAYS
Jacques Camatte

SPECTACULAR TIMES
Larry Law

FUTURE PRIMITIVE AND OTHER ESSAYS
John Zerzan

WIGGLING WISHBONE
Bart Plantenga

THE ELECTRONIC DISTURBANCE
Critical Arts Ensemble

X TEXTS
Derek Pell

WHORE CARNIVAL
Shannon Bell, ed.

CRIMES OF CULTURE
Richard Kostelanetz

INVISIBLE GOVERNANCE: ART OF AFRICAN MICROPOLITICS
David Hecht & Maliqalim Simone

THE LIZARD CLUB
Steve Abbott

CRACKING THE MOVEMENT: SQUATTING BEYOND THE MEDIA
Foundation for the Advancement of Illegal Knowledge

CAPITAL AND COMMUNITY
Jacques Camatte

AUTONOMEDIA BOOK SERIES

THE DAUGHTER
Roberta Allen

FILE UNDER POPULAR: THEORETICAL & CRITICAL WRITINGS ON MUSIC
Chris Cutler

CASSETTE MYTHOS: THE NEW MUSIC UNDERGROUND
Robin James, ed.

ENRAGÉS & SITUATIONISTS: THE OCCUPATION MOVEMENT, MAY '68
René Viénet

POPULAR REALITY
Irreverend David Crowbar, ed.

XEROX PIRATES: "HIGH" TECH & THE NEW COLLAGE UNDERGROUND
Autonomedia Collective, eds.

ZEROWORK: THE ANTI-WORK ANTHOLOGY
Bob Black & Tad Kepley, eds.

THE NEW ENCLOSURES
Midnight Notes Collective

MIDNIGHT OIL: WORK, ENERGY, WAR, 1973–1992
Midnight Notes Collective

A DAY IN THE LIFE: TALES FROM THE LOWER EAST SIDE
Alan Moore & Josh Gosniak, eds.

GONE TO CROATAN: ORIGINS OF NORTH AMERICAN DROPOUT CULTURE
James Koehnline & Ron Sakolsky, eds.

ABOUT FACE: RACE IN POSTMODERN AMERICA
Timothy Maliqalim Simone

HORSEXE: ESSAY ON TRANSSEXUALITY
Catherine Millot

DEMONO (THE BOXED GAME)
P.M.

FORMAT AND ANXIETY: COLLECTED ESSAYS ON THE MEDIA
Paul Goodman

THE NARRATIVE BODY
Eldon Garnet

THE DAMNED UNIVERSE OF CHARLES FORT
Louis Kaplan, ed.

BY ANY MEANS NECESSARY: OUTLAW MANIFESTOS & EPHEMERA, 1965–70
Peter Stansill & David Zane Mairowitz, eds.

THE OFFICIAL KGB HANDBOOK
USSR Committee for State Security

WILD CHILDREN
David Mandl & Peter Lamborn Wilson., eds.

AUTONOMEDIA DISTRIBUTION

FELIX
The Review of Television & Video Culture
Kathy High, ed.

LUSITANIA
A Journal of Reflection and Oceanography
Martim Avillez, ed.

DRUNKEN BOAT
An Anarchist Review of Literature & the Arts
Max Blechman, ed.

RACE TRAITOR
A Journal of the New Abolitionism
John Garvey & Noel Ignatiev, eds.

RADIO SERMONETTES
The Moorish Orthodox Radio Crusade Collective

AIMLESS WANDERING: CHUANG TZU'S CHAOS·LINGUISTICS
Hakim Bey
Xexoxial Editions

ALL COTTON BRIEFS: EXPANDED EDITION
M. Kasper
Benzene Books